Losing Face

A

Philip E. Lilienthal

Book

The Philip E. Lilienthal imprint
honors special books
in commemoration of a man whose work
at the University of California Press from 1954 to 1979
was marked by dedication to young authors
and to high standards in the field of Asian Studies.
Friends, family, authors, and foundations have together
endowed the Lilienthal Fund, which enables the Press
to publish under this imprint selected books
in a way that reflects the taste and judgment
of a great and beloved editor.

Losing Face

STATUS POLITICS IN JAPAN

Susan J. Pharr

University of California Press
Berkeley   Los Angeles   Oxford

To Robert Cameron Mitchell

University of California Press
Berkeley and Los Angeles, California

University of California Press, Ltd.
Oxford, England

© 1990 by
The Regents of the University of California

Library of Congress Cataloging-in-Publication Data

Pharr, Susan J.
    Losing face : status politics in Japan / Susan J. Pharr.
        p.   cm.
    "A Philip E. Lilienthal book."
    Bibliography: p.
    Includes index.
    ISBN 0-520-06050-4 (alk. paper).
    1. Equality—Japan—Case studies.   2. Social conflict—Japan—Case
studies.   I. Title.
JC599.J3P47   1989
306'.2'0952—dc19   88-31502
                                                                        CIP

Printed in the United States of America
1 2 3 4 5 6 7 8 9

CONTENTS

TABLES

PREFACE

No issue has been as central to twentieth-century democracies as that of equality. Most of the great struggles of this century have been waged in the name of equality: class conflict in Britain and elsewhere; the Third World struggle for independence from colonialism; demands in virtually all countries for the extension of suffrage to previously excluded people; pressures by women, minorities, and other disadvantaged groups for redress of their grievances; even demands for equity in taxation. In a broader sense, the ideal of equality has been basic to the notion of the modern state itself.[1] Certainly no major state, whether democratic, socialist, communist, or authoritarian, has been able to avoid confronting, and having in some way to address, demands from within society for greater equality and participation.

Yet from the standpoint of the state, no principle has been as thorny to deal with as this central issue of equality. Disparities in wealth, intelligence, talent, and all manner of other attributes are ubiquitous in social life. Moreover, people's consciousness of inequality has increased dramatically in recent years as a result of a broad range of factors, from improved communications that make inequities in the distribution of wealth, benefits, and privileges more visible to ideological changes that legitimate the struggle for greater shares of the pie. Indeed, some have argued that the "crisis of democracy," to the extent that one in fact exists, is due to a growing inability of democratic states to accommodate all the pressures from below by the many claimants who want more of whatever there is to get.

1. Dankwart Rustow, *A World of Nations: Problems of Political Modernization* (Washington, D.C.: Brookings Institution, 1967). See also Sidney Verba et al., *Elites and the Idea of Equality: A Comparison of Japan, Sweden, and the United States* (Cambridge, Mass.: Harvard University Press, 1987), for a major recent work on the centrality of equality as an issue.

According to a study by Michel Crozier, Samuel P. Huntington, and Watanuki Joji, the failure of the state to cope effectively with the challenge posed by people's wholesale pursuit of equality and freedom had by the mid 1970s resulted in a delegitimization of authority and an erosion of popular trust in leadership.[2] Serious ills in socialist systems revived faith in democracy and the free market in the late 1980s, but democratic systems had yet to overcome their basic problems.

This book explores the problem of equality in one country: Japan, heralded today as the site of an economic "miracle" and a state with an enviable record of stability and effective rule. It looks at how struggles over equality are waged in Japan and how authority responds to them. Because inequalities take various forms, the focus of this book is on disparities in social status based on age, gender, ethnicity, caste background, and other attributes beyond the powers of the individual to change. I call struggles over such inequalities "status politics."

The issue of equality has special importance in Japan today as a result of value changes that have occurred there, particularly since the end of World War II. Some 120 years ago, centuries after feudalism had ended in most of Europe, Japan was still a feudal society characterized by hierarchical status relations and a traditional Confucian ideology that saw inequalities in social relations as natural and legitimate. Although communitarianism at the village level, where most of society lived, provided a basis for solidarity and resistance to higher authority when conditions became unbearably oppressive, profound status differences were taken as given. These traditional norms and values persisted relatively unchallenged up to the end of World War II, legitimizing the many prerogatives exercised by status superiors over their inferiors and teaching inferiors to defer to those above them and to accept their lot. From the time of the Allied Occupation (1945–1952), however, as democratic values have been introduced into the legal system, the schools, and other institutions and Japan has become increasingly internationalized, the situation has undergone major change. Indeed, the past forty years have seen a marked increase in popular consciousness of inequalities in Japanese life, and today status inferiors seeking to alter the terms of social relationships can call on the counter-ideology of egalitarianism to support their demands.

This book focuses on three specific protests over issues of equality that have arisen during the past few decades. The cases involve groups who

2. Michel Crozier, Samuel P. Huntington, and Watanuki Joji, *The Crisis of Democracy* (New York: New York University Press, 1975), 3–9.

traditionally have been assigned positions of social inferiority and who, in the postwar period, have sought to improve their lot in the name of equality: young people, former outcastes, and women. By examining a series of status-based conflicts, we will explore the conditions that generate such conflicts, the various ways the status-deprived express their grievances, how they mobilize and organize, and the goals they seek.

These questions are important from the standpoint not only of assessing the successes and failures of status-based struggles in Japan, but also of examining Western theories regarding how interest groups arise and seek legitimacy in democratic societies. Implicit in the work of numerous writers who have studied the rise of interests in democracies—from E. E. Schattschneider to Mancur Olson and Terry Moe—is a developmental model the end products of which are relatively permanent, highly professionalized, and institutionalized "organized interests" of the kind able to play a role in policymaking.[3] Less organized interests—including relatively amorphous, impermanent groups or movements—are seen as less stable, and therefore less significant, forms of political life that may or may not survive a transition (generally assumed to be desired by the members) to such an end condition. Organized interests, in contrast, are viewed as inherently expansionist in their drive to maximize resources, from money to members.

Behind this developmental model lie many assumptions, first and foremost of which being that organized interests can, by maximizing their resources, gain access to policymaking. "Access to policymaking" itself is thought to involve the active participation of organized and bureaucratized interest groups, operating through their professional staffs, in the actual decision-making process, whether by influencing legislation, as in the United States, or by joining in corporatist arrangements, as in Sweden. In Anselm Strauss's terms, organized interest groups become involved in the actual "negotiations," or bargaining, of policymaking.[4]

The case of interests in Japan, I will argue, calls this developmental model into question and challenges the assumptions on which it rests. Although organized economic interests, including big business and the agricultural lobby, enjoy an astonishing level of access to policymaking in

3. Terry M. Moe, *The Organization of Interests: Incentives and the Internal Dynamics of Political Interest Groups* (Chicago: University of Chicago Press, 1980); Mancur Olson, *The Logic of Collective Action* (Cambridge, Mass.: Harvard University Press, 1975); E. E. Schattschneider, *The Semi-sovereign People: A Realist's View of Democracy in America* (New York: Holt, Rinehart and Winston, 1967).

4. Anselm Strauss, *Negotiations: Varieties, Contexts, Processes, and Social Order* (San Francisco: Jossey-Bass, 1978), 1–7.

Japan, when it comes to noneconomic interests the story is quite different. Given their limited access to policymaking at the national level, less organized interests such as social protest groups may have little incentive to become more institutionalized. In a society in which the dominant positive response of authorities to interest-group claimants is likely to be unilaterally granted concessions rather than actual admission to the bargaining process, there may be little to gain from amassing the staff or other organizational resources needed to play a role in policymaking. Indeed, at least in some cases, less organized interests may find it more advantageous to *minimize* their resources, to limit their group to those most committed, and, through various strategies, to present themselves as victims in order to trigger a paternalistic response on the part of the authorities. Certainly the study of how and why interests arise, organize, and pursue their goals in Japan poses important challenges to theories of interest groups and the assumptions that underlie them.

After focusing on the protest groups in chapters 3 through 7, I will turn in chapter 8 to an examination of how authorities respond to conflicts over equality as they unfold, and the consequences of that pattern of response, as a way of assessing how well Japan is coping with an issue that has proven so difficult for most states in the twentieth century.

In addition to exploring the question of equality in Japan, a major aim of this book is to look at how, in a broader sense, the Japanese deal with social conflict. Social protest may arise over many issues, ranging from quality-of-life concerns to economic ones. Status-based conflicts, for many reasons to be set out here, constitute a "worst case" of protest in Japan, both from the standpoint of persons attempting to press their grievances and in the view of authorities who must in some manner respond. Issues of equality are difficult to resolve in any country, but especially so in Japan, for in their essence all status-based protests involve an assertion of self, claims of entitlement, and demands for oneself and one's group that fly in the face of the Japanese "ideal model of protest," according to which some kinds of protest are judged to be more acceptable than others. Thus protesters face major obstacles in pressing their case, and authorities may in response bring into play a full range of conflict-management strategies, from "soft" backstage acts of appeasement to "harder" methods of social control. By studying Japanese struggles over equality, then, we can look both at how one country is dealing with a challenge that is felt worldwide and, at the same time, at how Japanese authorities approach the problem of social conflict in general.

The response of authorities to protest has an important bearing not only on the particular developmental pattern that interests will undergo in society but also on our understanding of how democracy works in practice. Conflict theorists and many political scientists—Schattschneider and Giuseppe DiPalma are two examples—have long upheld the value to political systems of allowing social grievances to be aired and of creating and maintaining institutionalized channels for the resolution of social conflict, arguing that openness to conflict and responsiveness to new interests assure the long-term health, viability, and stability of democratic systems.[5] Protest movements, some hold, advance the "statemaking" process itself. In Western democracies, moreover, these views of social scientists are generally backed by both average people and public officials (even though official support sometimes proves more rhetorical than real when actual social protests arise).

Authorities in Japan, as we shall see, take a dramatically different view of social conflict and protest, and of what should be done about it. The legacy of Confucianism, with its emphasis on harmony as a social good, causes even rhetorical tributes to the value of airing social grievances to be rare. Meanwhile, the tests that a social protest must meet if it is to be judged legitimate by the watching public and potential supporters are rigorous. If social conflict cannot in the end be avoided, authorities in Japan seek to contain it to the extent possible, using strategies that tend to marginalize protesters and to keep the protest outside existing channels and institutions of conflict resolution and policymaking.

At the same time, however, in what is a crucial part of the "Japanese formula" for handling social conflict, authorities do address—if less adequately than protesters generally would like—the issues raised as a means of heading off future conflicts. In daily life the unilateral granting of preemptive concessions is powerfully supported by societal norms that enjoin status superiors to avoid abusing their authority, to anticipate the needs of inferiors, and to be sensitive to how their behavior is viewed by the watching public. At the national level these same norms, which combine elements of paternalism and of communitarianism, have translated into a society in which social welfare measures compare favorably with those in place in the United States, and where the gap between the rich and the poor ranks Japan near Sweden as one of the more egalitarian nations—economically speaking—in the world. Given the country's extraordinary record of stability and governability in the postwar era, Japan's approach of privatizing social conflict while granting preemptive concessions challenges the assumptions of many conflict theorists and invites examination

5. Schattschneider, *The Semi-sovereign People*; Giuseppe DiPalma, *The Study of Conflict in Western Society* (Morristown, N.J.: General Learning Press, 1973).

by scholars and policymakers alike. Yet it is important to look as well at the costs of this approach, its consequences for the overall pattern of interest-group representation in society and the conditions on which it rests, and at how and why the Japanese approach to social protest may be changing in Japan today and in the future.

I am indebted to a great many people and institutions for their help while I worked on this book. Fieldwork was conducted in Tokyo and Kyoto in 1978 with the generous assistance of the Japan Foundation, and in a follow-up visit in 1985. Sakamoto Yoshikazu was kind enough to arrange for my affiliation with the Faculty of Law of the University of Tokyo for the earlier period, and I am grateful to him and to other faculty members and staff there for the aid they offered me.[6] Ishida Takeshi, then of the University of Tokyo and now retired, extended to me the same willing assistance, insightful comments and suggestions on my work, and warm hospitality that he has extended to so many other American scholars working in Japan.

My research in Japan could not have gone forward without the generous help of Uchida Mitsuru, of Waseda University, and Muramatsu Michio, of Kyoto University. Akamatsu Ryoko, former director-general of the Women's and Young Workers' Bureau of the Ministry of Labor, and her husband, Hanami Tadashi, of the Faculty of Law, Sophia University, both of them friends for some twenty years, provided many helpful suggestions and a number of introductions to informants, as well as a home where I have always felt welcome in Japan.

Each of the case studies brought me in contact with dozens of persons without whom I could not have pursued my research and whom I regret that I cannot acknowledge individually. I am deeply grateful to the headquarters staffs of the Liberal Democratic party and of the New Liberal Club for their extensive help with background material and for arranging interviews with Diet members. The Public Employees' Union office of Kyoto and Sakai Sadako of the regional office of the Women's and Young Workers' Bureau in Kyoto helped me immeasurably on the case study of gender-related politics. A great many people and organizations likewise provided generous assistance on the case study involving the problems of former outcastes in Japan, for which I am most grateful; these include the staffs of the Buraku Liberation League's offices, branches, and research institutes in Kyoto, Osaka, Kobe, and the Tajima area of Hyōgo Prefec-

6. Throughout the text of this book, personal names of Japanese individuals are given in Japanese fashion, that is, family name first. In the bibliography and notes, authors of works published in English are generally cited Western-style; authors of works published in Japanese are cited Japanese-style.

ture; the Buraku Problems Research Institute in Kyoto; the town office in Tajima; Yōka Senior High School; and a great many other organizations in the Tajima area, Kobe, Osaka, Kyoto, and Tokyo.

I am grateful to several institutions for support at all phases of the writing of this book. The Woodrow Wilson International Center for Scholars in Washington, D.C., provided a highly congenial and stimulating setting in 1981–1982 for me to begin to write up my research, which I then continued with summer support from the University of Wisconsin. A year in 1984 at Harvard University as a visiting faculty member in the Department of Government and in what is now the Reischauer Institute saw completion of the first draft, and I finished the book as holder of the Japan chair of the Center for Strategic and International Studies in Washington, D.C.

Colleagues from a broad range of fields provided comments and suggestions on all or part of the manuscript throughout the writing process. I would like to express appreciation to John Campbell, Gary Allinson, T. J. Pempel, Ellis Krauss, Muramatsu Michio, Ishida Takeshi, Murray Edelman, Richard Merelman, Emiko Ohnuki-Tierney, Crawford Young, Herbert Passin, George DeVos, James White, Frank Upham, Ezra Vogel, Thomas Rohlen, John McCarthy, Patricia Steinhoff, Chalmers Johnson, and Tsurumi Shunsuke for their many helpful remarks. I am especially grateful to David Titus for his detailed and astonishingly insightful comments on the completed manuscript.

I express my sincerest appreciation to Satō Ikuko and Mori Shizuko, who were unfailingly helpful as research assistants in Japan, and to Kishima Takako and Oyadomari Motoko for research assistance as graduate students at the University of Wisconsin. Special thanks go to Kishima Takako, who is now a research associate at Harvard University, for her many valuable comments at all stages of preparation of the manuscript. No one I have named, of course, bears responsibility for my mistakes, but all have contributed greatly to my work.

I am grateful to Jim Clark, director of University of California Press, for his patience and encouragement, and to Betsey Scheiner and Anne Canright of the Press and Frank Schwartz of Harvard for their superb editorial efforts. I would also like to thank Joanne Klys, Mary Mulrenan, and Susan Scott for the care they took with many drafts of the manuscript.

Finally, I would like to express my gratitude to my husband, Robert Cameron Mitchell, for his help as I worked to complete the book. My marriage to him in 1983 brought not only the strongest possible support and encouragement in the pursuit of my work, but deep bonds of intellectual companionship as well.

1

Status Politics in Japan

In the mid 1970s, Michel Crozier, Samuel Huntington, and Watanuki Joji issued a report on behalf of the Trilateral Commission which argued that the United States, Western Europe, and Japan were in the grip of a crisis of governability: social demands were rising, outstripping the capacity of the state to respond, while authority was on the decline.[1] When they compared the situation in the three regions, however, the authors found that in terms of success rates for governability, Japan came out ahead—in a sense foreshadowing the current "Japan boom," led by writers such as Ezra Vogel, in which Japan's accomplishments in everything from industrial organization to crime control have become the subject of Western study and admiration. Chalmers Johnson spurred further acclaim for Japanese governmental performance in 1982 by heralding Japan as the ultimate "developmental" state; whereas the bureaucracy has provided the driving force behind the economic miracle, the politicians, he said, "create space for bureaucratic initiative" by successfully handling, among other things, disaffection and social protest.[2]

By the late 1980s, many observers were arguing that the "crisis of democracy" had been overstated and that democratic governments and capitalism itself were showing resiliency in all three regions.[3] Indeed, market-

1. Michel Crozier, Samuel P. Huntington, and Watanuki Joji, *The Crisis of Democracy* (New York: New York University Press, 1975), 3–9, 161–170.

2. Chalmers Johnson, *MITI and the Japanese Miracle* (Stanford: Stanford University Press, 1982), 316.

3. See, for example, Hans Daalder, ed., *Party Systems in Denmark, Austria, Switzerland, the Netherlands, and Belgium* (New York: St. Martin's Press, 1987); Joseph LaPalombara, *Democracy, Italian Style* (New Haven: Yale University Press,

oriented economic reforms in the Soviet Union and China, and pressure for greater democratization in socialist countries as well as in authoritarian systems such as those of South Korea and Taiwan, suggested that capitalism and democracy were proving their superiority over alternative arrangements. Within the democratic camp, however, Japan's superior record of economic success and governmental stability continued to stand out. Even as Japan became a target of steady Western criticism because of conflict over trade and investment issues, the country's political, social, and economic systems continued to be the object of Western fascination and study.

Japan's record of success in governing is all the more striking because this continuity has been maintained despite regular tests of the authority of those in power by political parties, protest groups, and opposition movements.[4] Japan has four major opposition parties, two of which, the Japan Socialist and Communist parties, pose fundamental ideological challenges to rule by the conservative Liberal Democratic party (LDP). The percentage of popular votes cast for all opposition parties has surpassed that cast for the LDP in numerous postwar elections. Indeed, as of 1989 the LDP has failed to capture a majority of seats in three out of five of the most recent lower house elections; only through postelection overtures to non-LDP conservatives was it able to secure a working majority.

In the area of mass movements, Japanese labor has successfully organized more workers than has the U.S. labor movement.[5] Unions, some of which are quite radical by American standards, annually engage in nationwide mass demonstrations, as well as in "offensives" against both the government and employers.[6] Citizens' movements demanding that the government cope with Japan's environmental pollution problems were a major phenomenon of the late 1960s and early 1970s. Indeed, according to

---

1987); Eva Kolinsky, ed., *Opposition in Western Europe* (New York: St. Martin's Press, 1987); and Inoguchi Takashi, ed., *Shin hoshushugi no taitō* (The rise of neo-conservatism), *Leviathan*, no. 1 (special issue) (Tokyo: Bokutakusha, 1987).

4. A valuable survey of the changing pattern of protest activities is found in Michitoshi Takabatake, "Mass Movements: Change and Diversity," in *Annals of the Japan Political Science Association 1977: The Political Process in Modern Japan*, ed. Japan Political Science Association, 323–359. (Tokyo: Iwanami Shoten, 1979). See also James W. White, "Civic Attitudes, Political Participation, and System Stability in Japan," *Comparative Political Studies* 14 (October 1981): 371–400.

5. In 1986, 28.2 percent of Japanese workers were in unions, as compared to 18.0 percent in the United States; *Japan 1988: An International Comparison* (Tokyo: Keizai Kōhō Center, 1988), 73.

6. See Solomon Levine, "Labor in Japan," in *Business and Society in Japan*, ed. Bradley M. Richardson and Taizō Ueda, 29–61, (New York: Praeger, 1981).

one estimate some seventy-five thousand complaints over pollution were lodged with local governments in 1971, and in 1973 antipollution groups sparked as many as ten thousand local disputes over environmental issues.[7] In the postwar era vast numbers of protesters have been mobilized at peak periods by peace movements and student movements, and in recent years conflicts over land use at Narita Airport, over property and people affected by extension plans for the bullet train (shinkansen), and over nuclear power plant siting have commanded national attention. Recent protests over proposed expansion of U.S. military facilities in Zushi and Miyakejima follow in the same tradition.[8] Certain watershed protests, notably the struggles in 1960 and 1970 against the United States–Japan Mutual Security Treaty, have been mammoth in scale: for the antitreaty protest on 23 June 1970, for example, almost three-quarters of a million people took to the streets.[9] Other advanced industrial democracies have seen relatively few protests of comparable magnitude and intensity over the past three and a half decades.[10]

A critical view of the social order under the LDP is echoed in the opinions of many ordinary people, as reflected in numerous survey results. At the same time that the foreign media were conveying images of the happy and productive Japanese worker adjusting ably to rapid technological change, the majority of Japanese were voicing a deep-seated malaise about the nature and quality of life and work in Japan. Between 1958 and 1973, for example, a steadily increasing percentage of young people in the twenty-to-twenty-nine-year age group—well over the majority of them by 1973—agreed that human feeling is lost with the development of science and technology.[11] An eleven-nation survey conducted by the Manage-

7. Ellis S. Krauss and Bradford L. Simcock, "Citizens' Movements: The Growth and Impact of Environmental Protest in Japan," in Political Opposition and Local Politics in Japan, ed. Kurt Steiner, Ellis S. Krauss, and Scott C. Flanagan (Princeton: Princeton University Press, 1980), 187.

8. See New York Times, 5 March 1986, A32, for an account of a citizens' protest over a U.S. Navy housing project in Zushi; and Daily Yomiuri, 11 February 1986, 5, concerning a protest in Miyakejima over a proposed U.S. Navy landing strip.

9. Ellis S. Krauss, Japanese Radicals Revisited: Student Protest in Postwar Japan (Berkeley and Los Angeles: University of California Press, 1974), 1, uses that figure; Asahi Shinbun, 24 June 1970, 1, gives the figure as 770,000.

10. The nearest thing in Europe may be protests over nuclear issues. See Dorothy Nelkin and Michael Pollak, The Atom Besieged: Extraparliamentary Dissent in France and Germany (Cambridge, Mass.: MIT Press, 1981).

11. Chikio Hayashi, "Changes in Japanese Thought During the Past Twenty Years," in Text of Seminar on "Changing Values in Modern Japan," ed. Nihonjin Kenkyūkai (Tokyo: Nihonjin Kenkyūkai, 1977), 10–11, 48.

ment and Coordination Agency in 1988 showed that the percentage of Japanese youth expressing satisfaction with society had increased substantially compared to five years earlier, but that Japanese youth ranked only seventh, well behind the young people of Singapore, Sweden, and West Germany, in their overall satisfaction level.[12] Political alienation is also common. The belief that government is unresponsive to the electorate and that it is run primarily for the benefit of big business is frequently expressed, and even before the Recruit Cosmos scandal of late 1988 and 1989 brought approval levels to an all-time low, negative evaluations of the Diet and cabinet were widespread.[13] Levels of political dissatisfaction are seemingly at least as high as in the United States. Indeed, in 1989 discontent with everything from an unpopular consumption tax to the sexual misconduct of Prime Minister Uno Sousuke gave the opposition parties an unprecedented victory in the July upper house elections.[14]

Few would argue that the alienation and dissatisfaction expressed regarding the policies and priorities of the government in power and the nature of Japanese social and political life in general mean that the overall level of discontent is higher in Japan than elsewhere in the industrial capitalist world. But the record certainly does not suggest that Japan's stability and governability are attributable to a lack of social and political protest or to mass quiescence. How, then, do we explain the seeming paradox of high governability in the face of relatively high levels of protest and alienation? Given the strong authority of the state as reflected in Japan's long record of stable one-party rule, under what conditions does protest arise, and what factors constrain its impact? What is the response of Japanese authorities to social conflict and protest, and to the rise of new interests and issues in society more generally?

These questions provide a beginning point for the study of one particular type of protest in Japanese society—protest over the issue of social equality. At one level, this book explores sources of protest in today's Japan

12. The survey, conducted every five years since 1972, was of youth eighteen to twenty-four years old in Japan, the United States, Britain, West Germany, France, Sweden, Australia, Singapore, South Korea, China, and Brazil: see *Japan Times*, 15 January 1989, 2; and *Nihon Keizai Shinbun*, 15 January 1989, 31.

13. Scott C. Flanagan and Bradley M. Richardson, "Political Disaffection and Political Stability: A Comparison of Japanese and Western Findings," in *Comparative Social Research*, ed. Richard F. Tomasson, vol. 3 (Greenwich, Conn.: JAI Press, 1980). In the wake of the Recruit Cosmos scandal, in which many of Japan's leading politicians were implicated in a shady stock deal, public approval ratings for Prime Minister Takeshita and his cabinet dropped to 4 percent (*Asahi Shinbun*, 25 April 1989, 1).

14. *Asahi Shinbun*, 25 July 1989, 1.

by looking at "status politics," that is, the struggles of people attempting to challenge the terms of their ascribed status—younger generations, women, and former outcastes. It studies the conditions that give rise to conflicts over status issues, the ways that protesters organize and articulate their grievances, and the obstacles they meet along the way; it examines as well the goals of protesters and looks closely at how the issue of status inequalities is seen in Japan, a society with long-standing hierarchical traditions.

At another level, the focus is on how authorities respond to a status-based struggle as it develops, and the consequences for the protest movement of that pattern of response. The aim here is to explore the broader questions of how Japan remains governable, even in the face of considerable disaffection and protest at the grass roots, and of what costs the nation incurs from its particular formula for managing social conflict and responding to new interests in society.

In this larger sense, the present volume is aimed at taking Japan's measure as a democracy. Like all democracies, Japan faces at least two major challenges: first, to provide an efficient and stable government capable of generating policies that address the country's economic and social problems; and second, to satisfy the public that the state is sufficiently responsive to its diverse needs and interests. The outpouring of books on Japan as a model of economic success and efficient governmental performance suggests that Japan scores high on the first task. This book assesses Japan's formula and record in dealing with the second challenge.

On the Nature of Status Politics

Status-based conflict, or status politics, arises from the efforts of persons of a given social status to adjust their status position vis-à-vis those above them. In the broad sense in which leading theorists discuss such conflicts, the root cause may be attributable to many different types of status-related grievances, such as the type dealt with by Joseph Gusfield, in which a conflict arose when a given social class attempted to recoup a loss of achieved status.[15] Here, however, the term is limited to status conflicts in which the statuses of the two parties are ascribed—that is, are dictated by age, sex, caste background, and other attributes that are beyond the powers of the individual to change.

15. Joseph R. Gusfield, *Symbolic Crusade: Status Politics and the American Temperance Movement* (Urbana: University of Illinois Press, 1966). For Japanese status politics issues more specifically, see Taketsugu Tsurutani, *Political Change in Japan* (New York: David McKay, 1977), 51–53.

Singling out status-based conflicts as the focus of analysis recognizes their significance not just in Japan, but in advanced industrial societies more generally. No issue has been as central to democracies—and indeed, to virtually all forms of political systems—as that of social, economic, and political equality. In the twentieth century nearly every major political system has been forced, in varying ways and to varying degrees, to come to terms with societal pressures for greater equality and participation. Such pressures, of course, take many forms. One quest has been for political equality according to the "one person, one vote" principle, a struggle that has been successfully concluded in most parts of the world. Another goal has been a reduction in income disparities within and between entire categories of people. The complexity of the problem of inequality has been well demonstrated by writers from Plato and Aristotle to Douglas Rae.[16] Within this domain, status-based conflicts constitute one expression of the overall struggle for social equality in this century.

In the United States and other countries, some of the most visible status-based struggles have arisen over the issue of race and ethnicity, with the U.S. civil rights movement and protests waged by immigrant ethnic groups in European countries with migratory labor populations as major examples. Outside the advanced industrial societies, too, the problem of race and ethnicity continues to be central.

Status-based struggles have also arisen over generational issues in a great many countries. The work of Ronald Inglehart, Scott Flanagan, Samuel Barnes and Max Kaase, and many others points to such cleavages as being key factors in the differentiation of value and attitude patterns in advanced industrial nations and in the structuring of political participation as younger generations demand a greater say in what issues are included on the political agenda.[17] These overarching concerns, writers like Claus Offe have argued, have underlain the numerous protests led by younger generations in Western Europe, Japan, and the United States over such

16. See Douglas Rae, *Equalities* (Cambridge, Mass.: Harvard University Press, 1981), for a discussion of the many dimensions of equality.

17. Samuel H. Barnes, Max Kaase, et al., *Political Action: Mass Participation in Five Western Democracies* (Beverly Hills, Calif.: Sage, 1979); Ronald Inglehart, *The Silent Revolution: Changing Values and Political Styles Among Western Publics* (Princeton: Princeton University Press, 1977); Ronald Inglehart, "The Silent Revolution in Europe: Intergenerational Change in Post-industrial Societies," *American Political Science Review* 65 (December 1971): 991–1017; and Scott C. Flanagan, "Changing Values in Advanced Industrial Societies: Inglehart's Silent Revolution from the Perspective of Japanese Findings," *Comparative Political Studies* 14 (January 1982): 403–444.

diverse issues as nuclear power plant siting, defense and peace issues, and environmental protest.[18] An even more obvious form of intergenerational struggle in the post–World War II era has been manifested in student movements that have challenged authority and the allocation of power in political, social, and economic decision making even as they have targeted particular issues for protest.

The other major form of status-based protest is that waged over gender. Few nations of the world have been exempt from pressures by women for greater political participation, and—led by countries with major feminist movements such as the United States and Sweden—redress of inequities in social, economic, and political life.[19]

Status issues are important, it may be added, not only because so many manifestations of status-based protest have actually emerged, but also because the interests of status groups—women, youth, and ethnic, racial, and other minorities—cut across the lines of cleavage represented by such identities as class, religion, and region. A key issue for both the present and the future is the degree to which those interests will become organized and will vie for political expression.

Students of value change in advanced industrial societies and of the issues surrounding postindustrialism have argued that we may be experiencing a profound shift away from an era in which class-based economic interests overshadow all other concerns, to one in which numerous other issues, such as status and quality-of-life questions, vie for attention.[20] Other writers, however, have challenged this view, noting a reemergence of economic issues in the capitalist democracies, despite their greater affluence, in today's climate of fiscal uncertainty.[21] One recent study of the equality issue in the United States, Sweden, and Japan concluded that the "forward motion of equality slowed" in the economic climate of the

18. Claus Offe, "New Social Movements: Challenging the Boundaries of Institutional Politics," in *Changing Boundaries of the Political*, ed. Charles Maier (Cambridge: Cambridge University Press, 1987).

19. See Susan J. Pharr, *Political Women in Japan* (Berkeley and Los Angeles: University of California Press, 1981), 170–177, for a discussion of these pressures.

20. Inglehart, "The Silent Revolution in Europe"; and Nobutaka Ike, "Economic Growth and Intergenerational Change in Japan," *American Political Science Review* 67 (December 1973): 1194–1203. See too Ronald Inglehart, "Changing Values in Japan and the West," *Comparative Political Studies* 14 (1982): 445–479; and Flanagan, "Changing Values."

21. See, for example, Peter Hall, *Governing the Economy* (Cambridge: Polity Press, 1986), 3, on the reemergence of economic issues for a current generation.

1980s.[22] And yet in the United States, even in the "conservative era," the issue of comparable worth, the debate over the gender gap in presidential elections, the serious consideration of women, blacks, and members of ethnic minorities for high political office, and protests staged by largely female work groups such as nurses and clerical workers all suggest that status will be of continuing importance in the 1990s. Given broad trends in this century of increased pressure by disparate groups worldwide for social, political, and economic equality, there is every reason to believe that status-based concerns are here to stay.

Struggles for equality in Japan unfold against the backdrop of Japan's feudal past. The legacy of a caste system in which styles of dress and speech were rigidly prescribed and even punishment for crime was mediated by status is a social structure where considerations of rank and status continue to loom large, despite the phenomenal changes that Japanese society has undergone since the feudal era ended in 1868. The persistence of status inequalities as a major characteristic of the Japanese social system has been recognized in virtually all studies of the society, from Ruth Benedict's early analysis of 1946, to popular accounts today directed at American managers hopeful of doing business in Japan, to works by contemporary social scientists.[23] Generally, these analyses all discuss status inequality in terms of the importance that inferior-superior (or junior-senior) relationships and other rank and status considerations are accorded in the ordering of social relationships in Japan. Some years ago the prominent Japanese social anthropologist Nakane Chie drew much attention with a work treating the pattern of Japanese status inequalities somewhat more systematically in which she concluded that Japan is in fact a "vertical" society.[24] Challenging her work is a significant body of literature that stresses the importance of horizontal ties in Japanese society and of indigenous sources of egalitarianism, both historically at the village level and

22. Sidney Verba et al., *Elites and the Idea of Equality: A Comparison of Japan, Sweden, and the United States* (Cambridge, Mass.: Harvard University Press, 1987), 271.

23. Ruth Benedict, *The Chrysanthemum and the Sword* (Boston: Houghton Mifflin, 1946). See William Duncan, *Doing Business with Japan* (Epping, Eng.: Gower Press, 1976); Herman Kahn, *The Emerging Japanese Superstate: Challenge and Response* (Englewood Cliffs, N.J.: Prentice-Hall, 1970); Rodney Clark, *The Japanese Company* (Tokyo: Charles E. Tuttle, 1979); and K. John Fukuda, *Japanese-Style Management Transferred: The Experience of East Asia* (London: Routledge and Kegan Paul, 1988) as examples.

24. Chie Nakane, *Japanese Society* (Berkeley and Los Angeles: University of California Press, 1970).

within groups in many settings today.[25] Examples of such "horizontal alliances" abound, from peasant uprisings against outside authorities in Tokugawa Japan to grass-roots citizens' movements against polluting companies in the 1970s. Some writers have gone so far as to argue that to "persist in the fatalistic notion that Japan is a country of vertical relationships" in the face of such examples is "blindness."[26] But such a conclusion is hardly warranted. As Louis Dumont has argued, "homo hierarchicus"—the ordering of social relations based on hierarchies—is prevalent in all societies.[27] Challenges to authority mounted by grass-roots groups in Japan hardly alter the basic status-linked distribution of power in society. Indeed, Tsurumi Kazuko has argued that "co-equal" patterns of relations in many cases actually sustain and reinforce hierarchy, even if they may at the same time have a transforming or humanizing effect on authority relations.[28]

Most analyses of the hierarchical features of the Japanese social order have emphasized their positive merits for promoting social integration, consensus, and harmony (for example, by showing how the smooth functioning of inferior-superior relations in the workplace contributes to worker satisfaction and productivity).[29] It is clear, however, that conflicts or breakdowns in such relationships potentially have major consequences for the level of social conflict in Japan, for the very reason that status relationships are such key adjustive mechanisms in the social structure.

In recent years scholars have reported and analyzed numerous conflicts

25. See, for example, Amino Yoshihiko, *Nihon chūsei no minshūzō* (Tokyo: Iwanami Shoten, 1980); Kurimoto Shin'ichirō, *Gensō to shite no keizai* (Tokyo: Seidosha, 1980), 216–235; Hayashiya Tatsusaburō, "Chayoriai to sono dentō," *Bungaku* 19 (May 1954): 34–40; Hayashiya Tatsusaburō, *Nihon geinō no sekai* (Tokyo: Nihon Hōsō Shuppan Kyōkai, 1973); Kawashima Takeyoshi, *Nihon shakai no kazokuteki kōsei* (Tokyo: Nihon Hyōronsha, 1950); and Takako Kishima, "Political Life Reconsidered: A Poststructuralist View of the World of Man in Japan," Ph.D. diss., University of Wisconsin–Madison, 1987.

26. Daikichi Irokawa, "The Survival Struggle of the Japanese Community," *Japan Interpreter* 9 (Spring 1975): 466–494, esp. 490.

27. Louis Dumont, *Homo Hierarchicus* (Chicago: University of Chicago Press, 1966).

28. Kazuko Tsurumi, "Social Structure: A Mesh of Hierarchical and Coequal Relationships in Villages and Cities," part 1 of a 3-part series, "Aspects of Endogenous Development in Modern Japan," Research Papers of the Institute of International Relations, Sophia University, Series A-36 (Tokyo, 1979), 22–23.

29. James C. Abegglen, *The Japanese Factory* (Glencoe, Ill.: Free Press, 1958); Robert E. Cole, *Japanese Blue Collar* (Berkeley and Los Angeles: University of California Press, 1971); and Lewis Austin, *Saints and Samurai: The Political Culture of American and Japanese Elites* (New Haven: Yale University Press, 1975).

over status inequalities in Japan, including all three types dealt with in this study: intergenerational conflict, gender conflict, and conflict arising out of hereditary caste distinctions. Thus, conflicts involving inequalities in authority based on age have received much attention in the literature, not only for their impact on social value change and on youth (as manifested in the student movements of the 1960s),[30] but also for their bearing on conflict within Japanese political parties and in organizational life more generally between Young Turks and the senior generations in whose hands power is concentrated.[31] Similarly, conflicts involving the efforts of women to improve their status vis-à-vis men in the family, in the workplace, and in politics have been closely studied,[32] as have those involving some two million persons, referred to as *burakumin*, who today suffer discrimination in marriage, employment, and other circumstances as a result of their hereditary membership in a former outcaste group.[33] Although these various conflicts have been treated as discrete phenomena, all are in fact different forms of status-based conflict.

Why has conflict over status issues been a continuing feature of life in postwar Japan? To answer this question, one can consider the phenomenon in light of broader worldwide trends, as already discussed. But another explanation more specific to Japan entails our viewing the rise in status-based conflicts as the product of an ideological clash in the postwar period

30. Ike, "Economic Growth and Intergenerational Change"; Krauss, *Japanese Radicals Revisited*; and Takahashi Akira, "Nihon gakusei undō no shisō to kōdō," *Chūō Kōron* 5 (May 1968), 6 (June 1968), 8 (August 1968), and 9 (September 1968).

31. See, for example, Mainichi Shinbunsha Seijibu, *Seihen* (Tokyo: Mainichi Shinbunsha, 1975).

32. See, for example, Frank K. Upham, *Law and Social Change in Postwar Japan* (Cambridge, Mass.: Harvard University Press, 1987); Takie Sugiyama Lebra, *Japanese Women: Constraint and Fulfillment* (Honolulu: University of Hawaii Press, 1984); Alice H. Cook and Hiroko Hayashi, *Working Women in Japan: Discrimination, Resistance, and Reform* (Ithaca, N.Y.: Cornell University Press, 1980); and Pharr, *Political Women*.

33. The best-known work in English on the burakumin is George DeVos and Hiroshi Wagatsuma, *Japan's Invisible Race: Caste in Culture and Personality* (Berkeley and Los Angeles: University of California Press, 1966). See also Roger I. Yoshino and Sueo Murakoshi, *The Invisible Visible Minority: Japan's Burakumin* (Osaka: Buraku Kaihō Kenkyūsho, 1977); Hiroshi Wagatsuma, "Political Problems of a Minority Group in Japan," in *Case Studies on Human Rights and Fundamental Freedom*, ed. by William A. Veenhoven and Winifred Crum Ewing, 3:243–273 (The Hague: Martinus Nijhoff, 1976); Eugene E. Ruyle, "Conflicting Japanese Interpretations of the Outcaste Problem (*buraku mondai*)," *American Ethnologist* 6 (February 1979): 55–72; and Mikiso Hane, *Peasants, Rebels, and Outcastes: The Underside of Modern Japan* (New York: Pantheon Books, 1982).

between democratic values and the traditional value structure mediating human relationships. Designating this clash as a post–World War II phenomenon is, of course, an overstatement. Democratic values have had an impact on institutions in Japan ever since the modern period began in 1868, and have been available as a counterideology to those challenging traditionally ordered social arrangements. In addition, Japan has its own indigenous sources of grass-roots democracy. But following World War II, as a result of the Occupation (1945–1952), *demokurashii* was elevated to the status of official ideology. Democratic values have gained even further authority as Japan's contact and identification with the liberal democracies have increased in the postwar period. As a result, democratic ideology— incorporated into the Japanese constitution, spread by a mass educational system, and supported both by internal socioeconomic changes and by the process of Japan's internationalization—now implicitly challenges the legitimacy of the authority exercised by status superiors in social relationships and provides an ideological basis for status inferiors to improve their lot through protest. Thus in everyday life, those attempting to exercise status-based prerogatives derived from the traditional normative system may find the legitimacy of their claim to power questioned.

At the micro-level, this book is concerned with how individuals and groups respond to value change, with how they organize to pursue their grievances, with the cultural legacy constraining and shaping the protest, and with the goals they seek. Such a focus makes it possible to study the nature of equality-based struggles in Japan and their prospects for success in the future. At the macro-level, this book examines how Japan as a state, and Japanese authorities more generally, respond to the rise of new interests in society and to protests over those interests, and what the advantages and costs are of the Japanese approach to social conflict management.

This latter focus is especially important if we are to bring research on Japan into a comparative framework. Western social scientists have long argued, and both the rhetoric of politicians and public officials in many industrial democracies and the popular lore surrounding conflict have suggested, that addressing conflict directly is a good thing: bitter medicine though it may be, conflict, so long as it is actively confronted, is somehow good for the body politic. Opening up conflicts, allowing grievances to be aired, and creating and maintaining institutionalized channels for the resolution of social conflict, they say, are steps that contribute to stability and governability in democratic political systems.

The Japanese approach to social conflict challenges virtually all these assumptions. As this study will show, authorities in Japan view social conflict negatively and, seeing it as disruptive, have evolved an approach to social conflict management that, generally speaking, seeks to avoid and to contain social conflict. The conflict strategies they use make it difficult for protests to gain legitimacy in the eyes of potential supporters and the watching public, thereby effectively precluding a broader base of support. In the aftermath of conflicts authorities use preemptive concessions to address, at least to some degree, the issues that provoked the protest in the first place and thereby head off future conflicts. But in a way that challenges the assumptions of many Western writers about democratic policy-making and successful conflict management, authorities make relatively little show of direct "responsiveness" to protesters; instead they work to keep the troubles outside established conflict-resolution channels, and they remain reluctant to include the protesters in any bargaining over concessions. This Japanese approach to conflict helps explain why, despite recurring protests and the rise of new interests, the overall conflict level in Japan has remained manageable. Clearly the formula entails numerous consequences for protestors and their causes. At the same time, Japan's record of stability and governability suggests that the approach has certain advantages as well, which policymakers and conflict theorists alike would do well to study.

The Study

The methodology of this book has involved the assemblage of data on three cases of status-based conflicts, each of them involving inequalities produced by different ascriptive attributes. The data were gathered over a seven-month period in Japan in 1978, with follow-up work in 1985, and involved over 120 interviews with parties or observers to the conflicts, along with extensive analysis of primary and secondary materials.

In a study of social conflicts it is possible to study protests at many levels, from micro-protests between individuals in daily life to broad-based social movements directed at the state. Two major reasons can be stated for the focus here on organized protests at the grass-roots level. First, given the image that many observers have of Japan as a country with a strong record for containing social conflict, it is important to understand how authorities in that country actually respond to conflicts when and where they first arise. Second, because I had as a major aim the study of the numerous symbolic and psychological as well as instrumental goals involved in status-based conflicts, it made sense to locate conflicts in which these dimensions were obviously present and could be more easily examined.

All three of the conflicts investigated here involve micro-politics—protests that, because they are organized and involve readily identifiable goals, are above the level of interpersonal social conflicts but nevertheless are below the highest level of protest, that of broad-based social movements involving numerous parties. The case study involving former outcastes, it is true, may be seen as merely one conflict episode of a more comprehensive postwar burakumin protest movement, yet it can be studied on its own as well. All three protests unfold within some sort of organizational setting: in Japan's largest and ruling political party, in one division of a public bureaucracy, and in a public senior high school. It is in such settings that the ideological clash providing the dynamic for status-based struggles is most visible, since in each case the "official" ideology is explicit. The way in which conflicts in such organizational settings are resolved, I will argue, has major consequences for the kind of society Japan is and will become.

The first case involves the ascriptive attribute of age. The conflict in question arose within the Liberal Democratic party and resulted, in 1976, in the formation by a group of younger LDP members of a splinter party, the New Liberal Club (NLC). Although several of the LDP members involved in the breakaway, as well as a number (though still a minority) of persons who subsequently ran on the New Liberal Club ticket, were, even by Japanese standards, not young, the leaders of the NLC and most of its members were in their thirties and forties, and they left the LDP at the culmination of a conflict involving numerous grievances associated with their status as juniors in an age-graded party hierarchy. As is the case with most complex intergroup conflicts, numerous causative factors were involved; yet the intergenerational component loomed large.

The second case involves burakumin, a large group that continues to suffer discrimination on the basis of their former outcaste status. As with the Untouchables of India, outcaste status was originally assigned to burakumin (a word meaning literally "people of the village," a reference to the fact that, prior to their official emancipation in 1871, they were required by law to live in segregated villages) because they handled the killing and butchering of animals, tanning of hides, leatherwork, and other tasks regarded as impure and despicable under the tenets of Buddhism. In the post–World War II era, however, long after the legal basis for their outcaste status was removed, the burakumin continued to be exposed to various forms of status-based discrimination. As a result of many centuries of acquiescence to their inferior status vis-à-vis all other social groups, numerous members of this group have risen up against the system in movements that affect both local and prefectural policy and politics in Japan, especially in regions of the country where burakumin are heavily concentrated. Moreover, because both the Communist and Socialist parties of Japan vie for their support, conflicts arising from burakumin activism have had a bearing on prospects for an opposition party coalition at the national level as well.[34]

The particular conflict analyzed here arose in 1974 over the demands of a group of burakumin high school students—backed by the Buraku Liberation League, a militant group with links to the Japanese Socialist party—to organize a study group on burakumin problems in their school in Hyōgo Prefecture near Osaka in central Japan. This conflict culminated in a violent physical confrontation between teachers, who through their union were linked with the Japan Communist party, and members of the league. In 1983 thirteen league members were convicted on charges relating to the dispute; their conviction was upheld in March 1988 and is now being appealed to the Supreme Court.[35]

The third case concerns the ascriptive attribute of sex and focuses on a small group of female civil servants who formed a movement to protest a specific duty assigned to them purely on the basis of sex, that is, the making and serving of tea several times a day for co-workers in their Kyoto office. Conflict between the sexes is central to any study of Japanese status politics, for women, a majority of the population, continue to be treated differently in numerous social contexts strictly on the basis of status. The case selected for study here holds particular interest because it involves conflict over an activity—the serving of tea—that is a significant symbolic act tied to the traditional status of women, and thus provides a close look at the subtle psychological and symbolic issues that characterize status-based conflicts. The conflict is of special significance as well because of the larger issue it raises: namely, whether the state, speaking through the rules, regulations, and employment practices of public bureaucracy, can continue to support an ideology of meritocracy and egalitarianism while its daily routines defy these ideals. How this larger issue, one that arises in most societies today in the values and practices of both public bureaucracies and the private sector, is resolved worldwide has profound consequences for contemporary social arrangements.[36]

34. See Thomas P. Rohlen, "Violence at Yoka High School: The Implications for Japanese Coalition Politics of the Confrontation Between the Communist Party and the Buraku Liberation League," *Asian Survey* 16 (July 1976): 682–699.

35. *Asahi Shinbun*, 30 March 1988, 22.

36. See Alexander Szalai, *The Situation of Women in the United Nations*, Research Report no. 18 (New York: UNITAR, 1973).

2

Contemporary Japan as a Setting for Social Conflict

Few societies offer, in a legal and institutional sense, as free a setting for political participation and for social protest as contemporary Japan. For all their shortcomings up until 1945, the formal institutions of democracy, including competitive elections, a bicameral legislature, and constitutional government itself, have been in place for a century in Japan, dating from the constitution of 1890. These institutions experienced a democratic overhaul in the immediate postwar period as a result of reforms introduced during the Allied Occupation (1945–1952). The constitution and laws that emerged from that period closely resemble those of the United States, especially in the domain of civil liberties, where guarantees mirror those in the U.S. Bill of Rights. In some cases, measures in the Japanese constitution of 1947 go beyond those found in the U.S. constitution. For example, the Japanese constitution had the equivalent of an Equal Rights Amendment—an explicit guarantee of women's equality—even before American women began their postwar struggle (as yet unsuccessful) for such a constitutional provision.[1] Labor's right to organize and strike is likewise well established; except for a "red purge" in 1950 initiated under pressure from the U.S. Occupation forces, labor in Japan has had as free a hand, legally speaking, as in most other major Western countries.[2]

Apart from what the laws say, few critics would hold that in Japan basic democratic rights and civil liberties guaranteed by law are denied in practice through repression. Amnesty International, for example, gives Japan, almost alone among the major countries of Asia, a clean bill of health in its

1. See Susan J. Pharr, "The Politics of Women's Rights," in *Democratizing Japan: The Allied Occupation*, ed. Robert E. Ward and Sakamoto Yoshikazu, 221–252 (Honolulu: University of Hawaii Press, 1987).
2. Public employees, however, are forbidden to strike.

observance of basic human rights. Indeed, the country has been a major staging area for protests over the fate of dissidents in other Asian nations, such as Korea and Taiwan. The postwar Japanese state has a record of restraint in the use of police coercion against those who would engage in violent conflict, a record that compares favorably with that of most Western countries. Police are seldom charged with brutality. In the normal course of their duties they do not carry guns, and incidences of police corruption and bribe-taking are rare.[3] The *kidōtai*, the specially trained police who confront mass demonstrations from behind long shields, are not armed with guns and are known for their tight discipline under pressure. The external constraints on protest, in a legal or coercive sense, are thus relatively limited. Even if one advanced a radical critique and argued that all capitalist democracies tightly control protest groups and movements through some form of surveillance and coercion, it would be hard to show that the situation in Japan is worse than elsewhere; indeed, one could justifiably argue on a number of counts that the situation there is, relatively speaking, somewhat better.[4]

Given the relatively free climate in which protest operates today, then, what are the major constraints that serve to structure and set limits on protest? Japan makes an instructive focus of study in this respect, for, as noted in chapter 1, Japan has been widely recognized as a country with manageable levels of social conflict. Two major explanations address that phenomenon.

The first explanation sees the key to the lack of social strife in the nature of Japanese political culture, the basic values and beliefs of which not only affect would-be protesters themselves, their potential allies, and the watching public, but also work to prevent a protest from emerging in the first place, or at least from winning support if its emergence is unavoidable.[5] The second explanation emphasizes the role of authorities in re-

3. David H. Bayley, *Forces of Order* (Berkeley and Los Angeles: University of California Press, 1976).

4. The level of violence directed by police at antiwar protesters, militant black groups, and other activists in the United States suggests such a conclusion, as do accounts of exchanges between terrorists and the police in Germany, Italy, and elsewhere. As far as surveillance is concerned, a valuable account by Gary Marx of the methods the FBI used under Hoover make Japanese methods sound tame in comparison. See Gary T. Marx, "External Efforts to Damage or Facilitate Social Movements: Some Patterns, Explanations, Outcomes, and Complications," in *The Dynamics of Social Movements*, ed. Mayer N. Zald and John D. McCarthy, 94–125 (Cambridge, Mass.: Winthrop, 1979).

5. The numerous characteristics that operate to discourage social protest in Japan are well summarized in Margaret A. McKean, *Environmental Protest and Citi-*

sponding to protest when it arises.[6] Even if Japan today provides a relatively free environment from the standpoint of coercive or legal methods of protest control, the role exercised historically by authorities in relation to protest was highly repressive; not until quite recently—that is, until the end of World War II—did this situation change. Writers who emphasize this second line of argument often portray the relatively manageable levels of protest in Japan today as reflecting a lag effect.[7] In other words, with the lid of repression now off, protest and grass-roots political participation more generally are only now catching up to the levels found in other advanced industrial democracies, which (except for Germany and Italy) lack a comparable recent history of coercive repression. This "lid-off" theory has long been used to explain developments in the prewar era as well; thus, when legal restrictions (for example, peace preservation laws) and coercive measures were employed to discourage protest at key intervals before the war, the level of protest dropped, but when these restrictions were lifted, as during the early to mid 1920s, democracy flourished and the level of protest increased.[8]

Both lines of explanation are basically correct; but their complementary nature is frequently overlooked. Writers who espouse the political culture approach frequently underestimate the role Japanese authorities played historically in constraining social protest, whereas those who focus on the repressive role of the state and authority typically underplay the effects of political culture in limiting protest. Yet both explanations, I would argue, are crucial for understanding how protest arises in Japan, in the past as well as today. Both, moreover, require further elaboration before they can be used to show how the larger environment impinges on particular protests. As suggested, scholars who emphasize authority have typically focused on the state's intermittent use of coercion and legal restrictions to contain conflict; thus their line of explanation comes to a halt at the end of World War II when these types of repressive measures for the most part

---

zen Politics in Japan (Berkeley and Los Angeles: University of California Press, 1981).

6. Johnson, *MITI and the Japanese Miracle*, is an example of a recent study that emphasizes the role of the state, notably the LDP, in containing protests and thereby enabling the bureaucracy to do its work.

7. See, for example, the line of reasoning advanced in Robert A. Scalapino, *Parties and Politics in Contemporary Japan* (Berkeley and Los Angeles: University of California Press, 1962).

8. Robert A. Scalapino, *Democracy and the Party Movement in Prewar Japan: The Failure of the First Attempt* (Berkeley and Los Angeles: University of California Press, 1953).

disappeared. (In chapter 10 I will extend that reasoning into the postwar era to show how the particular pattern of response to protest, whether coercive or not, serves to structure the environment in which protest arises.) The political culture explanation also falls short when it comes to showing the actual effect of that culture on conflict, for typically it fails to explain how protest can arise in the first place.

In this chapter I propose to show through an analysis of the "political culture of protest" how the political culture impinges on protest when it first emerges. Indeed, not only does the political culture of protest constrain conflict, but it also generates sets of standards about the relative acceptability of various protest behaviors, strategies, and goals. What emerges is an "ideal model of protest," according to which certain forms of protest are judged to be more acceptable than others; in effect, it limits the chances for success of all protest that fails to meet its standards. At the same time, however, the particular ideal model of protest operating in any given national setting offers a set of potential resources to those who would engage in protest. Such a model, with all the rich symbolic meanings and historical associations that surround it, thus provides activists with opportunities to present or "package" the protest—consciously or unconsciously—in ways that maximize its appeal to potential participants, close observers, and the public at large. The notion of an ideal model of protest, then, is offered as an analytic device that is potentially useful for determining which types of protest and protest strategies are likely to work in a given national setting. Indeed, without such a tool many of the conflict behaviors that emerge in protests in Japan—from a seeming "contest to be the victim" characteristic of many exchanges between authorities and protesters, to the use of the radical tactic of *kyūdan* (denunciation sessions) both historically and today by the burakumin rights movement, to the ritualization of many types of protest behavior in Japan—are extremely hard for the outside observer to comprehend.

The remainder of the chapter examines Japan's historical legacy of protest in an effort to clarify the historical relation of Japanese authority to protest and the nature of a political culture in Japan that discourages conflict. A discussion of the resulting ideal model of protest will conclude the chapter.

A Historical View of Protest

Charles Tilly has argued that it is the nature of the state's response to protest that in fact structures protest over time.[9] Seen from that perspective,

9. Charles Tilly, *From Mobilization to Revolution.* (Reading, Mass.: Addison-Wesley, 1978); and Charles Tilly, "Repertoires of Contention in America and Brit-

the picture of Japan is of a society long ruled from above, with all the legal guarantees of civil liberties and free political participation that have become a part of the system since World War II being in fact alien to the Japanese tradition of rule and established authority relations. During the two and a half centuries of centralized feudalism prior to 1868, a system of government evolved that placed the right to rule squarely in the hands of a samurai elite and assigned to those below the duty not only of obeying but also of deferring in a highly ritualized manner to their superiors. The ideological basis for rule, neo-Confucianism, saw virtue in the benevolent conduct of superiors, but it left it to the elites themselves to define what constituted virtuous behavior; those below were in turn enjoined to be dutiful, submissive, diligent, and self-denying—at least with regard to their dealings with authority figures.

Officials occupying positions of power in Tokugawa Japan set severe limits on dissent or opposition; indeed, according to the dominant code of values, conflict had no place in society. Feudalism, as much as neo-Confucianism, may have been responsible for this view. Ralf Dahrendorf, writing about feudalism in Germany, notes that in "the ideology of feudal society there is no conflict between lords and subjects. For the lords, the subjects are but children who need a mixture of paternal severity and paternal care." [10]

Certainly the consequences of protest in feudal times were grim. Today samurai dramas on television and in movies explore the problem of social control and individual freedom in Japanese society by focusing on intra-elite struggles of the Tokugawa period, in which samurai retainers, ensnared in situations of seemingly hopeless injustice, reach their breaking point and protest to their superiors, knowing full well that such an act could result in death, either by ritual suicide on the order of the superior or in a violent fight to the finish. [11]

Peasant protests were also risky undertakings. Such writers as Aoki Kōji, Roger Bowen, Irwin Scheiner, William Kelly, and Stephen Vlastos have made a major contribution to the study of Japan by gathering considerable evidence on peasant uprisings (*hyakushō ikki*) and other protests, which oc-

---

ain, 1750–1830," in *The Dynamics of Social Movements*, ed. Mayer N. Zald and John D. McCarthy (Cambridge, Mass.: Winthrop, 1979), 153–154.

10. Ralf Dahrendorf, "Conflict and Liberty: Some Remarks on the Social Structure of German Politics," in *State and Society*, ed. Reinhard Bendix (Boston: Little, Brown, 1968), 378.

11. Examples include the Kobayashi films *Hara Kiri* (Seppuku) and *Samurai Rebellion* (Jōiuchi), on which see Joan Mellen, *The Waves at Genji's Door: Japan Through Its Cinema* (New York: Pantheon Books, 1976), 86–90.

curred relatively often even in heavily regulated Tokugawa society.[12] Bowen, for instance, records six distinct forms or levels of peasant protest, ranging from a "legal gathering of a crowd" for the purpose of voicing discontent to an illegal "violent movement" organized around broad goals,[13] and arising generally out of dire economic conditions brought on by excessive taxation or high corvée demands. As Vlastos notes, most involved "little obvious disorder or destruction of state property";[14] rather, villagers would submit a petition for redress of grievances to successively higher officials up to the domain level, and when the petition process failed to bring results, they would stage a nonviolent protest—such as a sit-in at the domain office or a verbal denunciation of officials.[15] What stands out is that despite the modest and nonviolent nature of such protests and the dire economic situation that triggered them, authorities almost invariably treated them as illegal activity. Although punishments varied and were sometimes quite lenient, a death sentence remained a possibility for the ringleaders. The disincentives for engaging in protest were thus staggering. In the absence of a legal appeals procedure, there was no formal way in which one could win in a contest with higher authorities. Even when authorities conceded to some or all demands in the wake of the protest, the leaders of the movement were at risk of being treated as criminals and punished accordingly.

There are many ways to gauge the success of a protest act. One crucial measure (to be much discussed in this volume) is the extent to which protesters are able either actually to achieve a victory within the established channels for conflict resolution or to open up such channels for the settlement of future conflicts. Whatever else they may achieve in the way of symbolic victories, protesters cannot hope to meet the ultimate test of success unless they manage to create a "shared universe of discourse" between

---

12. See Roger W. Bowen, *Rebellion and Democracy in Meiji Japan* (Berkeley and Los Angeles: University of California Press, 1980), esp. 70–125; Aoki Kōji, *Hyakushō ikki no sōgō nenpyō* (Tokyo: San'ichi Shobō, 1971); Irwin Scheiner, "Benevolent Lords and Honorable Peasants: Rebellion and Peasant Consciousness in Tokugawa Japan," in *Japanese Thought in the Tokugawa Period, 1600–1868*, ed. Tetsuo Najita and Irwin Scheiner, 39–62 (Chicago: University of Chicago Press, 1978); William W. Kelly, *Deference and Defiance: Nineteenth-Century Japan* (Princeton: Princeton University Press, 1985); and Stephen Vlastos, *Peasant Protests and Uprisings in Tokugawa Japan* (Berkeley and Los Angeles: University of California Press, 1986). Using Aoki's data, Bowen calculates that there were "no less than 6,889 peasant uprisings" during the Tokugawa period (*Rebellion and Democracy*, 72).

13. Bowen, *Rebellion and Democracy*, 72.

14. Vlastos, *Peasant Protests and Uprisings*, 3.

15. Upham, *Law and Social Change*, 68.

the opposing parties, thereby achieving legitimacy for the right to protest and gaining admission to the social process of "negotiation."

Given the continuing illegality of protest in Tokugawa society, outcomes that involved these kinds of adjustments in social arrangements and in the distribution of power were well beyond the protesters' grasp. From this tradition, then, has come a pattern of social conflict management in which authorities seek to retain control of their prerogatives, avoid the creation of legitimate channels for resolving conflict, and marginalize protesters. Such a pattern allows authorities to grant concessions on their own terms and thus to control the pace of social change.

If the state in Tokugawa Japan created a context in which protest was constrained from above, the society had its own powerful set of constraints on the articulation of grievances, born of the same value system that legitimized the official use of severe forms of coercion to limit protest. As Mayer N. Zald and John D. McCarthy note, it is "the social fabric of a society, the structured social relations between individuals and groups," that provide "the backdrop to any attempts at collective action."[16] In a broader sense, social control is a mix of the various methods by which societies regulate themselves and arrive at the measure of agreement necessary to make life in the society possible, whatever the difference of interests.[17] Of these various methods, none is more powerful than reliance on the subtle codes, cues, and expectations set out in daily life to guide us to virtuous and acceptable human behavior.

The dominant values of the Tokugawa period taught Japanese that virtue lay in obedience and deference not only to superiors in face-to-face relations but also to those unseen superiors higher still in the universally accepted, hierarchical ranking system that ordered daily life in feudal Japan. In contrast to Western tradition, in which it is considered reasonable and legitimate that those below must watch out for their own interests, Japan's tradition of rule from above charged the superiors with protecting the interests of their subordinates. Protest on the part of inferiors was thus not only a violation of the proper distribution of duties and responsibilities in human relations; however expressed, it carried as well the implicit charge that superiors had failed to act wisely or fairly in carrying out a commission that was naturally theirs. The fact that the actions of any given superior were likely to be dictated, at least in part, by factors outside the knowledge of his inferiors and arising from the superior's own obliga-

16. Mayer N. Zald and John D. McCarthy, "Epilogue: An Agenda for Research," in *Dynamics of Social Movements*, ed. Zald and McCarthy, 238.

17. Morris Janowitz, "Sociological Theory and Social Control," *American Journal of Sociology* 80 (July 1975): 88.

tions to higher-ups no doubt rendered such a charge all the more inappropriate and unwarranted.

Ideally, of course, superiors did take care of inferiors and preserve their interests, and they had many incentives for doing so: the high value placed on social harmony, the need to preserve good feeling in a society with low mobility, community and peer pressures on superiors to behave acceptably, and economic ties that often bonded inferiors and their immediate superiors together (farmers and a village head, for instance) in meeting responsibilities (such as rice quotas) vis-à-vis those higher up. In villages, bonds of blood, marriage, or tenancy linked larger landowners and agricultural laborers in fictive kinship relations.[18] Better-off landowners, in their role as village officials, often saw their duty of representing the community's interests against domain leaders as something tantamount to parental responsibility, even when, as suggested earlier, the costs could be high.[19] Meanwhile, inferiors, through a variety of methods ranging from displays of loyalty and deference to gift-giving rituals, tried to maximize their chances for favorable treatment from superiors.

In that sense, neo-Confucianism did provide an ideological basis for protest when the principle of reciprocity inherent in superior-inferior relations was transgressed. Faced with extreme violations, peasants considered it morally acceptable—even virtuous—to criticize authority for failing to take care of them.[20]

This legacy of grass-roots protest in Japan is important for understanding social conflict today. It has made available to activists of today a powerful range of symbols and strategies, as well as an ideological justification for protest that predates the influx of Western notions of democracy following the Tokugawa era. At the same time, however, a conflict tradition born in an era dominated by neo-Confucian values sets formidable standards for protest to meet if it is to be judged acceptable—a point to be explored in a moment.

Ostensibly, neo-Confucianism, with its emphasis on social harmony, offers little ideological support for protest. How, then, are we to explain the numerous uprisings that occurred in Tokugawa society, which some writers see as evidence of a long-standing indigenous democratic tradition in

18. See Bowen, *Rebellion and Democracy*, 83, for a discussion of such *oyakata-kokata* (parent-child) relationships.

19. See Thomas C. Smith, *The Agrarian Origins of Modern Japan* (Stanford: Stanford University Press, 1959), 69.

20. See chapter 9 for a discussion of protesters' demands in the context of paternalistic relations.

Japan? Within villages, Irokawa Daikichi and others note, horizontal relations predominated as peasants worked together in a shared struggle for survival. Irokawa sees these peasants' protests against the oppression of higher authorities as clear evidence that the neo-Confucianism promoted by officialdom did not penetrate deeply into village society, where the vast majority of people lived out their lives.[21]

Quite striking, however, is the degree to which such protests accepted the terms of hierarchically based social relationships. Tokugawa-era protesters on the whole accepted the rights of authorities to exercise power over them and, indeed, to punish them for protesting. In many ways, their protests were pleas for greater paternalism—based on their conceptions, derived from neo-Confucianism, of how superiors should behave.

In the Meiji period (1868–1912), profound changes occurred in the environment surrounding protest. One critical act involved the abolition of the caste system that had placed the samurai on top, and along with this system the rigid prescriptions governing people's behavior, dress, and geographic mobility. In effect, this move constituted a challenge to hierarchy itself as the dominant principle of social ordering.

Economic shifts were less sudden, but nonetheless central. In the last one hundred years of the Tokugawa period and into the early Meiji, numerous socioeconomic changes, from the rise of merchant guilds to the increased concentration of land in fewer hands, operated to undermine close community bonds, as did new conditions in the Meiji era, including conscription and rising tenancy due to heavy taxation.[22] In the first years of the Meiji era, protests by farmers and by former samurai left out of the Meiji settlement were more frequent than in the past. Partly to channel social conflict into nonviolent forms and partly to create a state capable of winning the respect of the West, Japan in 1890 introduced limited suffrage; although initially confined to 1 percent of the population, by 1925 this franchise had expanded to include all the adult male population. Even if opportunities for political participation were modest, they offered at least some possibility for formal influence on decision making from below.

Meanwhile, new ideological forces, operating in a society long insulated from world intellectual currents by a Tokugawa-era policy of national isolation, began to challenge Confucian notions of hierarchy and of social harmony as the highest good. The works of Mill, Spencer, Tocqueville, Vissering, and other Western writers underlay the forging of a Japanese individual-rights doctrine, which in turn provided a new ra-

21. Irokawa, "The Survival Struggle of the Japanese Community," 466–494.
22. See Bowen, *Rebellion and Democracy*, 92.

tionale for protest.[23] Economic forces also mounted a challenge to the traditional patterns of relations between inferiors and superiors. Bowen, for example, holds that the "early market liberalism" of the Meiji era allowed the rise of a democratic consciousness, since market contracts, based as they are on a notion of "equal and free parties in terms of stated rights and duties," are in basic opposition to the feudal covenant between those who are legally unequal.[24]

These changes cannot be assessed without reference to the power of the state and its use of ideology to countermand and limit their potential impact on basic values and the conditions surrounding social protest. The Meiji state—for which fundamental social change was never a goal— stepped in immediately to revamp and reinforce Confucian principles of social harmony and relations to meet the challenges of the new era. Even as a modern market economy took shape in Japan, the traditional small shops and family-run industries offered an environment in which an older formula for social relations based on hierarchy could be easily applied. At the same time, the new factory managers of industrializing Japan drew on Confucian values to construct an ideology for monitoring and directing behavior in the workplace.[25] And the emperor-centered ideology eventually promoted through state Shintoism gave average people a system of meaning congruent with the past to help them cope in a turbulent period of change.

The new constitution that brought the Imperial Diet into being carried forward Tokugawa social principles by stating subjects' duties while failing to guarantee their rights. The basic values that in Tokugawa Japan had defined the boundaries of obligation and responsibility in human relationships continued to be based on hierarchy and natural inequality in social relations. Indeed, in the Meiji-era "samuraization" of society sponsored by the ex-samurai elite who led the country, a warrior-caste ideal of duty to superiors became a part of the national ideology. The newly created public education system affirmed, through its "morals" course, a hierarchical social order in which superiors exercised authority on behalf of their inferiors and inferiors showed them deference; final authority, of course, was vested in the emperor at the top of the social pyramid. While it is true that

23. See Scalapino, *Democracy and the Party Movement*, 71–78; also Bowen, *Rebellion and Democracy*, 182–212.

24. Bowen, *Rebellion and Democracy*, 124.

25. Andrew Gordon, *The Evolution of Labor Relations in Japan: Heavy Industry, 1853–1955* (Cambridge, Mass.: Harvard University Press, 1985).

the state itself occasionally used Western notions for its own ends (conscription, for example, which farmers fiercely resisted when it was first introduced in 1873, was promoted as an extension of "freedom and equality to all"),[26] in general the state actively promoted the traditional ideology of social relations, as reflected in the Meiji constitution, up until the end of World War II.

Meanwhile, the resources available to the state for meeting the ideological and other challenges of the new age increased. Thus, although the first years of the Meiji era saw a rise in the number of protests by farmers, former samurai, and others opposed to the regime, as the Meiji leadership consolidated its power and used a newly conscripted army to put down conflict, mounting major social protests became increasingly difficult.

Conditions improved in significant ways in the Taishō era (1912–1926). "Taishō democracy" made it possible for proletarian parties, unions, and other movements, including social movements such as early women's rights and women's suffrage groups and the buraku liberation movement (Suiheisha, or the "Levelers'" Association), to organize and, in the case of the proletarian parties, to compete in elections. At the same time, however, through a variety of noncoercive methods, authorities responded to protest in ways that had the effect of co-opting or discrediting protesters and marginalizing protest itself. (See chapter 8 for more on these methods with respect to contemporary Japan.) Coercive measures were also resorted to on occasion. Even in this most democratic period of the prewar era the state sometimes used the police to break up protest meetings (or to stand back and allow right-wing groups to do so), enforce censorship, maintain surveillance on political activists associated with proletarian parties or movements, and force a change of attitude and belief in radicals who had become enamored of revolutionary ideologies.

By the late 1920s, ever-mounting restrictions on protest had brought an end to the brief interlude of Taishō democracy. Subsequently, although the political party system remained in place through the 1930s, mass arrests and forced "conversion" (tenkō) of communists and other radicals made open protest activities virtually impossible until after World War II.[27]

Through the turbulent first three decades of the twentieth century, certain types of social protest unquestionably were gaining an increased le-

26. Hane, *Peasants, Rebels, and Outcastes*, 18.
27. See Scalapino, *Democracy and the Party Movement*, chaps. 8 and 9, for a discussion of the protest climate in prewar Japan.

gitimacy. Certainly the overall level of overt social and political protest was far higher than at any time in the Tokugawa period. Nevertheless, the disincentives were staggering. Waves of coercive acts by state authorities made it clear that many forms of social protest were deemed illegitimate—indeed, potentially dangerous. And traditional values governing relations between inferiors and superiors were gaining even greater moral force through their new linkage to a nationalistic, emperor-centered ideology.

Through the changes in Japan following World War II, democracy and egalitarianism gained powerful new underpinnings. As indicated earlier, both principles guided the revision of the constitution and other laws, as well as the reform of public institutions: by fusing with indigenous traditions of grass-roots democracy and communitarianism they became, in effect, the "official" ideologies governing social relations. Numerous other factors (apart from democratization itself) have also operated to support ideological change and to erode the traditional framework of hierarchically ordered social relations. Internationalization, for one, has validated egalitarianism and human rights as desirable principles. Increased economic prosperity likewise has eroded the dependency that is the basis for inferior-superior relationships, thus presenting the individual with more options for self-advancement. Higher education levels have had the same effect. The nuclear family has removed the constraints placed on the individual to meet the expectations of an extended family—expectations that often entailed great personal costs. Urbanization has had a similar influence, by removing the individual from the strong community pressures characteristically found in Japanese rural life.

Despite these changes, the ideological reality in postwar Japan is complex on this score. In effect, democracy and egalitarianism as ideologies vie for cultural support with a traditional ideology based on hierarchy and status that continues to have strong backing from older generations in positions of power. Although communitarianism, another important current of the traditional ideology, does operate within groups to create a basis for cooperation across status lines, it does so in a way that preserves hierarchy; indeed, according to its tenets an assertion of rights is judged to be fully acceptable only under extreme conditions. In many areas of Japanese life, such as the private business sector, public bureaucracy, and rural community, a hierarchically grounded ideology of social relations operates as the "real" ideology, even if the "official" ideology, as set forth in public pronouncements, is based on democracy and egalitarianism.

A gap between the ideal and the actual exists in all societies, of course—as Gunnar Myrdal, for example, long ago argued with respect to the issue of equality.[28] (Indeed, even in the American South prior to the civil rights movement, blacks could advance by enjoining white southern Americans to live up to their democratic ideals.) But in Japan the gap is not one between deeply held, *indigenous* ideals and the reality of their application to certain groups (as in the case of the American South). Despite a grass-roots tradition of communitarianism that, scholars argue, has many egalitarian and democratic elements, most Japanese continue to view the official ideology, with its linkage to a notion of individual rights, as basically "Western." Thus in Japan the gap is one of *foreign* ideals as official ideology versus practice with respect to *all* groups.

From the standpoint of status inferiors in Japan, however, the implications of the complex ideological changes that have occurred since 1868, and especially since World War II, are far-reaching. Democracy and egalitarianism together have become a viable counterideology for individuals dissatisfied with the traditional ways of resolving conflict who are prepared to engage in overt protest to try to improve their lot. Especially for the younger generations, democracy and egalitarianism represent not only the "official" ideology but increasingly the "real" one as well. Yet because senior Japanese educated at least in part before or during the war still dominate in business, bureaucracy, and elsewhere, the values of younger people often conflict with those of the organizations in which they find themselves. The situation is even more complex because the youth of today, even as they learn democratic principles in school, are socialized into traditional patterns of deference behavior as well; they must therefore operate within a dual ideological system.

Numerous factors in Japan constrain the emergence of democracy and egalitarianism as both the "real" and the "official" organizing principles in social relations. A key factor, as noted earlier, is that elites in Japan, who as status superiors enjoy the largest share of prerogatives, clearly have little to gain from actively promoting and legitimizing a social ideology that does not favor their interests. But other elements operate as well. As Takie Lebra has argued, Japan is a society in which the importance of social relations predominates over abstract principles.[29] It is therefore hard for a set of abstract principles that many people see as "Western" to become efficacious.

28. Gunnar Myrdal, with Richard Sterner and Arnold Rose, *An American Dilemma: The Negro Problem and Modern Democracy*, 2 vols. (New York: Harper, 1944).

29. Takie Sugiyama Lebra, *Japanese Patterns of Behavior* (Honolulu: University of Hawaii Press, 1976).

The People's Republic of China (PRC) provides an important contrast with Japan in this respect, since both countries have had a traditional social ideology based on Confucianism that emphasizes social harmony and hierarchy. Although support for a new ideology in the PRC has come from the state in the context of a major social revolution, numerous accounts nevertheless reveal a continuing struggle to render its adoption "real." In Japan, since the same process has gone on without a revolution and with relatively weak support from the state, it is little wonder that the "official" ideology has been so slow in becoming "real."

Another factor supporting ideological duality in Japan may be the cultural tendency to maintain seemingly conflicting sets of beliefs simultaneously, an attribute of what Tsurumi Kazuko has called the "many-layered" personality of the Japanese.[30] Finally, because Japanese often ignore nominal rules in favor of informal approaches to problem solving, new rules gain currency only with difficulty. This tendency, which is reflected in many areas of life—for example, in contract negotiations, where the practice of overlooking legalisms and of resorting instead to informal understandings is widespread—clearly makes the process of incorporating new abstract principles into the domain of everyday life a slow one.

Ideological shifts occurring over the last century, then, have laid the groundwork for major changes in protest behavior in Japan. Even if democracy and egalitarianism lack full acceptance as principles governing social relations, they have relatively strong support in the culture, and thus have become an important counterideology for status inferiors who wish to improve their position through protest.

The Political Culture of Protest in Japan

Given the tradition just described, it is easy to see that many characteristics of the mass political culture of contemporary Japan pose barriers to those who would engage in conflict: deference to authority; hierarchy as the dominant ordering principle in social relations; a strong antipathy to overt expressions of conflict; a preference for consensus and compromise in the name of maintaining social harmony, even if compromise masks fundamental disagreements or inequities in benefits among the parties involved; a "longer view" in the approach to social problems, in which long-term, evolutionary solutions are favored over outcomes that necessitate

---

30. Kazuko Tsurumi, *Social Change and the Individual: Japan Before and After Defeat in World War II* (Princeton: Princeton University Press, 1970), 13.

immediate remedies in an atmosphere of open conflict; and a view that under all but a handful of conditions denies protest basic legitimacy.

The "passive" or "parochial" nature of Japan's political culture has been revealed in numerous surveys and studies and may be seen in a close examination of the political landscape in Japan, despite the various manifestations of protest behavior and attitudes described at the outset of chapter 1.[31] The political parties are not mass-based. In 1986 the largest opposition party, the Japan Socialist party, had only eighty-six thousand members, giving it one of the smallest bases of any major socialist party in the democratic industrial world.[32] And although the Liberal Democratic party claims well over a million members—who, through payment of modest dues, may vote in elections for party president whenever these are held— the flow of organizational efforts and funding in the party is top down. Volunteeristic, grass-roots participation is decidedly not the rule.

Meanwhile, although the labor movement has been more successful at organizing workers than have unions in the United States, most of these workers belong to enterprise unions, which, constrained as they are by close labor-management relations, are inherently more conservative than craft and industrial unions. Similarly, although some peak protests, such as that over the United States–Japan Mutual Security Treaty, have won broad public sympathy and support for a time, few protest movements have managed to overcome the public's "passive formalist" approach to politics, whereby most people confine their political participation to such mainstream acts as voting and eschew protest activities. Only a small minority of Japanese feel called upon to participate in politics more actively, especially in relation to national political or social issues. Although the Japanese are joiners, with a rate of membership in groups of various kinds that is one of the highest in the world, their participation in political groups is another matter: only 13 percent of the total population, according to one study, belong to political organizations—the lowest figure for any nation studied except India. Furthermore, even most of these memberships grow out of the individual's far deeper attachment to some nonpolitical group.[33] Those who challenge authority figures and organize

31. See Bradley M. Richardson, *The Political Culture of Japan* (Berkeley and Los Angeles: University of California Press, 1974).

32. See J. A. A. Stockwin, *Japan: Divided Politics in a Growth Economy* (New York: W. W. Norton, 1982). The 1986 figure for the JSP membership is from *Asahi Shinbun*, 24 October 1986, 2.

33. Sidney Verba, Norman H. Nie, and Kim Jae-on, *Participation and Political Equality: A Seven-Nation Comparison* (Cambridge: Cambridge University Press, 1978), 100–102.

to press for their demands in Japan thus confront strong currents of resistance from those around them; typical Japanese, even if they may approve of the *idea* of political and social participation, strongly oppose open manifestations of conflict and are predisposed to accept authorities' view of protest.

The political culture surrounding protest greatly constricts and weights the options available for challenging unsatisfactory authority relations. In issues involving unequal distributions of resources between two parties, for instance, historically four choices have been open to individuals or groups in the weaker position. First, they could attempt to improve the situation through the use of traditional formulas open to persons in a position of dependency, including displays of loyalty and gift-giving rituals. Second, they could adapt, and merely endure the unsatisfactory terms. Third, they could engage in covert protest, perhaps by failing to engage in expected behavior (in the protocol of greeting a superior, for example) or meeting expectations minimally. Ideally the superior, alerted to the inferior's dissatisfaction, would then take steps to remedy the situation; in an organizational or community context, such methods often worked by bringing collective pressure to bear on the superior. Finally, status inferiors could engage in numerous overt forms of protest, ranging from direct complaints to the superior regarding their grievances to collective action.

The political culture of protest pressed the individual or group to explore the first three routes and to turn to the fourth only as a last resort. Certainly, if trying to improve the situation through traditional formulas failed, the social rewards for adapting to the situation could be substantial. The frequent use in Japan of the expression *shikata ga nai* (it can't be helped) reflects the view that resignation is a reasonable response to unsatisfactory circumstances, while film and fiction continue to suggest that those who accept their lot in a spirit of self-sacrifice deserve high rewards for virtuous behavior.

Implicit in these choices is an ideal model of how conflict is to be avoided or resolved in a hierarchical society, with the following key tenets:

1. Superiors have the initiative in the relationship: ideally they anticipate an inferior's grievances and address them in the interest of preserving harmony.

2. Collective pressures, such as from the community or company, act as a check on unacceptable behavior by superiors toward inferiors.

3. Homogeneity (based on shared experience, attitudes, language, and

so forth) operates to insure that superiors understand the vantage point of inferiors and take their position into account.

4. A long-term perspective in social relations means that it is in the superior's interest to make accommodations now in order to insure good relations in the future.

5. An inferior may let the superior know that the latter's behavior toward the inferior is unacceptable so long as the methods of relaying this information are consistent with the goal of maintaining social harmony.

6. When the various correctives on a superior's behavior fail to bring about a desired result, the inferior must adjust to the situation—and there are payoffs for doing so.

Numerous factors both historically and today have supported this neo-Confucian model for dealing with protest. In a group-oriented society, the force of collective pressure in the community or other social group, on both superiors and inferiors, proves a powerful corrective on unacceptable behavior and on the emergence of conflict itself. James S. Coleman found in the United States, for example, that webs of affiliation had numerous effects on conflict behavior: persons with extensive community ties are, he discovered, less likely to engage in overt protest behavior, whereas the more "apart" individuals are from social networks, the greater the chances are that they will behave with violence.[34] Moreover, when organizational density (that is, density of the network of organizational affiliations) is high among potential participants in a conflict, it is likely that the whole community (or organization) will be pulled in—yet another powerful constraining effect on conflict.

In the case of Japan, its very homogeneity—the common language, shared history, and extraordinary sense of "we-ness" that Japanese people feel—creates a strong basis within inferior-superior relationships for status inferiors to believe superiors capable of understanding their situation, a basis that is often missing in societies with major language, religious, ethnic, or other differences. Various historical forces in the broader environment as well have supported or promoted the view that self-sacrifice and acceptance are appropriate responses to all but the most oppressive conditions. In the prewar era, for example, an emperor-centered nationalistic ideology asserted that sacrifice and delayed gratification were necessary in the name of Japan; the larger goals connected with nationalism and the need to keep pace with the West should, it was held, take

34. James S. Coleman, *Community Conflict* (New York: Free Press, 1957).

precedence over individual needs—and in any case, the cultural emphasis on the group over the individual made individual claims uncompelling.

The Challenge for Status-based Struggles:
The Problem of Legitimacy

Independent of the role played by the state in containing protest, then, the political culture itself sets constraints in defining what forms of conflict are acceptable. These operate on protesters, potential recruits to a social movement, and the public alike. The psychological factors that impinge on those with social grievances who must decide whether to incur the risk of actively trying to improve their lot make the formation of a protest difficult from the outset. In all countries the gap between an experienced sense of injustice or of opposition to the terms of social arrangements, on the one hand, and the actual organization of a protest, however modest, on the other, is great, but in Japan, with its particular political culture of protest, these steps are especially difficult to take. Even the acutely alienated individual recognizes how vast the gulf is between a grievance and an overt protest over its cause. Similarly, once an individual has overcome such constraints and joined in a protest, a strong wave of self-doubt with regard to the appropriateness of the protest may cause that person to drop out. The same factors serve to limit the appeal of the protest in the eyes of potential supporters and the public.

The success of social protests in complex industrial societies stands or falls largely on the organizers' ability to build networks of supporters and allies and to win the sympathy of the watching public. When protest itself is seen as basically disruptive, undesirable, or even selfish, independent of the merits of its cause, this task becomes all the more onerous. The historical legacy of protest in Japan thus structures not only the prospects for what can be achieved through protest but also the very nature of protest itself.

The central problem of Japan's particular legacy is that protest, so long repressed or constrained both by the state and by dominant social values, is far from achieving full legitimacy. As studies conducted in other countries suggest, social protest gains public acceptance in any given setting only gradually, with many setbacks along the way (see chapter 10 with regard to Germany and England). Gaston Rimlinger, for example, traces the long and difficult struggle of labor in Germany and in Britain to legitimate their protests; fundamental changes, he shows, had to occur not only in the attitudes of employers and government officials but in labor's own attitude and outlook as well—a process that took several centuries to complete.[35] In Japan, with its long history of suppressed social protest and a dominant political culture strongly antagonistic to overt conflict, the struggle to legitimate protest continues.

A study of the extensive literature on social protest suggests the existence of four distinct types of social conflict (see table 1), all of which have had numerous expressions in Japan, both before and after World War II. Class-based conflicts waged for material benefits have particularly long roots going back to the peasant uprisings of the feudal era and traceable in the twentieth century in the growth of the labor movement and in farmers' protests. Value-based conflicts also have a long history in a country where much protest has been justified in the name of the emperor, a potent moral symbol. Nationalism—in the Meiji period, in the late 1920s and 1930s, and sporadically since then—has given rise to numerous protests (those of the 1930s led often by military men) that relied on the emperor as a legitimating symbol and were guided by a belief in a superior national destiny for Japan. Conflicts over status and quality-of-life issues, in contrast, represent a "new politics" in Japan, even if (as was shown above) both have, to a more limited extent, historical roots of their own. Quality-of-life issues have come to the fore quite recently as a major locus of social conflict. The prominence of citizens' movements to fight industrial pollution and government land-use policies (for example, those concerning Narita Airport and disputed land in the path of the *shinkansen*, or bullet train) reflects changes in consciousness and basic values that are occurring in many increasingly affluent societies. Certainly, the greater importance accorded quality-of-life issues closely parallels Japan's own rising status as a major economic power. Status politics has been similarly spurred by postwar changes in values and consciousness, although the history of status-based struggles reaches back to the Meiji period.

In any society, certain types of social protest will be seen as more appropriate than others. Labor activism, for example, has gained a relatively high degree of legitimacy today in most industrial democracies owing to the long history of unionism in those countries, even if potential supporters and the public may disagree with the specific goals of individual labor actions. As suggested above, social conflicts focused on material or moral issues have particularly long roots in Japan and so have gone further in achieving acceptance. Indeed, social conflict over material issues represents the single greatest tradition of protest coming out of the Tokugawa period, when the peasantry often suffered extreme economic hardship,

35. Gaston V. Rimlinger, "The Legitimation of Protest: A Comparative Study in Labor History," in *Protest, Reform, and Revolt*, ed. Joseph R. Gusfield, 363–376 (New York: John Wiley, 1970).

Table 1. Types of Social Conflict

Type	Basis for Organization	Goals	Japanese Examples
Acquisitive	Class-based	To gain material benefits	Peasant uprisings (*hyakushō ikki*) in the Tokugawa era; farmers' protests, such as rice riots, in pre–World War II Japan; labor disputes
Quality of life	Issue-based	To redress specific problems external to the individual that affect living conditions	Citizens' movements and litigation over pollution or land use policies (anti-*shinkansen*, anti–Narita Airport); peace movements
Moral, religious, ideological	Value-based	To change others' behavior according to a set moral code	Right-wing nationalist protest in the 1930s and since; postwar protest of government corruption; political activities of new religions
Equal rights ("status politics")	Status-based	To address grievances arising out of unequal treatment of disadvantaged groups	Prewar suffrage and rights movements; prewar protests by Suiheisha (the Levelers); Meiji protests by dissident ex-samurai; women's movements; student movements and other struggles involving generational issues; postwar protests by burakumin, Koreans, and Ainu; protests by handicapped

and this trend was reinforced in Meiji Japan through such forces as the changing market economy.

The dominant mode of value-based conflict, for its part, in which protest was justified in the name of *bushidō* or in the name of the emperor and of the moral code he embodied, drew on values that were shared by both the elites and society at large, making its claim to legitimacy by far the strongest.

Status-based conflicts in Japan, I would argue, have had the weakest claims to legitimacy of all major types of protest. In the Tokugawa era, when the guiding ideology based social distinctions on natural inequalities, status-based protest had no real ideological underpinnings and was as a result virtually precluded. After the start of the Meiji period, however, ambiguity over the issue of status created conditions under which status-based protest could arise. The most important ideological basis for protest lay in the formal abolition of the caste system and in attacks, both implicit and explicit, on the notion of social distinctions, fueled by newly available Western ideas of democracy and socialism. At the same time, however, the old caste system was quickly replaced by a new version of hierarchy based on two ascriptive attributes—age and gender. And just as any hierarchical society needs an apex (in Japan, the emperor), so must some group be designated as occupying the bottom of the social pyramid. Thus burakumin found that despite the official end to caste distinctions, they, more than any other former caste, continued to be treated on the basis of their former status.

But the limited acceptance of the foreign ideologies, the powerful validation for the notion of social inequalities, and other factors continued to pose problems for the legitimation of status-based protest. Such movements as those for women's rights, women's suffrage, and burakumin rights early in the twentieth century challenged the very basis of Japanese social arrangements prior to World War II, and so could claim no more than the most limited popular support. Only in the postwar period, then, when democracy became the official ideology, has status-based protest enjoyed a serious claim to legitimacy; those questioning the terms of status relations thus have less of a tradition to call on than do more "mainstream" protesters. This situation in turn affects how status-based protest is viewed by the state and authorities more generally, the watching public, potential allies to the protest, and the participants themselves.

An Ideal Model of Protest, Japanese-Style

Although certain types of social protest have gone further than others in achieving popular acceptance, apart from the actual issues at stake in a given protest action (material, in the case of a class-based protest, for example, or over treatment of a given group in the case of a status-based protest), certain characteristics will maximize its chances of winning public sympathy. Charles Tilly has argued that any given cultural setting has a particular "repertoire of collective action," ranging from written requests for action to mass demonstrations, that protesters may call on; this repertoire derives from the conceptions of rights and justice that prevail in the population, the relevant population's prior experience with collective action, and so on.[36] Carrying that notion forward, I would suggest that a particular cultural setting can likewise be seen as generating a set of popular standards against which protest may be *judged*, and that these standards constitute an "ideal model of protest." In Japan, with its particular tradition of protest and dominant social values, the ideal model of social protest appears to have at least five characteristics:

1. *Only the most extreme situations of injustice or deprivation should give rise to protest.* Prevailing social values have stressed obedience, endurance, and self-sacrifice in the face of difficulties. Japan's dominant tradition of social protest has involved peasants, farmers, and blue-collar workers in situations of utter economic desperation due to food shortages, usurious interest rates, forced conscription, and oppressive working conditions, or intra-elite conflicts in which protesters could face death as a condition for waging the protest. Thus the bases for protest are held to rigorous tests of justification.

2. *Protests (other than those over survival issues) ideally are guided by a high moral purpose.* There is no greater test in Japan than that to determine whether protesters are "sincere," that is, guided by a high moral purpose and not just "selfish" personal considerations. This characteristic appears to arise out of the cultural emphasis on selfless duty to higher authority and to a higher code of behavior, as embodied in the protest behavior of samurai and, later, of right-wing nationalists. (Although other justifications for protests, such as those arising out of a sense of entitlement or a violation of individual rights, may be accorded some legitimacy, their cultural support is far weaker.)

3. *Commitment to the protest should be total.* Consistent with both cultural norms stressing enduring loyalties and strong sanctions for engaging in protest behavior, individuals ideally embark on a protest only when they are fully committed to the cause behind it and are prepared to devote themselves to it.

4. *Protesters ideally demonstrate a spirit of self-sacrifice.* Protest in Japan represents an assertion that the issue under dispute justifies a disruption of social harmony, a highly valued state in Japan. Protesters are thus expected to justify their disruption of the social order by using a culturally approved formula, self-abnegation. In a society in which the good of the group or community is given priority over the individual, displays of self-sacrifice in

36. Tilly, "Repertoires of Contention."

conflict behavior affirm such a value and, in effect, offer proof that "selfish" personal gain is not the motivating factor behind the protest.

5. *The protesters' chosen "repertoire of collective action" should be at a lower level of conflict than that used by the opposing party.* Given how very negatively overt expressions of conflict are evaluated in Japan, protesters generally must demonstrate an ability to contain their level of conflict in order to vie successfully for public support or else offer strong justifications for raising it. Whereas in certain societies activists may show their commitment to a cause by raising the level of conflict, so long as the cause appears justified to observers,[37] in Japan even protesters with aims that are otherwise acceptable to the public may lose support rapidly if they attempt such an action.

None of these features of the ideal model of protest is unique to Japan. In combination, however, what emerges is a set of standards that asks a great deal of protesters: full commitment, a willingness to engage in self-sacrifice for the cause, high moral purpose, and selfless goals for protest. And protests that do not meet these conditions encounter serious difficulties in the winning of public support, difficulties independent of the actual issues at stake in the protest.

This situation is especially problematic when it comes to status-based protests, which, almost by definition, involve certain goals that do not conform to the dominant ideal of protest. These goals are affective and symbolic as well as instrumental, and they entail implicitly—if not explicitly—a claim of entitlement and an assertion of self, running completely counter to the more culturally compelling justification of a "selfless" moral purpose. Similarly, the claim of dire necessity is difficult to make in many types of status-based protests: none of the central claims made in the three case studies in this book—for ending tea-pouring duties, for beginning a high school study group, for wanting a greater say in party decision-making—could be easily justified on such grounds. In contrast, movements launched by victims of severe environmental pollution or against the threat of nuclear war, to cite but two examples, have the advantage of many appealing, culturally compelling justifications working in their favor as a basis for building support.

This ideal of social protest in Japan has an important bearing on status-based protest specifically, not only because of the problems it presents for such actions, but also because its very existence in large measure deter-

37. France, contemporary Iran, and China during the Cultural Revolution are possible examples.

mines how a status-based conflict will proceed—what strategies protesters will use, what criticisms opposing parties will make to discredit their rivals, and so on. It offers resources to protesters and authorities alike. As will be shown later, conflict strategies such as a hunger strike used by burakumin student protesters become effective means of rallying support, consonant with a protest tradition that places a high value on self-sacrifice. Similarly, in our case involving intergenerational conflict, senior LDP leaders, via the media, played on Japanese notions of acceptable conflict behavior by charging that younger-generation Diet members were "not serious" or were "spoiled"—to their own ultimate advantage. The ideal model, then, provides numerous cues for interpreting Japanese conflict behavior in general and for understanding status-based struggles more particularly.

Conflicts are extraordinarily complex phenomena. Because their costs are so high in a society that strongly emphasizes social harmony and conflict avoidance, the key question to ask is why certain individuals, but not others, embark on a social protest in the first place. The next chapter explores this question by looking more closely at the nature of status relations in Japan and by exploring why and under what conditions groups form to challenge the terms of their social position.

3

Intergenerational Conflict: Status Politics in the Conservative Camp

In his autobiography Kurosawa Akira, Japan's internationally known prize-winning film director, fondly recalls his rise to prominence under the wing of his mentor, the director Yamamoto Kajiro. After he was assigned by his studio to serve as an assistant director in Yamamoto's group, he writes, "It was like the wind in a mountain pass blowing across my face. . . . The breath of that wind tells you you are reaching the pass. . . . When I stood behind Yama-san in his director's chair next to the camera, I felt my heart swell with that same feeling—'I've made it at last.'"[1]

Kurosawa's autobiography is filled with warm recollections of the long span of his career as a junior man under Yamamoto's tutelage. He marvels that unlike many film directors in their behavior toward subordinates, Yamamoto "would treat his assistant directors without regard for seniority, asking the opinions of all." The attributes of "Yama-san," as described in the book, are almost godlike: Yamamoto "never got angry. Even if he was furious, he never showed it." He was warm, empathetic, compassionate, and yet brought out excellence in his subordinates because they strove to please him. "How is it possible to express one's gratitude to someone so selfless?" Kurosawa wonders. Although Kurosawa is widely acknowledged as the discoverer of the great Japanese actor Mifune Toshiro, he modestly gives the credit to his mentor Yamamoto. Kurosawa's professional debt to Yamamoto he says, is beyond measure: "No matter how much paper I had, I could never finish writing down everything I learned from Yama-san."[2]

1. Akira Kurosawa, *Something Like an Autobiography* (New York: Alfred Knopf, 1982), 93.
2. Ibid., 97, 99, 100, 107.

The relationship between mentor and junior extended into many facets of life beyond the professional. Since Yamamoto was a gourmet, Kurosawa took up his interest in food. Yamamoto's fondness for antiques and folk art likewise became Kurosawa's. Yamamoto and his wife were the official matchmakers for Kurosawa's marriage. In an autobiography in which Kurosawa at seventy-two makes only the most passing and impersonal references to his wife of thirty-seven years—a film actress who gave up her career to marry him—many pages are devoted to moments he shared with Yamamoto, listening to him, learning from him, drinking with him, sitting at his sickbed.

Those moments when he earned Yamamoto's disapproval are recorded with sorrow. Of one such reprimand Kurosawa writes: "These words have stayed with me; even now I can't forget them."[3] Kurosawa's profound respect for and gratitude to his mentor and his desire to please him are perhaps best summed up in an incident that is quite remarkable by Western standards. During an outing on the town, Yamamoto suggested to Kurosawa and another assistant director that they stop in a movie theater to see a film that they had all worked on together. At one point in the film an error appeared—a mistake for which the two assistant directors were responsible. Yamamoto turned to the two sitting beside him in the darkness and chided them jokingly, whereupon—to the wonderment of the audience sitting behind them—the two junior men sprang to their feet in the darkened theater and, bowing humbly to Yamamoto, offered their profoundest apologies.[4]

Few subjects so warm the hearts of Japanese people as a successful inferior-superior relationship. In such a relationship inferiors display loyalty that is heartfelt, going far beyond the call of duty in performing whatever work is required of them; in this way they gain a sense of meaning and purpose that fills their lives. In return they receive the love, protection, and care of one who has their interests at heart. Kurosawa's account of his debt to his mentor is a story retold countless times in Japanese fiction, drama, and film. Japan's greatest epic tale, *Chūshingura*, is the story of forty-seven *rōnin*, or masterless samurai, who turn their backs on wives, children, aging parents, and other loved ones to avenge the unjust death of their young lord, knowing that they will die as a result of their actions. The tale, retold in numerous film versions and known to every schoolchild, carries the message that there is no higher calling than service to a

3. Ibid., 101.
4. Ibid., 100.

superior, and no greater duty than that of an inferior to the one served. Although a subordinate may sometimes be caught between the contrary pulls of obligation to a superior and obligation to others (in this case, to family and loved ones), in the end honor and meaning go with putting the former before the latter.

A major part of socialization for Japanese children today, as in the past, is aimed at preparing them to participate in a society in which status differences are meticulously observed in social relations. Takie Lebra has noted that much socialization in Japan, even today, centers on "how to treat" seniors. The task goes beyond the general instruction in respect and courtesy toward adults that children in most countries receive. For one thing, the Japanese language is filled with status indicators that must be mastered, from verb endings to wholly different terms of reference depending on the relative statuses of speaker and addressee. For another, there are minute, status-based differences in bowing behavior, which must similarly be learned. Indeed, the various cues are so elaborate and intricate that two Japanese people previously unknown to each other who must suddenly interact socially may be at a loss on how to proceed until their relative statuses are sorted out in socially acceptable ways, such as through exchange of name cards or by asking a pointed series of polite questions. And gift giving in Japan is an art form in itself because of the need to determine the appropriate level of gift based on a complex calculus, with status considerations being paramount.[5] The socialization required to prepare children for proper conduct with superiors is aimed, as is socialization in all countries, at providing them with the keys to becoming "good" and successful adults, for the traditional ideology tells them that if they allow these rules of social behavior to guide their relations with the key superiors in their lives, they can expect to receive certain rewards, both affective and instrumental.

As Kurosawa's account of his relation with his mentor suggests, the sources of emotional gratification are numerous. The psychologist Doi Takeo holds that Japanese experience major emotional satisfactions from relationships in which their dependency needs are met—indeed, that they feel deprived if those needs are not met. For inferiors, he says, the warm good feeling that results from being protected and cared for is a major reward of a relationship. Doi has become well known for his analysis of the

5. For childhood socialization regarding seniors' treatment, see T. Lebra, *Japanese Patterns of Behavior*; and, on gift giving specifically, Harumi Befu, "Power in Exchange: Strategy of Control and Patterns of Compliance in Japan," *Asian Profile* 2 (December 1974): 601–622.

word *amae*, one widely used in Japanese culture, which he sees as capturing the sense of satisfaction that Japanese experience when they put themselves in the hands of another in the expectation that the superior will look out for their interests. Doi has argued that *amae*, an emotion characteristic of children's relations with their parents in all countries, extends widely into relations between adults in Japan and thus becomes a major affective reward for inferiors in social relations.[6]

Other types of emotional rewards occur as well. In a close relationship with a superior who is setting standards of performance and appraising the results, for example, the inferior experiences role satisfaction—feelings of pride and self-esteem—when the evaluation is favorable. Even when the evaluation is less than what was hoped for, duty to a superior carries a moral reward: the emotional satisfaction of having done one's best, and thus of being a virtuous and worthy person, even in adversity.

If the traditional Japanese ideology of status relations and the tales that surround them emphasize the affective rewards of service and loyalty, the instrumental rewards can be multifold. Many types of inferior-superior relationships present opportunities for apprenticeship under optimal conditions. In the contest of a close, affective relationship, the inferior, for example in the role of student or worker, learns and masters tasks and advances as a result. Experimentation is permitted, but in many situations it is the superior who takes responsibility for the most serious mistakes of his inferiors. Even traditionally, certain types of inferior-superior relations were understood to involve stress, such as that between the eldest son's bride (*yome*) and his mother if and when the younger woman went to live under the roof and tutelage of her mother-in-law. But these relationships, too, have had clear-cut instrumental rewards for the inferior: not only does the eldest son's family assume financial responsibility for the *yome* if she is living with them, but the young woman also knows that, by serving out her apprenticeship, she will eventually replace her mother-in-law as senior woman of the house.

Apart from affective and instrumental rewards, the ideal inferior-superior relationship has other attractive features. As with many social roles, lapses are permitted. Even if the demands on an inferior are ostensibly high, certain kinds of nonconformist behavior will be tolerated as a part of the license granted to dependents. For example, in relations between young people and their superiors, it is generally understood that youth are high-spirited and may have strong convictions. Within certain

6. Takeo Doi, *The Anatomy of Dependence* (Tokyo: Kōdansha, 1973).

limits, then, a "good" superior will tolerate or even mildly encourage im-
pulsive conduct, including protest behavior, as long as the behavior is
motivated by high ideals and does not challenge the terms of the relationship itself.[7] Similarly, in relations between males and females, females are
permitted under some circumstances to be more expressive and emotional
than are male subordinates in like situations, and in the workplace women
sometimes are allowed to be less serious about their work than men—an
employer attitude that would be a liability to a career-minded woman but
attractive to someone who wished to limit job commitment because of
family responsibilities.[8] Stress in inferior-superior relationships also has
outlets in the context of the relationship itself, moments of liminality
when inferiors are permitted to air their grievances without incurring
costs, such as through drinking rituals.[9]

Strains inevitably occur in all social relations, whatever the ideology
guiding them. A final reason why relations between superiors and inferiors
work as well as they do for subordinates involves the congruence between
the behavior expected of them in the relationship on the one hand and
dominant norms and values in society on the other. The traditional ideology of social relations based on hierarchy affirmed the prerogatives exercised by superiors and assigned value to the efforts of inferiors to conform
to expectations. Thus, still today, if an inferior finds himself caught in
an inferior-superior relationship that yields fewer rewards than were
hoped for, the traditional ideology gives meaning to perseverance and self-
sacrifice and legitimizes the inferior's acceptance of the terms of the
relationship.

From the standpoint of the inferior, then, the pattern of inferior-
superior relations in Japan and the expectations associated with the role
have held out key rewards for the individual, while cultural support for
accepting the terms of such relationships has been strong. The problem,
of course, is that all inferior-superior relationships do not yield the hoped-
for rewards, or, conversely, the costs of deference may be too high. All
social relationships hold the possibility of strain and ultimately conflict.
The key question, then, is, Under what conditions is conflict likely to sur-

7. Employers' tolerance for hiring students who had taken part in the student
movements of the 1960s would be one example; see Krauss, *Japanese Radicals
Revisited*.

8. See, for example, the discussion of neotraditional women in Pharr, *Political
Women*, 52–58.

9. Victor W. Turner, *The Ritual Process: Structure and Anti-Structure* (Chicago:
Aldine, 1969).

face in interstatus relations? To understand how and why status-based conflicts emerge, we must look first into the lives of individuals and the situations they were in when they embarked on a protest; then we may ask why the rewards inherent in the terms of status relations somehow failed to work for them.

The New Liberal Club Breakaway

On 14 June 1976, six members of the Liberal Democratic party (LDP), the conservative group in power, held a press conference to announce their intention to leave the party. A week later, with the press in tow, they appeared at LDP headquarters in Tokyo and formally resigned. Three days later, on 25 June, they announced the formation of a new conservative political group, the New Liberal Club (NLC). With the next election for the lower house of Japan's bicameral Diet slated for December at the latest, the NLC began a frantic effort to draw other conservatives to their cause. They managed to find the requisite twenty-five candidates willing to throw their lot in with the rebels,[10] of whom seventeen won seats in the lower house election on 5 December 1976—a showing that fell short of the twenty seats necessary to secure the NLC's full legislative status in the Diet but was nevertheless widely hailed as a stunning victory for the club and yet another blow to the beleaguered LDP.[11] Indeed, only through a postelection roundup of conservative independents were the Liberal Democrats able to hold their majority in the lower house.[12]

In the years following the New Liberal Club's breakaway from its parent party until its demise in August 1986 (after a poor showing in the lower house election the previous month), the road it traveled was a rocky one. For all the attention that the NLC commanded at the time of its debut, and despite massive media coverage in Japan of the club's attempt to secure a foothold in the political landscape, the party even in the best of moments met with only limited success, and their efforts ultimately proved insufficient to keep the group alive. By early 1979 the media assessment

10. To have the right to put forward candidates, a political group must offer a minimum of twenty-five candidates in a lower house election or ten in an upper house election; Wagatsuma Sakae, ed., *Roppō zensho* (Tokyo: Yūhikaku, 1967), 94.

11. To have the right to introduce legislation, and thus to fit the official definition of a party, a political group must hold at least twenty seats in the lower house and ten in the upper house; ibid., 62.

12. The LDP won 249 seats in the election, 7 seats short of a majority. When 12 independents joined the party following the election, the party's total increased to 261 seats, giving the LDP a 5-seat majority in the lower house.

was harsh. Summing up the view of many critics, the *Yomiuri Shinbun* observed that the club lacked the indispensable "3 S's"—*seisaku* (policy), *soshiki* (organizational structure), and *shikin* (funds)—necessary to survive as a party in Japan.[13] In the lower house election of October 1979, the NLC captured only four seats, and in November the party's leader, Kōno Yōhei, resigned to take responsibility for the defeat and to meditate on the group's future.[14] Demoralized by its loss of momentum after such a promising start and plagued by internal problems, the NLC for a time appeared to be near an end. Key members returned to the LDP. Although it partially recouped its losses by gaining twelve seats in the lower house election of June 1980, its showing in December 1983 was once again modest.[15] After gaining only seven seats in the July 1986 double election, in August the group ended its decade-long existence and, coming full circle in the protest, returned to the LDP fold.[16]

Why the quasi-party failed to take hold is less important, for our purposes, than why it arose in the first place. The club's electoral hold was minuscule; only occasionally in its decade of existence did it play a role of some significance in Japanese politics.[17] Its major claim to fame is that following the 1983 election it helped to form the only coalition government Japan has had since the LDP was established in 1955. Yet even this success was not the NLC's own making: the poor showing of the ruling party in 1983 sent the LDP once again scrambling for an infusion of outside conservatives to give it a working majority—thus bringing in the New Liberal Club, with six members. For its contribution, the club received a cabinet post in the new government.[18]

Let us now look more closely at the breakaway of the NLC. As suggested in chapter 1, protests are frequently spurred by an entire panoply of

---

13. *Yomiuri Shinbun*, 8 March 1979.

14. *Asahi Shinbun*, 27 November 1979.

15. For the state of the NLC following the 1983 election, see Maki Tarō, "Nakasone 'anrakushi' o takuramu Miyazawa vs. Takeshita no yamiuchi" *Gendai* 18 (March 1984): 122–139; Uchiyama Hideo, Uchida Mitsuru, and Iwami Takao, "'Hakuchū seiji' e no kitai to fuan," *Ekonomisuto* 62 (17 January 1984): 10–19; and Takabatake Michitoshi, "Jimintō gosan to jikai no kōzō," *Ekonomisuto* 62 (3 January 1984): 10–21.

16. One of the seven, former NLC chairman Tagawa Seiichi, held out; he formed his own one-member group, Shinpotō, in January 1987.

17. Prior to its gain in the 1983 election, the major example of NLC influence was in the election of Ōhira as prime minister in 1979, in which the NLC vote was decisive in Ōhira's win over Fukuda; see Gerald L. Curtis, *The Japanese Way of Politics* (New York: Columbia University Press, 1988), 32–33, 40–41.

18. Ibid., 33–34.

contributing factors, and this case is no exception. In some ways, the secession was only one of numerous creaks and strains that the giant LDP, with its many warring factions, was feeling in the 1970s. In an era when the party's base of support was steadily eroding, it was to be expected that internal conflicts would intensify in the tug-of-war over accountability for the party's decline and in disputes over how further losses were to be arrested. Policy disagreements fueled the conflict from the outset, but by the time of the break the central issue was the Lockheed scandal and the broader problem of "dirty money politics" in the LDP. The secession was also a power play—the effort of a small group of mavericks to jockey for a more advantageous position in the conservative camp's power arrangements. Interpersonal rivalries figured in the breakaway as well and had their own elaborate history, what with Kōno Yōhei's famous political family's own long postwar record of challenging conservative authority.[19] Even today reporters and scholars who have analyzed the rebellion are not in full agreement on why the Kōno group left the ruling party.

Whatever other more immediate motives may have spurred the protest, the break at a deeper level may be seen as an episode of status politics that focused on the distribution and prerogatives of authority based on seniority. Kōno Yōhei, his two chief lieutenants, and most of the men who subsequently joined the cause were in their thirties and forties. Significantly, the departure of the original six from the LDP came at the culmination of a conflict that involved both the dissenters' status as juniors in a party hierarchy determined largely on the basis of seniority and the nature of the leadership exercised by a senior generation of LDP members. Thus, the stage for the protest was effectively set by the terms of status relations within the Liberal Democratic party itself.

In party politics, as in Japanese organizational life more generally, the distribution of authority is weighted heavily in favor of more senior people who monopolize the stakes of power—in the case of LDP seniors, money and posts—and allocate them to their subordinates on the basis of rank.

19. In 1971 Kōno Yōhei's uncle, Kōno Kenzō, staged a revolt against then prime minister Satō Eisaku by successfully running against Satō's close associate, Shigemune Yūzō, for the chairmanship of the House of Councillors (see Hans H. Baerwald, *Party Politics in Japan* [London: Allen Unwin, 1986], 94–95). Yōhei's father, Ichirō, provides a much more dramatic example of defiance. In 1960, after the faction he headed failed to gain positions in the new Ikeda Hayato cabinet, he attempted to break with the ruling party by forming a "New Kōno party" (*Kōno Shintō*). When only five or six of his initial fifty followers stuck with him, however, he abandoned the plan (see Togawa Isamu, *Shōsetsu Yoshida gakkō*, vol. 2 [Tokyo: Kadokawa Shoten, 1980], 320–340; and Kishimoto Kōichi, "Kōnoke no hitobito," *Chūō Kōron* 91 [August 1976]: 200–208).

Within the LDP, juniors are expected to acknowledge—indeed, cele-brate—their superiors' authority through deferential behavior. As Takie Lebra has noted, for juniors, "not only *doryoku* ("strenuous effort") but *kurō* ("suffering") is expected of a young person who has ambition."[20] The payoff is long term: by punctiliously meeting role expectations, juniors can eventually enjoy power themselves.

Most legislative bodies employ some type of seniority principle in al-locating leadership positions to members. Even those that do not formally rely on seniority obviously consider experience to be a major prerequisite for high positions. In Japan, however, as a reflection of organizational principles that are widely in operation in everyday life, what is unusual is the *degree* to which the seniority principle guides the allocation of rewards controlled by the ruling party, the *degree* to which power is concentrated in age superiors, and the *degree* to which access to leadership is governed by factors that are beyond the powers of the individual to change—specifi-cally, political age (number of times elected) and, to a lesser extent, bio-logical age.

The distribution of posts and other rewards by the LDP to its members is handled through the five to ten factions into which the party has been divided at any point since its founding, each of which is presided over by a senior LDP Diet member. Because the factions exist outside the formal organizational structure of the party, the allocation process occurs without resort to formal party rules through informal negotiations among status superiors. Although the LDP's official position as a party has been to re-gret and deplore—and, depending on the political mood of the moment, on occasion to outlaw—these factions, they remain the key unit by which the party distributes posts. Party, Diet, and cabinet positions, including the prime ministership, are parceled out on the basis of factional strength. Each faction head then distributes the faction's share of positions to the members waiting below.

Nathaniel Thayer describes the evolution of factions in the Liberal Democratic party after its creation in 1955; in so doing he sets out the terms of the party reward structure:

> As the formal structure began to emerge, it also became hierarchi-
> cal; politicians standing at the peak of the hierarchy got first shot at
> the cabinet and favored party posts. Position in the hierarchy was
> ultimately determined by the faction leader. He gave consideration
> to age and to the number of times a Dietman had been elected,
> common standards that are used throughout the party. But more

20. T. Lebra, *Japanese Patterns of Behavior*, 75.

important criteria were length of time in the faction and degree of service to the faction. A new faction member started at the bottom of the pecking order.[21]

As Thayer notes, position in the hierarchy of a given faction is determined by an intricate set of calculations that take into account political age, biological age, and performance criteria. Figuratively speaking, each newly elected LDP member is assigned a number within his faction and then waits in a queue until his number is called; he may be moved up in line on the basis of performance, but the queue itself is fundamental to the structure of authority within the LDP, and there is no way to avoid it entirely, no matter how faithful one's service to the faction.

The relation between biological age and political age is complex in the case of the Diet. Normally in Japanese organizations, biological age and time in service are congruent considerations. At the top of the organizational pyramid are the oldest persons, who also have the most experience; at the bottom are those who, in terms of both age and grade, are the most junior. This complementarity of attributes is maintained by hiring people of approximately the same age and educational background, who thus begin their ascent up the organizational ladder from a common base point. Because of the nature of Diet membership, however, which is almost never a first career for anyone, biological and political age are often out of sync, particularly in the case of persons who enter parliament in their late forties or early fifties after a long period in the bureaucracy and thus are senior biologically but junior in terms of experience. This incongruence is resolved by assigning priority to political age—specifically, the number of times elected to the Diet—and then further differentiating on the basis of biological age and service to the faction.[22]

The seniority principle has been in place throughout the LDP's history. Indeed, most observers agree that it is far more institutionalized now than in the past. In the 1960s, for example, LDP members with outstanding backgrounds in business or the bureaucracy were occasionally appointed to the cabinet after having served fewer than five terms in parliament; today members routinely must serve six terms before being assigned cabinet posts.[23] Because so many LDP politicians are waiting in line, moreover, reshufflings occur regularly so that virtually all six-termers will get a chance at a cabinet post (in fact, the average period of service in the cabinet today

21. Nathaniel B. Thayer, *How the Conservatives Rule Japan* (Princeton: Princeton University Press, 1969), 23.

22. LDP Diet member Ōtsubo Kenichirō, interview with author, 4 June 1978.

23. Curtis, *Japanese Way of Politics*, 88–90.

is only 278 days).[24] As in all systems based on seniority, these arrangements represent great fairness and even-handedness from many standpoints. All incoming LDP members know that over the first fifteen or so years of their careers in the Diet, regardless how meager their talents, they will hold a succession of posts and will almost invariably serve at least once, if briefly, in the cabinet. In effect, then, the seniority principle presents a minimum guarantee of rewards.

The problem, of course, is for more ambitious politicians who wish to maximize rewards immediately. For them, there are few shortcuts to positions of power and responsibility, no matter how great their talents and abilities or impressive their background. Furthermore, beyond minimal assurances of posts, advancement within the party to the highest levels of power depends on accepting the terms of junior-senior relations and excelling within that framework.

The top power holders are members senior in political as well as (normally) biological age. This top group includes the faction heads, former prime ministers still in the Diet who have transferred factional leadership to junior men, and a few other senior men who function as power brokers in the party. To become a contender for prime minister generally requires ten terms in office, or some twenty-eight years of service, which puts most leaders well into their sixties or seventies before they are seriously considered. Although a few younger men have become top party leaders, their situation is unusual—the most prominent example in recent years being Nakasone Yasuhiro, who became a faction head at the early age of forty-seven upon the sudden death of his predecessor, Kōno Ichirō. Nakasone was not young in political age, however, having served eight terms at the time of his elevation.

Seniority in political or biological age is no guarantee of a top role in the LDP, of course; many senior members, after securing the minimal rewards of the system, are never contenders for a greater share of power. (As Satō Seizaburō and Matsuzaki Tetsuhisa note, only 40 percent of LDP members are ever reappointed to a cabinet post.)[25] Political and biological age (typically both) *are*, however, the essential preconditions to power.

The advice to junior men wanting to ascend the ladder to the top, then, is "Matte, matte" (Wait, wait). Besides waiting, the other key to success is service to the faction, a performance criterion shaped by the very nature of status relations in Japan's ruling party. LDP juniors are expected to ac-

24. Ibid., 90.
25. Satō Seizaburō and Matsuzaki Tetsuhisa, *Jimintō seiken* (Tokyo: Chūō Kōronsha, 1986), 48.

knowledge their status superiors' authority in a number of ritualized ways: by employing a language of deference, bowing respectfully, and displaying an attitude of alertness to the expectations, both expressed and unexpressed, of superiors. For men older biologically but young in political age, the terms of behavior are adjusted somewhat, but some display of deference is required. For men who are junior in both senses, though, "service to the faction" becomes crucial if any advancement beyond the minimum rewards is desired.

Numerous forces operate to make the terms of performance acceptable. A major factor is the high degree of legitimation that traditional authority arrangements enjoy within the LDP. The ruling party (together with its predecessor conservative parties in the prewar period) has embodied and actively promoted traditional norms in junior-senior relations, extolling workers for loyalty to employers, housewives for service and devotion to their families, children for obedience to their parents, and Japanese people in general for work and sacrifices in the furtherance of national goals. Few institutions are thus as committed to a traditional ideology based on hierarchy as is the LDP itself—and the instrumental and affective rewards for accepting these codes have been considerable.

One immediate reward, crucial to junior men for political survival, is funds. Many young faction members state openly that they belong to a faction primarily to get the funds that the faction head distributes to members for campaign and other political expenses. A critical gain for political hopefuls is the LDP endorsement of their candidacy, which, as many writers have pointed out, is an enormous advantage given the complexity of Japan's multimember, single-ballot constituency system. Factional membership provides as well a concrete basis for participation in the political life of the Diet. As veteran LDP member Matsuda Takechiyo once noted, young Diet members "have no [other] way of learning their trade. . . . They have no forum for their ideas. They get no important assignments because they have no political experience. They have nothing to do. Nothing to do and no place to be. It's no wonder they drift to factions."[26] And of course, factional alliance means posts, the promise that, with the passage of time, minimal positions of leadership—and perhaps, further down the road, top positions—will at last be passed out to those loyal members waiting in the queue.

The affective rewards may also be high. As several junior Diet members interviewed for this study pointed out, the LDP is too large a group to relate to on a face-to-face basis. Factions break the whole into manageable

26. Quoted in Thayer, *How the Conservatives Rule Japan*, 40–41.

Table 2. Age Distribution Within the Liberal Democratic Party, 1956–1987
(in percentages)

Generation	1956	1966	1976	1987
Senior (60 and over)	28.6	39.0	40.6	44.3
Middle (50–59)	41.4	39.4	33.6	33.6
Junior (under 50)	30.0	21.6	25.8	22.1

Source: Nihon Seikei Shinbun, ed., *Kokkai binran* (Tokyo: Nihon Seikei Shinbunsha, 1956, 1966, 1978, and 1987).

units and provide a framework within which the individual can fit psychologically. Certain members gain additional affective rewards because of long-standing personal ties with the faction leader through family or earlier political connections.

When we consider that factional membership offers all these immediate financial, political, and psychological rewards, that it holds out the promise of still greater benefits in the future, and that no clear-cut way to gain these benefits exists within the present order except through the factions, then the practical constraints on objecting to the terms of factional membership seem powerful indeed. Given the present distribution of party authority, which grants so little power to junior members, it seems at first glance remarkable that a small group of juniors would have been prepared to defy the terms of party hierarchy and strike out on their own, renouncing all these seeming benefits. Why, then, did the LDP in the mid 1970s become a forum in which status-related grievances found expression?

First, age-structural changes in the party appear to have exacerbated the tensions of waiting to gain political seniority and privileges, for the LDP itself had been aging (see table 2). Following the postwar purges of conservatives and the general shake-up in Japan's leadership during the Occupation, the dominant generation within the LDP when it was formed in 1955 consisted of men in their fifties; in 1956 this group represented 41.4 percent of the party's membership, as opposed to less than 5 percent for the seventy-and-over group. By 1976, however, 40.6 percent of party members were sixty and over (and by 1987, 44.3 percent), with almost 12 percent of total membership made up of men in their seventies. Meanwhile, under-fifty membership increased in the 1970s as compared to the 1960s, leaving more age juniors waiting in line for future rewards.

Moreover, whereas in the 1950s and 1960s an ambitious LDP politician could hope to advance to the cabinet and to other key positions more quickly than his less motivated peers, by the 1970s routinized promotion practices were becoming entrenched.[27] Younger men were waiting for the opportunities to be had when a middle generation of men in their fifties moved up; but with so many posts held by older generations, there was nowhere for the middle generation to go. From the junior men's standpoint, the more fluid system of the past was giving way to a rigid arrangement with a guaranteed minimum of rewards but diminished opportunity for anything more. The mid-1970s media were attentive to this shift, thus mirroring the perception among the party's junior membership that the LDP leadership was dominated, and the reward structure therefore controlled, by a generation of grandfathers.[28]

Second, reward-structural changes in the 1970s were at the same time causing considerable discontent. As discussed above, factional membership carries distinct financial, political, and psychological rewards that can offset whatever dissatisfactions juniors may feel regarding party status relations. Maximum benefits seem to be realized when a number of conditions are met. The financial advantages of factional membership, for example, are of greatest significance when the Diet member must rely on factional monetary assistance to support his campaign. The more financially independent the junior is, or the fewer the resources that the party is offering, the less advantageous factional membership will appear. The same argument holds for the political rewards represented by LDP endorsement and active campaign support as well as for the psychological benefits of factional membership, that it provides a meaningful basis for participation in the political life of the Diet: if endorsements do not promote electoral success, or if alternative opportunities exist for parliamentary participation, then factional membership clearly has less significance. Finally, a key benefit of factional membership exists in the form of future posts. To the extent that junior members believe in the senior generation's ability to command and to distribute these rewards, this factor obviously has great meaning.

When these conditions are considered, it is possible to see why LDP juniors in the early 1970s could have been experiencing less satisfaction from the terms of factional arrangements than in the past. Recent changes in the law had raised questions about the ability of the faction heads to keep up steady financial support for their members. The Political Funds Control Law passed during Miki Takeo's prime ministership forced disclosure of the names of contributors to the party and set limits on individual and corporate donations. In 1976, the year of the breakaway, the vari-

27. Satō and Matsuzaki, *Jimintō seiken*, 42–44.
28. For an analysis, see, for example, *Ekonomisuto*, 7 July 1977, 31.

ous factions raised only half the amount they had collected the previous year, and the LDP itself raised only 7.8 billion yen (30.6 million dollars), down 32 percent from 1975.[29] Although today we can see that the law has in fact had little effect on money levels in political campaigning, which have ballooned in Japan as elsewhere, to politicians in 1976 there was good reason to believe that the financial rewards of factional membership might well be reduced in the future.

The political benefits of LDP endorsement had become increasingly questionable in the wake of the Lockheed scandal and the accompanying issue of party corruption, both of which reduced the value of having famous party members, often the faction head, stump on a candidate's behalf. The psychological benefits may likewise have lost some meaning as additional avenues for participating in the political life of the Diet became available to juniors. In the 1970s, for example, a number of study groups made up predominantly of junior representatives emerged in the Diet. These included the Shinpū Seiji Kenkyūkai (New Breeze Political Study Association), established in 1971, the Hirakawa Society and Seirankai, both founded in 1973, and Kōno Yōhei's Political Engineering Institute (see chapter 6). Study group membership was in no sense a substitute for factional affiliation, since the factions still handled the distribution of posts, but it may have reduced some of the psychological dependence on the faction.

Finally, the future political benefits of factional membership were thrown into question in the mid 1970s by the Lockheed scandal, the party's declining base of popular support, and increased media speculation that the LDP would lose its parliamentary majority. As Kōno Yōhei noted, the faction's counsel to junior members of "Wait, wait" (*matte, matte*) had meaning only when the listener believed that waiting would pay off.[30] But with the LDP's own future uncertain, the party's ability to command and distribute government posts fifteen years down the road was subject to doubt.

All these changes affected the context in which junior LDP members found themselves just before the New Liberal Club breakaway in 1976. To understand why these particular juniors and not others were prepared to strike out on their own, we must look more closely at the rebels themselves.

The secession was led by Kōno Yōhei, who in 1976 was thirty-nine, and his two chief lieutenants, Yamaguchi Toshio, thirty-six, and Nishioka

29. Derek Davies, "Japan's Great Debate," *Far Eastern Economic Review* 98 (4 November 1977): 20–25.

30. Kōno Yōhei, interview with author, Tokyo, 5 June 1978.

Takeo, forty. Kōno and Yamaguchi were both in their third term of office; Nishioka was in his fourth. In addition to their youth, the men shared certain important characteristics. First and foremost, all three were *nisei*, that is, second-generation politicians, either the sons of famous political fathers or with other close relatives in the LDP. Kōno's father, Kōno Ichirō, was an especially famous LDP politician; although he never became prime minister, at the time of his death in 1965 he headed one of the party's most powerful factions. The implications of being a *nisei* in Japan's political system are great, since voter loyalty, developed over a long period of time in a politician's electoral stronghold (*jiban*), is generally transferable to a designated successor; thus, men who follow in the footsteps of famous politician fathers normally inherit safe seats. (Indeed, so marked are the advantages of being a second-generation politician that by the 1986 election, fully 38 percent of successful candidates were *nisei*.)[31] Kōno, Yamaguchi, and Nishioka all enjoyed financial independence as well, having comfortable personal incomes derived from family resources, let alone the financial connections that went along with an inherited seat.[32] In this regard they contrasted with most young Diet members, who typically are preoccupied with raising funds to survive in hotly contested races.

The fact of being *nisei* had the further advantage of greater media coverage than was devoted to most junior Diet members. Kōno Yōhei's situation is of special note. Following his first election to office in November 1967, two years after his father's death, Kōno joined the faction headed by Nakasone Yasuhiro, who had inherited leadership from Kōno's father. This situation, in which the natural heir of a famous Diet member came under the care and tutelage of the same member's political heir, was the subject of much media interest. How would Nakasone treat the son of the man to whom he owed so much? Given Nakasone's own relative youth, could the young Kōno ever hope to gain control of the faction that had once been his father's? The media found ample material with the political emergence of Kōno Yōhei, then only thirty years old.[33]

One final characteristic results from the three men's shared situation as sons of politicians. Because they had inherited safe seats, all had run successfully for the Diet for the first time when quite young. Whereas at the

31. Curtis, *Japanese Way of Politics*, 96.
32. For a probing look at Kōno Yōhei's finances, see Kase Hideaki, "Kōno Yōhei ni aete tou—Anata no kinmyaku wa yogorete inaika?" *Gendai* 11 (May 1977): 56–79.
33. See, for example, Akasaka Tarō, "'Kōno shintō' hataage no shokku," *Bungei Shunjū* 54 (August 1976): 254–258.

time of the breakaway most Diet members in the same age range (forty and under) were in their first or, in a few cases, second term, these three men were ahead for their years.

In light of these shared characteristics, then, Kōno, Yamaguchi, and Nishioka had less to lose than other junior LDP men from engaging in status politics vis-à-vis those above them. Owing to their relative financial independence, the major attraction for factional affiliation diminished—all the more so because their inherited safe seats made their financial needs less serious, not to mention more predictable, than those of the average Diet member who is trying to build a political base from the ground up. Their safe seats also reduced the political benefit of LDP endorsements and help at election time. Kōno is a case in point: in his first electoral attempt, with his father's name behind him, he ran first among the five candidates in his five-member district in Kanagawa Prefecture; from the outset of his political career, then, his need for party assistance was minimal. Other factors associated with being *nisei* surely reduced these men's psychological reliance on the factional tie as well. For one, media attention gave them visibility and identity independent of their factional identity; for another, their intimate familiarity with the political landscape almost certainly made them less reliant on the factions as a way of relating to the party.[34]

Finally, these three must have viewed the promise of future posts in return for accepting the terms of LDP status relations with particular ambivalence. Whereas most young Diet members in the early 1970s—obscure, with few political or financial resources of their own—saw meticulous service to the faction and waiting as the only possible route to otherwise wholly unattainable leadership posts, such a course, with its promise of only minimal rewards, no doubt seemed arduous, frustrating, and interminable to juniors with so many initial assets. The privileged route that these "heirs apparent" followed into the Diet, moreover, surely made the terms of factional membership, with its emphasis on ritualized deference behavior, most difficult, if not actually painful. A general's son is, after all, in a special position to know and feel the agony of being a private.

The process by which Kōno Yōhei came to be dissatisfied with the party and reached the point of organizing a group in response was of long duration. On being elected to the Diet, Kōno, like almost all newly elected ju-

34. For analyses of the NLC candidates that weighed such factors, see Hosojima Izumi, "Hoshu yurugasu Kōno shintō," *Ekonomisuto* 54 (29 June 1976): 10–14; and Hashimoto Akikazu, "Kōno shintō o sasaeru kiban wa aruka: 'Kikentō' no konnichi teki bunseki," *Asahi Jānaru* 18 (2 July 1976): 12–16.

nior members, had quickly aligned with a faction. Within this faction, however, Kōno soon began to feel increasingly discontented with both the way the party was run and his own prospects within the prevailing authority structure. As Kōno puts it in an account written at the time of the breakaway, the doubts had been there from the very beginning: "In January 1967 I received the official approval of the Liberal Democratic party and became a member. In the nine and a half years since then, these very basic doubts have remained like dregs in my heart."[35]

Kōno's criticisms of the leadership and authority relations within the LDP were directed at its most basic features. For one, he objected to how leadership was exercised within the party: its overconcentration in the hands of a small number of senior men; the lack of turnover in the uppermost echelons; the top leadership's domination of party posts; the rivalry within the elite ranks for key posts, a rivalry impervious to the influence of other party members; and the types of decisions made at the top, which, according to Kōno, were announced with no explanation of the logic or rationale involved and without reference to any coherent set of policies or principles. Another charge of special interest was that major generational differences in thinking—a kind of "perception gap"—divided the junior and senior members of the party, and that the senior leadership's way of thinking was alien to those below: "There is a large wall within the Liberal Democratic Party. . . . It seems to loom thick and high in front of us, blocking us." To portray this difference, Kōno cites a phrase from the party platform: whereas Kōno and his age peers would want to call for "the creation of a new ethics," the LDP senior leadership still talked in terms of "the establishment of national morals"; in other words, they used language that echoed the prewar world in which they had been educated.[36]

All these objections can be seen as attacks on the closed nature of decision making within the party and on the terms of junior status. Kōno notes the frustration and sense of hopelessness among juniors who voiced dissatisfaction with party policies or called for reforms, and the leadership's intolerance of dissent in the name of party unity. "I see democracy within the party," he writes, "become more and more limited each day."[37] And he observes the lack of channels for input by party juniors into matters of personnel or internal policy. Most observers hold that Kōno had problems with the terms of factional politics from the beginning and was never an

35. Kōno Yōhei, "Jimintō yo saraba: Hyaku no giron yori mo mazu kōdō o—sore ga wareware rokunin no shinjō da" *Bungei Shunjū* 54 (August 1976): 94–102, esp. 96.

36. Ibid., 97.

37. Ibid.

enthusiastic member of the Nakasone camp.[38] This dissatisfaction with the Nakasone faction arose from various causes, including the faction's history, ideological differences (Nakasone was considered a hawk whereas on defense-related issues Kōno advocated restraint), and disagreement over specific policy positions (Nakasone supported Satō's second- and third-term reelection as party president, while Kōno did not).

The point at which Kōno's discontent with the party and factional arrangements began to be expressed in conflict behavior, together with the steps ultimately leading to the breakaway, will be explored in chapter 7. Behind that process, however, we consider briefly the broader changes taking place at the ideological level in Japanese society which support and, indeed, may spur changes in individual consciousness.

During the years prior to the New Liberal Club's secession in 1976, it was common for the media to decry "party gerontocracy." The LDP leadership, said the respected journal *Ekonomisuto* at the time of the breakaway, was a "group of grandfathers" whose views were no longer those of the nation.[39] Younger Japanese—LDP members, business people, and the public alike—applauded the departure of Kōno Yōhei and his colleagues from the LDP, and surveys confirmed that the NLC had strong initial support among younger voters. This evidence suggests that the problems inherent in junior-senior relations in the party, and in organizational life more generally, are widely perceived in today's Japan; the public, especially younger voters, understood the rationale for the break well enough to support Kōno and his five associates. It appears, then, that the "awareness process" by which inherent tensions over status inequalities manifest themselves is well advanced in society at large, particularly in cases involving intergenerational conflicts, which have their own long history in Japan. As the NLC's troubled path since the breakaway indicates, public comprehension of the issues at stake in a status-based struggle is no guarantee of continued support, but the larger process of ideological transformation is a powerful force, one supportive of change in individual consciousness.

Junior status and the problems surrounding it are readily comprehensible to the great majority of Japanese. Not only is every individual at any given moment junior to many people, but Japan's leaders, who have articulated and supported the traditional ideology of social relations, have themselves been juniors as well. Other types of ascribed status, however, do not

38. Suzuki Tsuneo, former newspaper correspondent and secretary to Kōno, interview with author, Tokyo, 29 May 1978.

39. *Ekonomisuto*, 7 July 1977, 34.

have this advantage for attracting public empathy and support. Japan's leadership has been overwhelmingly male and majority Japanese. Thus, the conditions for status-based protest on the part of other groups, notably women and burakumin, have been somewhat different, even if all forms of such dissent are profoundly affected by the broad ideological changes just discussed. In the next chapter we shall consider the inherent conflict in status relations involving gender, by focusing on the protest of one small group of Japanese women civil servants regarding a duty assigned to them on the basis of sex: that of serving tea to their office mates.

4

Gender-based Conflict:
The Revolt of the Tea Pourers

On an ordinary day in the fall of 1963, a small group of women civil servants launched a protest that is well remembered by senior male bureaucrats in the administrative offices for the city of Kyoto. The form of the protest was hardly dramatic. Acting on a plan worked out among the women and then communicated to a union section made up of the younger men in the office, women employees of the Housing Division, in accordance with their usual routines, prepared the morning round of tea for everyone in the division. But then, in an act akin to a declaration of war in this orderly world of the Japanese office, the women failed to pour and carry the tea, cup by cup, to the employees of their particular sections; instead they took a cup for themselves (and, in several cases, one for their immediate boss) and returned to their desks. Several younger men, by prior agreement, came forward to serve themselves—but for the most part, the great container of tea was left to steam soundlessly into an office whose rituals had been rent asunder.

According to the participants in the struggle, none of the more senior men ever said anything about the protest. Yet days after it began, women from among the small band of protesters began to backslide and resumed their tea-pouring duties. The most telling evidence of the charged climate of feeling at the time was the way my questions were received *nine years later* when I first interviewed high-ranking bureaucrats in the city office about the protest: their faces visibly darkened, and their tone as they spoke

Portions of this chapter appeared in Susan J. Pharr, "Status Conflict: The Rebellion of the Tea Pourers," in *Conflict in Japan*, ed. Ellis S. Krauss, Thomas P. Rohlen, and Patricia G. Steinhoff, 214–240 (Honolulu: University of Hawaii Press, 1984).

of the "anti–tea pouring struggle" (*ochakumi hantai tōsō*) can only be described as one of outrage. Several years after the protest, tea-serving rituals, even in the Housing Division, were back in place, the key participants having either left to get married or been transferred to other divisions.

The struggle over tea-serving duties was the culmination of a long process, dating from 1957, by which fourteen women had gradually become aware of certain problems they faced as female employees in the city office and had banded together to attempt to change those conditions. In the many meetings that preceded their protest, grievances other than those relating to tea pouring were aired. One problem was the women's need for a changing room. As is the custom in many Japanese offices, city office employees wore uniforms, and the women felt the need for a place to change into and out of their uniforms, comb their hair, touch up their makeup, eat their lunch, or lie down on an off day, especially during their menstrual period or during pregnancy. There was no place for any of these activities because the restrooms in the city office, again following Japanese custom, were for both men and women. Although hypothetically the restrooms were "shared," in practice they represented male turf; a woman might scurry past men lined up at the urinals to get to a cubicle, but she was not going to tarry long enough to comb her hair. Another topic of discussion was the unpleasant chore of cleaning the tops of the men's desks and emptying ashtrays brimming with stale cigarette butts. Still another issue centered on the problem of menstruation leave days. According to Japanese labor law provisions in place until 1986, women workers were entitled to up to two days of "menstruation leave" each month.[1] Women found it difficult to take the leave, however, for office procedure required that employees asking for time off state the reason on a publicly displayed sign-up sheet. Most women were too embarrassed to request their leave days, or suffered feelings of dread before they did so.

These various issues starkly reveal the harsh terms of status relations in the Housing Division in the 1960s. Along with the issue of tea pouring itself, all were linked to the condition of status inferiority. They were so

1. See Cook and Hayashi, *Working Women in Japan,* for discussion of this and other protectionist measures that were a legacy of the Occupation reforms. The Equal Employment Opportunity Law, which took effect on 1 April 1986, abolished the menstruation leave, rejecting the premise that work is harmful to women during their menstrual period; now women may request and be granted leave during menstruation, but it is treated as sick leave. See also Hanami Tadashi and Akamatsu Ryōko, with Watanabe Mayumi, *Josei to kigyō no shinjidai* (Tokyo: Yūhikaku, 1986), esp. 154–159 and 190–198 (appendix: "Equal Employment Opportunity Law"); *Asahi Shinbun,* 10 March 1986, 2.

intimate, so rooted in fundamental biological and cultural differences dividing the sexes, that collective action on the part of the status group was mandatory if these conditions were to be acted on at all. Although the women's struggle was in every sense a micro-protest arising out of everyday office life, the issues it raised are symptomatic of the broader problems that all Japanese women face, both in the workplace and in other areas of life.

Recent works place Japan squarely in the front ranks of the postindustrial, "information" societies, and argue that Japan presents even the most advanced countries with "lessons" to be learned—social and political as well as economic. In the area of women's rights, however, few would offer Japan as a model. Japanese women today, despite major gains since World War II resulting from Occupation-era social reforms and more recent social and economic changes, still confront many of the problems that limit women's life chances in virtually all societies, whatever the level of economic development: underrepresentation in political life at all levels; an extraordinary degree of sex-role stereotyping in the media, advertising, and education; and, our concern here, highly discriminatory conditions in the workplace. An important book on Japanese working women concluded with the following appraisal: "Many norms that are used to describe the nature and scope of women's work in the national economies of the industrial nations . . . do not apply to Japan. . . . The Japanese employment system probably exploits women more extensively than is the case in any other industrialized country." [2]

Japan, then, is an important reminder that national economic development and improvements in women's status in the workplace do not automatically go hand in hand. Even spectacular economic performance in a "model" information society is no guarantee of fundamental change in the nature and conditions of women's work, or of redresses for stark inequities in the distribution of power between the sexes.

The problems confronting women today in the workplace are an extension of status relations as they have applied to Japanese women throughout history. Under the terms of status arrangements in place before World War II, women, by both law and custom, were considered dependents of male family heads who represented the family's interests to the outside world. Thus, upper-class married women played few roles outside the home and immediate neighborhood. And although gender-role distinctions were less pronounced among the working classes, where women and men labored side by side in the shop or field, the work of women in home

2. Cook and Hayashi, *Working Women in Japan*, 1–2.

enterprises or in the mills and factories of prewar Japan was regarded as an outgrowth of their primary commitments to their father or husband. No wonder, then, that their wages were less than half those of men, and their status in the workplace exceedingly low.[3]

The traditional view of women's status and roles was challenged on many fronts after 1945. Not only did the constitution of 1947 give women a "Japanese ERA"—a provision that explicitly forbade discrimination on the basis of sex—but reform of the civil code altered the legal basis for women's dependence within the family as well.[4] The 1947 Labor Standards Law affirmed the principle of equal pay for equal work and introduced a number of measures aimed at improving the situation of working women. Meanwhile, increased prosperity, urbanization, and rapidly rising education levels in Japan have brought opportunities for daughters as well as sons, greater freedom for women in the nuclear family, and greater educational access for women (as evidenced by the thirty-two-fold increase in the number of women in institutions of higher education between 1950 and 1982).[5]

The legacy of the prewar era continues to affect women's status in the workplace, however. In 1987, women's wages were only 52.3 percent of those for men;[6] indeed, Japan is the only industrial country in which the differential between men's and women's wages has actually been increasing in recent years.[7] Better-educated women in particular have difficulty finding suitable jobs that offer them work on the same basis as male employees and a chance for advancement. A survey of companies in 1981 revealed that only 27 percent were prepared to hire women for positions requiring a university degree, and 45 percent indicated that they did not promote women to supervisory (*kakarichō*) positions.[8] Of particular interest in rela-

3. For sources on the situation of women in prewar Japan, see Susan J. Pharr, "Japan: Historical and Contemporary Perspectives," in *Women: Role and Status in Eight Countries*, ed. Janet Z. Giele and Audrey C. Smock (New York: John Wiley, 1977), 219–255; and Pharr, *Political Women*, chap. 3.

4. See Pharr, "Japan: Historical and Contemporary Perspectives," 231–234; and Pharr, "The Politics of Women's Rights."

5. Japan, Ministry of Labor, Women's and Young Workers' Bureau (hereafter WYWB), *The Status of Women in Japan* (Tokyo, 1983), 7.

6. Calculated from the figures presented in Japan, Management and Coordination Agency, Statistics Bureau, *Statistical Handbook of Japan 1988* (Tokyo, 1988), 109. In 1987, the average annual earnings of regular male employees were ¥4,796,184, compared with ¥2,508,756 for women.

7. *Asahi Shinbun*, 31 March 1986, 3.

8. Japan, Ministry of Labor, "Survey on Personnel Management of Women Workers" (Tokyo, 1981); cited in Tadashi Hanami, "Equality and Prohibition of Discrimination in Employment—The Japanese Case" (photocopy).

tion to the present case study, only 1.7 percent of managerial positions in civil service jobs were held by women—even in 1980. That figure in 1960, in the period of the tea pourers' rebellion, was a mere 0.8 percent.[9]

The problems for women workers are rooted in the basic employment pattern for women in Japan, and in the way companies have dealt with it. The pattern resembles an M: typically, women work for several years from the time they complete their education until they marry or have their first child; they return to work in their mid to late thirties, once their children are well on in school. This second peak in women's employment has grown in recent years, greatly swelling the number of married women in the work force. Whereas in 1962 married women made up only 32.7 percent of the female work force, in 1986 they constituted 68.2 percent.[10]

This employment pattern has put women at a distinct disadvantage in a system that distinguishes sharply between "permanent" employees—who receive superior wages, benefits, training opportunities, promotions, and wage supplements (such as family and housing allowances)—and "temporary" or "part-time" employees, whose wages and benefits (if any) are far inferior. Temporary or part-time status often has little to do with the hours worked or how long the worker is prepared to continue employment; many "part-timers" work more hours than regular employees and may stay at the same job indefinitely. Generally, women's participation as permanent employees in such a system is confined to the first years of their working life, before they leave to marry or have children. Even as "permanent" employees, however, they fare less well than men because they are not eligible for the housing and family allowances that raise men's pay, and they normally have far fewer opportunities for promotion or training, on the grounds that they will soon be leaving the work force. When they return to the labor market after raising families, they are seldom eligible for permanent employee status and so typically continue their working life as temporary workers or part-timers, with all the disadvantages that such a status entails.

To employers, of course, this pattern of utilization offers major advantages. For one thing, top wages and benefits can be reserved for a relatively small portion of the work force, almost entirely male, from whom a high level of commitment to the firm is expected in return. For another, because women usually leave their "first-phase" permanent positions before their pay level rises substantially, their replacement by new low-paid young female workers represents substantial savings for the company. Fi-

9. WYWB, *The Status of Women* (1983), 17.

10. Japan, Ministry of Labor, "The Labor Conditions of Women 1987—Summary" (Tokyo: Foreign Press Center, 1988), 7.

nally, the growing number of married women who return to work after their children are in school provides a source of cheap labor and a major "safety valve" in the Japanese economy; in periods of recession or retrenchment, they can be laid off at will while the "permanent" work force remains intact.

Over the postwar era, consciousness of women's problems in the work force has increased. In a survey conducted by the *Yomiuri Shinbun* in 1988, over 80 percent of respondents agreed that discrimination against working women exists in employment and promotion practices, job assignments, and wages. At the same time, the majority of Japanese still see women's work for wages as secondary to their home responsibilities—a view that does not translate into strong support for improving women's career opportunities or the terms of their employment. In the same survey, 65 percent of respondents agreed that "it is more important for women to back up their husbands than to have work of their own."[11] Another major factor standing in the way of change, however, is the attitude of employers and of the ruling party. As Sidney Verba and his co-researchers found in a three-country study of equality issues, business leaders and ruling-party politicians in Japan were "far more conservative" than their counterparts in the United States and Sweden when it came to women's concerns.[12]

The status-based conflict that I call the "tea pourers' rebellion," then, began in the objective conditions that define the status of women in the Japanese workplace—or more specifically, that defined the status of women in a particular public bureaucracy in the early 1960s. These conditions were (and are) inherent in the tension between the official ideology of the workplace, which forbids discrimination on the basis of sex and upholds the principle of equal opportunity, and the informal ideology, derived from traditional norms, which structures women's work roles and opportunities according to their ascribed status as women. The protest involved the problems that women face in the workplace, even those who enjoy the privileged status of permanent employees in Japan's dual economy.

The key issue at the Kyoto city office was "job content"—specifically, the requirement that women civil servants perform various extra custodial duties, including serving tea in the office. Indeed, so extensive were their tea-serving duties in this large bureaucracy that the average female civil servant was preparing and serving over one thousand cups of tea each

11. *Daily Yomiuri*, 8 May 1988, 2.
12. Verba et al., *Elites and the Idea of Equality*, 257.

month, in addition to performing her regular workload. Other issues fell in the domain of working conditions. In lodging a formal protest, then, the women presented their superiors with a series of demands on specific issues, including their need for a changing room and their right to take menstrual leave. On these issues they scored success. The problem of tea-pouring duties, however, proved most intractable—and thus our focus on it here.

Tea-pouring duties are a metaphor or "condensation symbol" for traditional expectations regarding women that run counter to the official ideology.[13] These activities thus distill the larger objective conditions of the workplace, which structure the lives of all working women in Japan (and, indeed, to varying degrees in all societies) into the familiar rituals of daily life. The tea-pouring rituals had been practiced in the Kyoto city office throughout the postwar era, and in that sense the objective conditions that gave rise to the tea pourers' rebellion had been in place for some time. Before exploring the various issues in the conflict and the question of why a protest arose at the particular time it did, we must look at tea pouring itself—a set of rituals ubiquitous in Japanese organizational life.

It is a long-established tradition in Japanese offices that employees, even if their wages are low or the work unsatisfactory, are supplied with as much tea as they wish to drink. The central reality about this ritual is that all the activities relating to it except the drinking—heating the water, assembling the employees' personal cups, pouring and serving the tea (and remembering which cup belongs to whom), afterward gathering, washing, and arranging cups and cleaning the counter where the tea was made, and buying the tea or making sure that it is bought—are the assigned domain of women employees. It is true that many offices hire women who do little besides prepare tea; however, these women (known as *ochakumi*) are generally reserved for "up front"—that is, for serving tea to those high-ranking officials who are in regular contact with the public and to their guests. Quite apart from the *ochakumi* and their duties, it is the general expectation of everyone in the office that if a woman employee is present when male employees of equal or superior bureaucratic rank want tea, she will be responsible for its preparation.

The tea-making routines in the Kyoto city office were highly developed. In most sections, the women employees formed a pool and rotated the duty. In one Housing Division section, for example, there were four women among the seventy employees, and so each woman's turn came

13. See Mary Douglas, *Natural Symbols* (New York: Vintage Books, 1973).

once every four working days. On this day, the woman employee would arrive at work about twenty minutes early on her own time (that is, without compensation) to prepare the water for everyone's morning cup. An even earlier arrival time was necessary in the winter for bringing a large container of water to the boil, and likewise in the summer, when the tea had to be allowed to cool slightly once it was made. After the first morning round she would go about her regular office duties, only to drop them again shortly before noon and again at three to prepare the next rounds. At the end of the day, having served some 210 cups of tea, she made a final round of the office to collect the cups, wash and arrange them, tidy up around the tea preparation area, and check supplies. She then went home, free of all tea-making responsibilities for three days.

Legally or "officially" none of these duties existed. Nowhere did tea making appear on women employees' job descriptions. Even the tea itself was not paid for by the city office but by the employees themselves from a kitty collected for that and related purposes. Several of the women I interviewed reported that when they had gone to their section chief with problems arising from the competing demands of their regular jobs and their tea-pouring responsibilities, they had been told that nothing could be done, since tea pouring was not an official duty. They were told to manage as best they could, but that when it came to the allocation of official duties they would have to be treated equally with the men. Occasionally at this juncture they were reminded that Japan is a democracy and that women must accept equal responsibilities in exchange for their rights. At the same time, however, a number of women and several high-ranking men in the office told me that female job applicants, in the interview that follows successful performance on the civil service exam, were asked how they felt about serving tea to office mates, and that if they voiced objections there was little chance of their being hired. A personnel officer half-heartedly denied that this practice existed, but added that it was natural and proper for women to pour tea. Among the many male officials and employees interviewed, none could agree with the view that it was unfair for women to be required to pour tea for their male office mates, and most repeated the phrase often heard in Japan—that it is "women's duty to pour tea."

The serving of tea has profound symbolic meaning in Japanese culture. In a larger sense, it is a ceremonial or ritual activity aimed at opening up lines of communication between individuals. But what makes it so central to this inquiry is the asymmetry implied—indeed, ritualized—in the relationship between the server and the one served. The serving of tea fits comfortably within Erving Goffman's definition of "status rituals": "marks of devotion . . . in which an actor celebrates and confirms his relation to a recipient."[14] The implied relationship is reciprocal; in the status ritual of pouring tea, the social inferior expresses deference and dependence and is rewarded by the superior's protection. Indeed, the sociological and political uses of such ritual forms as tea pouring are profound, for by transmitting cultural formulas of appropriate social behavior they function to regulate and channel power itself.[15] In the terms of our earlier discussion on status politics, the tea-pouring ritual evokes the traditional normative code that regulates interaction between persons of different statuses, thus legitimating—even celebrating—status superiors' exercise of prerogatives over status inferiors.

One might argue that serving functions of all kinds—including the coffee-preparation duties of secretaries in Western offices—carry the same type of symbolic meaning. To a certain extent this is true. In Japan, however, where status is so crucial in the mediation of social relationships, these rituals are far more elaborate and central. In an office, tea is served not in a random fashion or on the basis of physical proximity to the server, but precisely according to status, from the highest-ranking person first right down to the lowest-ranking person last. In cases of equal rank—for example, three section chiefs (kachō) in one division—service will be according to length of time in that particular rank; and where promotions or appointments were concurrent, then age decides who is served first. Needless to say, having to master and retain the "hierarchy map" of the office and adjust it as personnel changes occur makes tea-pouring duties quite onerous, especially in a large office. The rituals, then, play a central symbolic role in maintaining status lines in Japanese society more generally.

As a ritual engaged in primarily by women, the serving of tea is a potent symbolic act expressing the asymmetry of the sexes. By pouring tea for men, women express their deference and inferiority to them. At the same time, the symbolic act of serving tea is linked to woman's role as nurturer, a gender-based function that appears in most of women's social roles. In this sense, the tea-serving ritual accentuates the differences in behavioral expectations for the two sexes while ceremonially acknowledging and approving their traditional functional justification.

For these reasons, the expectation that women employees will assume the duties of tea pouring clashes with the official ideology of public bureaucracy in Japan, which holds aloft the principle of achievement over

14. Erving Goffman, *Interaction Ritual: Essays on Face to Face Behavior* (Garden City, N.Y.: Anchor Books, 1967), 56–57.
15. Douglas, *Natural Symbols*, 30, 42.

that of ascription and explicitly forbids sex discrimination. Thus is laid the objective basis for conflict.

The process by which a small group of women in the Housing Division became "aware" of this basis for protest, one inherent in their daily routines, was a long one, just as it was in the intergenerational conflict examined in chapter 3. Whereas Kōno came to his views gradually over a nine-year period, for the women office workers the process took over five—from 1957, when a male union official in the division began to investigate some of the women workers' problems, to 1962, by which time the women workers had begun to discuss their problems and to contemplate concrete steps to remedy them.

In contrast to Kōno, who appears to have become conscious of status-based problems in the LDP on his own, the tea pourers were alerted to grounds for complaint by an outsider to the group of eventual protesters and, indeed, a man. This employee, Kawata,[16] was then in his late twenties and had become active in the public employees' union to which all regular employees in the city bureaucracy belonged. Kawata's initial concern was with the problems of young temporary workers, both male and female, and to address their needs he set about organizing union "youth and women's bureaus" (seinenfujin-bu) in various divisions of the city office— including his own, where he became the bureau head. Gradually his attention fell on regular women employees, who, although hired on the basis of performance on a standard civil service exam, had career paths wholly different from those of men: "The role of women was as men's assistants. They had the jobs of servants and maids—running errands for men who should have run their own errands, cleaning up the men's desks. . . . Their future was entirely different from men's. They were permanent assistants to men."[17]

It is impossible to establish how firmly Kawata held such views in 1958, twenty years before he expressed them in an interview. His own efforts continued to focus on issues relating to temporary workers. But the new union bureau did create a setting in which the objective terms of women's employment in the city office were exposed to scrutiny, and Kawata took it on himself to stir the women employees to action.

The Youth and Women's Bureau of the Housing Division was just being formed when Makino Yuriko, the woman who would lead the rebellion, came to work in the division. As a recent high school graduate

16. All names and certain details have been changed to protect the anonymity of the participants in the conflict.
17. Interview conducted in Kyoto, June 1978.

attending college classes at night, Makino was for four years only nomi-nally involved with the bureau. Then in 1962, soon after her March gradua-tion from college, Kawata approached her and asked whether she would be interested in forming a women's section within the bureau to deal with the special problems of women workers. Indeed, by both his account and hers he asked her many times to lead the undertaking. As Kawata remem-bers her, Makino was a most reluctant leader, fearful of criticism from the men in her section of the Housing Division if she asserted herself. Ac-cording to several female observers to the recruitment process, however, Makino stepped forward quite willingly. For these women, Kawata's role in instituting the new section figures less prominently than he himself indi-cates; meanwhile Makino, while acknowledging the importance of Kawata's role, claimed not to remember the details. Concretely, though, all do agree that for a period of at least a month in 1962, Kawata and Makino discussed the question of how to organize the women's section of the bureau.

It struck me in interviewing both leaders that neither remembered dis-cussing specific issues to be dealt with by the proposed women's section. Kawata explains this lapse by stating that his primary aim was to see the new group launched; he assumed that once the group was formed, it would identify specific problems for attention. Makino, who by then was eager to take the reins of leadership, reports that she did not see a need to spell out the issues to be taken up, preferring to concentrate on organizational questions instead.

Another interpretation, based on a close reading of both accounts, is that the two were engaged in conflict-avoidance behavior. While Makino, like the other female participants, reported the later conflict as a struggle centered primarily on the women's tea-serving duties, Kawata preferred to portray it as having larger aims and appeared embarrassed to hear it re-ferred to as a conflict over tea pouring. His verbal and facial responses gave every indication that he considered this label demeaning to the se-riousness of what he had been trying to encourage. It should also be re-membered that Kawata, despite the importance of his role as an agent of change and as a third party and ally once the conflict commenced, was a status superior whose tea the women poured every day. For both these reasons, then, if Makino had been planning to make tea pouring a cen-tral issue in the conflict to come, it seems doubtful that she would have brought the matter up with Kawata. For his part, Kawata, eager to make a leader out of someone he saw as reluctant to take on that role, would have had his own stake in conflict avoidance.

At the end of approximately one month of discussions with Kawata, Makino was prepared to call a meeting of women in the division to consider what to do. The gathering marked the beginning of a process by which awareness of the conflict situation inherent in the office set-up gradually was diffused from Makino herself, and a small group of fellow college graduates who soon rallied around her, to the other women. Ostensibly, the meeting was an informal social get-together held after work at a nearby restaurant. Little if anything was said about the problems of women in the Housing Division or the possibility of organizing a women's section. The tone of the meeting, by Makino's description, was "let's all get to know one another."

Following this dinner came a long period, nearly a year, devoted to what the Japanese call *nemawashi* (preparatory activity—literally, "preparing the ground," as when setting in a plant) and *hanashiai* (exploratory talk). Conflict theories based on Western experience allow that considerable time may elapse between the emergence of conflict and the initiation of conflict behavior; in Japan, however, there is often an intermediate stage that is manifested quite distinctly before the onset of face-to-face protest. The overall goal of this stage, which is characterized by numerous meetings, often with no explicit agenda relating to the goal, is seemingly to create a feeling of oneness among the participants and a sense that they agree—even though the exact terms of the agreement are not necessarily spelled out. Indeed, in the present case the individuals interviewed all had difficulty characterizing the nature or content of these meetings, except to say that the end result was a formal move to seek approval from the union for the creation of a women's section. These meetings, taken collectively, seem to represent the search for consensus so often described as characteristic of Japanese decision-making.[18]

In this early stage, then, some fourteen women from four of the five sections in the Housing Division began gathering more or less regularly. In the course of the year's meetings, numerous grievances related to tea pouring were raised. One problem was the quality of the tea-making equipment, which a number of women felt to be old-fashioned and unsafe, not to mention extraordinarily slow at heating water. Furthermore, two of the five sections had no tea-making equipment of their own; the women employees had to carry huge teapots of boiling water up a flight of stairs several times a day, a chore that was considered troublesome and even dangerous. A second issue concerned precisely what women's tea-pouring

18. See Michael Blaker, *Japanese International Negotiating Style* (New York: Columbia University Press, 1977); and Ezra F. Vogel, ed., *Modern Japanese Organization and Decision-Making* (Berkeley and Los Angeles: University of California Press, 1975).

duties should be, given what appeared to be general agreement that it was in fact their responsibility to make tea for the men in the office. The points of discussion centered on how often each day the tea should be prepared and whether it was incumbent on the women to pour and serve the tea as well as make it. Much talk was devoted to the need to "rationalize" the tea-pouring duties, although what this meant was often not spelled out in the discussions.

A final issue, one central to this analysis, was the attitude of the men in the office about being served tea. The Housing Division was a new division in the city bureaucracy, and its office routines were said to be unsettled. Everyone seemed rushed and on different schedules, with builders, architects, and planners always hurrying in and out. Some of the higher-status males, particularly the architects, apparently took personal services of all kinds for granted; often tea was set before these men without their giving so much as a flicker or grunt of acknowledgment. The younger men, whom the women knew better through the Youth and Women's Bureau of the union, had a much better attitude in general, and, significantly, many of the women did not mind serving them.

These discussions hold much of interest to the student of status rituals, particularly in view of the changes that were occurring in the city office workload in the early 1960s. On the eve of a decade of double-digit growth in Japan, the work of public bureaucracies was expanding, with divisions such as housing, linked as it was to the construction boom of the period, especially affected. The workload of all employees was increasing, but the men in supervisory positions gave little thought to how these changes affected women. Assignments were handed down without regard to potential conflicts with tea-making duties. A classic example was the decision to locate two sections of the Housing Division in upstairs rooms with no place to make the tea that all the men expected to drink.

It is clear that in the Housing Division during that period many of the conditions under which status rituals would have most meaning for those performing them were not being met. It can be hypothesized that optimal performance of status rituals like that represented by tea pouring occurs when four conditions are maximized: (1) when the deference behavior is warmly rewarded by reciprocal conduct; (2) when the one engaging in the deference behavior feels it to be well deserved (for example, in the case of a military salute, the salute has more meaning and comes easier when the person saluted is a hero and general rather than a disliked or little-respected lesser officer); (3) when the required behavior is congruent with other expected behaviors; and (4) when the status differential due to sex is reinforced by other status differences (in bureaucratic rank, socioeconomic background, age, educational level, period of employment, and so on).[19]

In the case of women employees in the Housing Division, there had clearly been an erosion on all four fronts. In the hurried atmosphere of a new division, an absence of warmth in face-to-face relations drained deference behavior of its emotional rewards. The attitude of the older male professionals—their lack of basic courtesy and generosity and their failure to acknowledge favors—likewise made performance of the required rituals onerous. In addition, the nature of the workload for which female employees were held responsible was in flux in the early 1960s. Successive waves of postwar "rationalization" had increased women's share of the normal work of public bureaucracies without correspondingly decreasing the number of unofficial "women's chores"; consequently, there was a growing incongruence between the content of the tasks expected of them in their two roles—as workers on the one hand and as women on the other. Finally, the entry into the bureaucracy during this period of better-educated women, many of whom saw tea-pouring duties as beneath them, that is, as inappropriate to their level of training, experience, and skills, caused the status quo to be called into question for the first time.[20] For all these reasons, the status rituals expected of the women were losing their meaning, thus nullifying some of the factors that might otherwise have constrained conflict behavior.

The women's discussions continued for a year, forging the women's subjective awareness of their situation into a collective consciousness. The meetings also appear to have constituted an almost-formal prefatory stage prior to real action. And they made it possible for a distance to grow between the women and their male superiors. Locked into day-to-day relations with the targets of their anger, the female employees had to undergo a certain change of consciousness in which the ordinary Mr. Tanaka and Mr. Sakai of the office became cast as "the enemy." In status politics struggles that arise in close relationships, status superiors seemingly need to be objectified—blown up into larger-than-life caricatures and viewed collectively—before anger can be released on them.[21]

The process by which a group of women workers join together and contemplate taking active steps to change their working conditions is

19. See Goffman, *Interaction Ritual;* and Douglas, *Natural Symbols.*

20. See Pharr, *Political Women,* chap. 3, for a discussion of the impact of higher education on women's attitudes.

21. See Murray Edelman, *The Symbolic Uses of Politics* (Urbana: University of Illinois Press, 1964).

complex and difficult—more so than in forming a new political group, as in the case discussed in chapter 3. In politics, after all, the name of the game is power; the formation of informal but goal-oriented groups and open sparring for power and privilege are a regular part of the life of a political party. In most organizational settings, however, overt conflict is rare, and for this reason the steps that the Kyoto city office workers took toward protest were far more hesitant and cautious than were Kōno's early moves in breaking from the LDP. The need for validation from a higher-status third party to legitimize the protest, for preparatory meetings long before action was contemplated, for distancing—all reflect the greater constraints on engaging in protest in a public bureaucracy, with its emphasis on compliance, discipline, and conflict avoidance in interpersonal relations.

But the women workers' hesitancy is also a reflection of the greater force of the constraints involved in gender-based protest, as opposed to intergenerational conflict involving men. Traditionally women, more than men, have been enjoined to accept rather than protest, to endure rather than complain, to make sacrifices themselves rather than expect accommodation from others. For that reason, the cultural barriers to conflict behavior by women are extraordinarily high, and so it makes sense that the process of consciousness transformation would proceed slowly for women workers and that a higher-status authority figure—a male—would perform an important and perhaps necessary function by, in essence, legitimating their protest (to be discussed in chapter 7).

If status-based conflicts are supported by a common ideology of democracy and egalitarianism, each individual protest differs depending on the ascriptive group involved—its particular attributes and its own unique history of struggle. In the next chapter we will explore the third case, this one involving burakumin. Of the three groups examined here, burakumin are the furthest advanced in overcoming cultural obstacles to protest, but the problems they face arising from social inequities are also the most severe. Despite a century of status politics struggle, numerous barriers to full equality remain.

5

Burakumin Protest: The Incident at Yōka High School

At 9:30 A.M. on 22 November 1974, some fifty-two teachers at Yōka Senior High School in southern Tajima, an area in Hyōgo Prefecture, walked off the job, declaring that under the conditions prevailing in the school they were unable to teach. The immediate targets of their statement were members of a local branch office of the Buraku Liberation League (Buraku Kaihō Dōmei, referred to hereafter as the league). The league's student members at Yōka High School had been attempting since May to gain approval for a study group on burakumin problems at the school and at the time of the teachers' walkout were engaged in a hunger strike over the issue. Emerging from Yōka High into the bright sun of that Friday morning, the teachers encountered a large gathering of league members. Shouting that the teachers were abandoning their responsibilities as educators, league members blocked their exit and ordered them back into the school. As one league account later succinctly stated, "The teachers resisted, which resulted in chaos. In this struggle, many people were injured."[1] The "chaos" continued for some thirteen hours, during which time the teachers were forced back inside the school, formally denounced by the league, then compelled in extended sessions to acknowledge in writing that they had behaved discriminatorily toward burakumin. By the end of that long day, as many as sixty people, most of them teachers, had been injured, with forty-eight hospitalized.

1. *Yōka Kōkō sabetsu kyōiku kyūdan tōsō: Sabetsu kyanpein o haishi jijitsu o tashikameru tameni* (Kobe: Buraku Kaihō Dōmei Hyōgo-ken Rengō-kai, 1975), 48. The account of events is reconstructed from numerous sources, including *Akahata*, *Mainichi*, the Yōka student newspaper, and league publications. The figure for those hospitalized is from Rohlen, "Violence at Yōka High School," 685–686.

In the conflict referred to as the Yōka High School incident, the objective condition for a protest is located in the terms of status relations that persist between majority Japanese and burakumin, of whom there are an estimated 1.2 to 3 million today in Japan.[2] As in the case of the Untouchables of India, burakumin (literally, "people of the hamlet") were originally assigned outcaste status because of their occupations as butchers, tanners, and leatherworkers—tasks regarded as impure and despicable under the tenets of Buddhism. In Japan, Buddhist teachings on the evils of killing animals and eating meat fused with Shinto conceptions of *kegare* (impurity or defilement) and *imi* (avoidance connected with blood, dirt, and death). Historically, then, the burakumin were "specialists in impurity," in that they assumed occupational roles that protected the rest of society from having to deal with the impure.[3] In some cases they enjoyed elevated status as a result; temple sweepers and landscape architects, for example, "polluted" through their association with dirt, nevertheless had a privileged position in society.

Until well into the medieval period, from the twelfth to the sixteenth century, these "special-status people" were a loosely defined group of persons engaged in a broad range of occupations. During the latter part of the medieval era, however, occupational categories tightened, and those who dealt with pollution now came to be seen as polluted themselves. Laws enacted in the Tokugawa period required burakumin to live in segregated villages, and the deference behavior required of them likewise became increasingly extreme. When burakumin encountered a majority Japanese, for example, they were expected to move away or to prostrate themselves until the other had passed. Extraordinary restrictions on movement were sometimes instituted; in 1820 in the feudal domain of Tosa, for example, they

2. Determining or even estimating the number of burakumin in Japan is both a difficult and a sensitive task. Since the historical aim of at least one wing of the burakumin liberation movement has been for burakumin to merge with the majority population, it is considered inappropriate to ask people who live outside officially designated *buraku* (those villages that have qualified for compensatory measures under laws passed in 1969 and 1982) to identify themselves as burakumin in various government tallies. The Buraku Kaihō Dōmei estimates the number at 3 million, while the official figure from a 1985 General Affairs Agency survey was 1.2 million. The latter figure, however, includes only those burakumin living in officially recognized buraku districts (*Daily Yomiuri*, 6 December 1987, 6).

3. The term is from Dumont, *Homo Hierarchicus*, 48; cited in Emiko Ohnuki-Tierney, *The Monkey as Mirror: Symbolic Transformations in Japanese History and Ritual* (Princeton: Princeton University Press, 1987), 91. Ohnuki-Tierney (pp. 75–100, 140–144) provides an excellent discussion of the historical evolution of the social position of "special-status people" and of the cultural and symbolic meanings of purity and impurity in Japan.

were banned from walking in the street and from entering the city after 8:00 P.M.[4] When burakumin went to a majority person's home, not only were they not invited in, but they were expected to remove their headgear and footwear and to squat in the dirt-floored entryway before stating their business. They were forbidden to wear silk and were excluded from majority temples, shrines, and festivals.[5]

In 1871, in the wake of the 1868 Meiji Restoration, the caste system was abolished and burakumin subsequently could move about freely. Yet they nonetheless continued to be exposed to numerous forms of status-based discrimination. Mikiso Hane cites numerous examples of burakumin mistreatment, even by government officials. A handbook issued by the Ministry of Justice nine years after their "liberation" described burakumin as "the lowliest of all people, almost like animals."[6] In 1919 the government instructed an entire burakumin hamlet in Nara Prefecture to relocate because it overlooked an area considered sacred to the Japanese. Not until World War II was an effort made to end discrimination against burakumin use of majority temples; meanwhile, burakumin continued to be barred from hot springs and bathhouses.

No legal barriers restrict burakumin today. Indeed, article 14 of the Japanese constitution of 1947, which guaranteed equality to women, also forbade discrimination based on social status and family origin—wording designed to extend the measure to burakumin. Since burakumin are ethnically, linguistically, and in every other way indistinguishable from majority Japanese, the basis for discrimination against them is difficult for outsiders to understand. Discriminatory attitudes in the end spring from fears of pollution that have remained long after the religious taboos associated with eating meat and slaughtering animals disappeared, and after burakumin themselves, with all other Japanese, gained occupational freedom and mobility at the outset of the Meiji period.[7] Because of discrimination in employment and other spheres, economic status and educational levels have been lower and the crime rate higher among burakumin than among majority Japanese; these and other handicaps in turn lead to fur-

---

4. See Hane, *Peasants, Rebels, and Outcastes*, 142–143.

5. Ibid., 139–143; and DeVos and Wagatsuma, *Japan's Invisible Race*, 6–34. See also Harada Tomohiko, *Hi-sabetsu buraku no rekishi* (Tokyo: Asahi Shinbunsha, 1975); and Hijikata Tetsu, *Hi-sabetsu buraku no tatakai* (Tokyo: Shinsensha, 1973).

6. Hane, *Peasants, Rebels, and Outcastes*, 146.

7. According to anthropologist Emiko Ohnuki-Tierney (*Monkey as Mirror*, 100), the "symbolic structure of purity and impurity" that placed burakumin at the bottom of the social stratification system and, figuratively speaking, outside society has not fundamentally changed since the onset of the Tokugawa era.

Table 3. Discrimination Affecting Burakumin

Psychological Discrimination (latent in concept and consciousness)	Actual Discrimination (appears concretely in actual life)
Contempt	Refusal of employment
Prejudice	Low educational and cultural standards
Aversion	Inferior living environment
Refusal of social contact	Low income level
Cancellation of wedding engagement	Unstable occupations
	Petty scales of agriculture and small enterprise

Source: Akio Imaizumi, *Dōwa Problem: Present Situation and Government Measures* (Tokyo: Prime Minister's Office, 1977), p. 7.

ther discrimination, in a vicious cycle that affects disadvantaged groups widely, whatever the national setting.

Discrimination against burakumin is multifaceted (see table 3); however, the two most prevalent forms are in marriage and employment. When a marriage is contemplated with someone whose family is not known to the prospective bride or groom's parents, they commonly will hire a "marriage detective" to do a background check. If the prospective spouse's family is traced to a burakumin village, parents often will oppose or abort the marriage plans.[8] The same discrimination occurs in employment, where a person's burakumin origins may be traced to place of birth. Although the traditional Japanese family registry system included such information, in 1976 groups associated with the burakumin movement finally succeeded in restricting access to these records. Since then, "buraku place-name registers" (*buraku chimei sōran*), published commercially and sold surreptitiously to companies, marriage detectives, and others, have continued to allow interested parties to identify burakumin. Even though such books are outlawed by the Ministry of Justice as soon as they appear, new versions are quickly produced—evidence of the enduring intent to discriminate.[9] Moreover, discriminatory treatment is often quite different from

8. In a 1980s survey of married couples in which one partner was a burakumin and one was not, 37 percent reported that they had faced opposition to the marriage for explicitly discriminatory reasons (*Daily Yomiuri*, 6 December 1987, 6).

9. For an excellent discussion of the legal battles over such books, see Buraku Kaihō Dōmei, *Konnichi no buraku* (Osaka: Kaihō Shuppansha, 1987); and Frank K. Upham, "Ten Years of Affirmative Action for Japanese Burakumin: A Preliminary Report on the Law on Special Measures for Dōwa Projects," *Law in Japan: An Annual* 13 (1980): 39–73.

that experienced by a minority person whose race or ethnic identity is readily visible, and can come unexpectedly when the burakumin origins of someone thought to be a majority Japanese are suddenly discovered. In short, the informal exclusion of burakumin from many spheres of majority social life continues, thereby affirming the stigma that their status carries.

In contrast to youth and women in status-based relationships, burakumin do not confront a calculus of rewards under ideal conditions. Historically, it is true, burakumin did benefit from various protective measures that, in effect, compensated for their status inferiority and exclusion from society. In the Tokugawa period, for example, they enjoyed clear instrumental rewards in the form of an occupational monopoly on leatherwork and certain other "polluted" occupations. Indeed, burakumin were able to use their "polluting effect" to expand the monopoly to occupations that had formerly been neutral, such as straw-sandal making and basket weaving; thus burakumin had work even when other groups, such as *rōnin*, or masterless samurai, could find none. Other material benefits included tax-free use of land, and various benefits accrued as well to burakumin leaders, who were permitted to exercise rather complete control over their own communities, even to the point of having power of taxation.

With emancipation in 1871, however, burakumin lost these various forms of compensation for status inferiority, which Meiji policy considered special feudal rights; these included the tax exemption of their land, as well as the trade monopoly on leatherwork—and just when the demand for leather for boots, saddles, and other equipment for Japan's new conscription army was rising. The special power and prerogatives of burakumin leaders were likewise stripped away.[10]

Certain benefits did accrue to burakumin as a result of their earlier legal monopolies, however. Burakumin continue to figure prominently as butchers and middlemen in the beef industry and as merchants and manufacturers in the shoe industry. Indeed, they have used their political power effectively to lobby for protections of both industries against inexpensive imports.[11] Burakumin have also been aided by *dōwa*, or "integration," legislation of 1969, 1982, and 1987, with funds provided to improve living conditions in qualifying buraku. Yet despite the bitter criticism of many majority Japanese, to whom such measures represent "special treatment," the charge that burakumin as a group are better off than majority Japanese

10. See DeVos and Wagatsuma, *Japan's Invisible Race*, 17–34.

11. See John Longworth, *Beef in Japan* (St. Lucia, Queensland, Australia: University of Queensland Press, 1983), 70–75, for the role of burakumin in the beef imports issue. For their role in the leather and shoe industries, see *Asahi Shinbun* (evening issue), 24 December 1985, 3.

because of successes in a few occupations or the monetary benefits gained from recent legislation has little basis in reality. By virtually every measure, from health to status in the workplace, burakumin are significantly worse off. Few material or affective rewards have come to burakumin in exchange for accepting the status quo; indeed, the benefits they have gained—such as protection for the meat industry or special funds for buraku—have been the reward not of quiescence but of making active claims. Thus, for burakumin, the expectations that operate on women and juniors in a seniority system have not been a constraining factor. With so little to lose, it is no wonder that burakumin have picked up the pace of their protest in this century.

Like many social conflicts involving a large cast of characters and numerous charges and countercharges, the particular conflict that unfolded at Yōka High School is multidimensional. At one level it was the eruption of an ongoing ideological conflict between the Japan Socialist party (JSP), which has links to the Buraku Liberation League, and the Japan Communist party (JCP), to which most of the teachers were connected through their membership in the JCP-allied Hyōgo Prefecture High School Teachers' Union (Hyōgo-ken Kōkyōso). The political ideological dimensions of this conflict were manifest throughout. Indeed, sources identified with the JCP position in the struggle later argued that the real "minority" players in the Yōka incident were not the burakumin people or the league members but the teachers, who found themselves confronted with a JSP-dominated power structure in Yōka Town that backed the league because of its links to the Socialist party; in this view, the league members who participated in the struggle were little more than pawns in a game being played by the JSP.[12] Similarly, some league sources have charged that the teachers were hapless victims of their own JCP-dominated union, which was acting on its own party-dictated agenda. These sources, pointing to the dramatic success of the JCP in the local election held three months after the Yōka High School incident, argue that the Japan Communist party sent the teachers out on that November morning into waiting throngs of angry league members specifically to provoke an attack, knowing that the actions of the league, with its JSP ties, would discredit the town's Socialist administration and so cause its defeat in the upcoming election.

At another level, the Yōka incident was a manifestation of an inter-

12. Fujiwara Toshihiro, interview with author, Kyōto Buraku Mondai Kenkyūjo, Kyoto, 3 July 1978.

organizational conflict within the burakumin movement over who should lead: the Buraku Liberation League, which, with its prewar antecedents, has been the major burakumin rights organization, or a rival organization, the National Liaison Council for Buraku Liberation League Normalization (Buraku Kaihō Dōmei Seijōka Zenkoku Renraku Kaigi), formed in 1969 by communists who broke with the league. These two groups, though they share a commitment to improving the lives of burakumin people, have fundamentally different views on how to achieve that goal. The "normalization group," following the JCP line, sees the plight of burakumin in the context of the working-class struggle. In the key issue at Yōka, for example, they saw the purpose of a high school study group dealing with burakumin problems to be that of teaching the participants about the oppression not only of burakumin, but of labor and farmers as well, all in the context of a discussion of class struggle. The league, in contrast, has argued that a high school study group directed at burakumin problems should be aimed at raising burakumin people's consciousness of their own unique problems as an invisible minority.[13]

The difference in the approach of these two rival groups was even more profound in practice than in theory. A buraku problem study group formed at Yōka High School by the JCP had only one burakumin member at the time of the Yōka incident. According to its league critics, this group approached the problems of burakumin academically and from a historical perspective; its membership, they said, was made up of majority students who were there because of their commitment to the Japan Communist party, not because of an interest in the problems of burakumin specifically. The league-sponsored buraku liberation study group, in contrast, was composed entirely of burakumin, students who, by their own account, wanted a more "human" and personal approach to the problems of burakumin in which they could discuss the discrimination that they and their parents had faced. Yet such an approach, by JCP standards, offered students no real framework for understanding the problems of oppressed groups in general. At this level, then, Yōka High School was one of many arenas in which a long-term struggle between rival organizations with differing goals and approaches was being waged.

Finally, the conflict at Yōka High is a foremost example of a status-based conflict. Leaving aside for a moment the organizational and ideologi-

---

13. The league's position is well-described in Yoshino and Murakoshi, *The Visible Invisible Minority;* and *Yōka Kōkō sabetsu kyōiku kyūdan tōsō.* Both positions are delineated in Wagatsuma, "Political Problems of a Minority Group"; and Rohlen, "Violence at Yōka High School."

cal dimensions of the struggle, the fact remains that the two groups which met head on outside the school on that November day were made up of burakumin people on the one hand and majority Japanese on the other. The teachers were representatives of a majority culture in Japan that treats burakumin as social inferiors. Meanwhile, despite the support that the Buraku Liberation League had managed to gain from groups identified with the majority culture, it was burakumin themselves who engaged in the actual physical struggle with the teachers. Indeed, their circle of majority supporters soon fell away when the league suffered severe public criticism following the episode. The struggle, in short, is comprehensible only in the context of the problems that burakumin people face as a former outcaste group in modern Japan.

The problems of burakumin in Hyōgo Prefecture have been particularly acute, perhaps largely because Hyōgo has had the highest concentration of burakumin of any prefecture in Japan.[14] The conflict inherent in burakumin–majority Japanese relations became manifest in the Yōka High School case for several reasons. A major factor setting the stage for the struggle was the broad impact that burakumin liberation group activities have had in recent decades on the consciousness of both burakumin and majority Japanese with regard to issues of status. A second factor relevant to the Yōka case specifically was the special influence that the local Buraku Liberation League chapter had in the Tajima area owing to its efforts beginning in 1973 to recruit young people and encourage them to explore their position as burakumin. In a larger sense, the incident at Yōka High School was but one more episode in a long-term movement in which burakumin activists, their consciousness of discrimination raised long ago, continue to press for improved conditions. Unlike the two other conflict episodes described in chapters 3 and 4, the struggle at Yōka High School is part of a larger drama in which conflict has long been manifest and in which a highly visible protest movement presses for change.

Yōka High School, in existence for over eighty-five years, has been considered one of the top high schools in its area of Japan—a senior high school preparing students for Kyoto University, Tokyo University, or another of the prestigious national universities. Before World War II Yōka was a prefectural agricultural high school, oriented toward training stu-

14. In 1975 there were 4,374 *dōwa* districts in Japan. Nearly half were concentrated in the Chūgoku and Kinki regions, which include Hyōgo, Osaka, Kyoto, and Nara prefectures. Hyōgo Prefecture had the highest percentage of burakumin in the population. Akio Imaizumi, *Dōwa Problem: Present Situation and Government Measures* (Tokyo: Prime Minister's Office, 1977), 8.

dents for the silk industry. In the postwar period, however, it developed into a general high school, with the general college-preparatory course and vocational courses in such areas as stockbreeding, agriculture, and home economics coexisting under one roof.[15] Each year its best students excel on university entrance examinations that are Japan's entry to elite status, a fact that redounds to the credit of the school's dedicated teachers. To prepare students for the exams is a challenge to teachers and demands a major commitment of their energies. Several Yōka graduates (who were majority Japanese) described to me with great fondness and appreciation the amount of time and personal attention they had gotten from their teachers as the time of the university entrance exams approached. To do well on the exams was to do well not only for one's parents, but for Yōka's reputation and that of its teachers as well.[16]

The Tajima district from which Yōka students came in 1974 has a relatively high concentration of burakumin. Whereas in the nation as a whole an estimated 2 percent of the population are burakumin, in Yōka Town approximately 7 percent are burakumin, and in some nearby towns the percentage is as high as 9–10 percent.[17] Burakumin in the Tajima area have traditionally been concentrated in thirty-one buraku, typically in less desirable areas such as near the river or at the foot of mountains. Unemployment has been high. Those who do work are engaged in agriculture or as laborers or line workers in construction or manufacturing. Because land holdings are small and often far from choice, most agricultural workers engage as well in part-time work such as day labor to supplement their meager income. The buraku, compared to nearby nonburakumin villages, are overcrowded, have narrow roads, and often have drainage and landslide problems owing to their location.

Burakumin in the area have long been regarded—by themselves, by the organizations that represent them, and by the schools—as educationally disadvantaged. According to the league, at the time of the protest few buraku in southern Tajima had nursery schools, despite the high percentage of burakumin women who worked, and there were virtually no cultural or special-education facilities. Only a small percentage of burakumin in the

15. Following the incident the two tracks were separated and a Tajima Agricultural High School was established some two kilometers from Yōka High School. Both league members and teachers held that this action by the Hyōgo prefectural Board of Education was a direct result of the incident.

16. Interviews with graduates of Yōka High School who were students at the time of the struggle, Yōka Town, August 1978.

17. Unpublished data provided by the Office of the Mayor, Yōka Town, August 1978.

area went on to the university; quite the contrary, a disproportionately large number, relative to nonburakumin, ended their education before graduating from high school, and most male burakumin students who did finish went through the vocational course. Burakumin school performance in general lagged well behind that of majority Japanese. Data show that among elementary and junior high school students, 10.5 percent of burakumin students were academically in the bottom group in the schools, whereas only 3.3 percent of majority Japanese students fell in that group. Among second- and third-year junior high school students, 44 percent of the burakumin youngsters had what would be the equivalent of a "below C" average in the United States, as opposed to only 24 percent of the majority Japanese.[18]

In 1974, of the twelve hundred students at Yōka High School, fifty-three were burakumin. Reflecting the educational handicaps faced by burakumin throughout Japan, the students who later became involved in protest activities reported that upon entering Yōka they experienced extreme cultural shock and an educational gap vis-à-vis their majority classmates. The fact that they were burakumin was well known to the other students because of their residence in separate villages. For most, entry into a large high school drawing its students from a broad area was their greatest exposure to date to majority culture. Most of the incoming students, especially the boys, headed immediately into the less prestigious vocational course, whereas exceedingly few became part of that top group of general-course students who are the object of particular teacher interest and attention.

The objective basis for conflict, then, existed in the simple reality of the burakumin students' presence at Yōka High School as a distinct, identifiable minority whose school performance overall was below that of majority students. One of the eight burakumin students central to the Yōka protest, interviewed long after graduation, summarized the situation in explaining why he had wanted to join the league-organized study group when it emerged:

> Those of us who came from Sawa buraku, well, our performance was not too good at the beginning. . . . In middle school the buraku students were very active and had a [league] study group. We developed our self-awareness as burakumin, and we could help each other concretely with lessons and the problems we had being burakumin. Our performance really improved. When it came time to go to senior high school, though, we were scattered. I was the only student from Sawa buraku at Yōka. I felt very isolated. When I was

18. Unpublished data provided by the Hyōgo Prefectural Office, August 1978.

approached by [burakumin] seniors to join the new [league] study group I was happy. I had been lonely and timid up until then.[19]

While the specific grievances of the burakumin students at Yōka High School in 1974 are important for understanding the subsequent protest, the larger environment in which this handful of students became key actors is equally significant. Targeting Yōka for a protest effort was part of an overall strategy of a movement committed to ending discrimination, a movement that has long considered reform of Japan's education curriculum a key goal.

Burakumin liberation groups have been extremely active in postwar Japan. The two groups referred to earlier, the Buraku Liberation League and the JCP-organized "normalization" group, both claim large memberships, have research centers in the major areas of burakumin concentration, and carry on an extensive range of activities. The pace of such efforts increased after 1969, when a Law on Special Measures for Dōwa Projects was enacted by the Diet, making funds available for improving the conditions affecting burakumin. Indeed, much of the conflict between the league and the normalization group has been over which group should apply for and distribute these funds at the local level—in essence, which group is the legitimate representative of burakumin nationwide.[20]

A major area of dispute and competition between the two groups was education. In major cities such as Osaka, one consequence of the Special Measures Law of 1969 was affirmative action measures, backed strongly by the league, designed to improve the educational achievement of burakumin students. These measures, however, met with some resistance; in fact, they led to a confrontation in April 1969 between the league and several middle-school teachers—the "Yata incident"—that in many ways foreshadowed the Yōka conflict of five years later.[21] It was, however, in the

19. Comment by one person in interviews with Yōka graduates who were members of the league-organized study group at Yōka and participated in the hunger strike, Tajima regional headquarters, Buraku Liberation League, August 1978.

20. See Rohlen, "Violence at Yōka High School"; and Upham, "Ten Years of Affirmative Action."

21. The measures included extra counseling, remedial classes, upgrading of facilities, and a prohibition on cross-district registration to prevent majority students from switching out of school districts with large burakumin populations. In the Yata incident, the league forcibly detained and denounced several middle-school teachers for supporting the JCP candidate in the Osaka Teachers' Union election of March 1969 and for repeatedly refusing to meet with league representatives to discuss a pamphlet, which the league said was discriminatory, circulated by the candidate. League leaders forced the teachers to attend a public denunciation session in the citizens' hall of a Yata buraku in Osaka. After the session, which

early educational initiatives that the league's dominant role in assimilation education became well established.

Developments in the Tajima area of Hyōgo Prefecture mirrored the changes and tensions taking place in the major cities where burakumin are concentrated. By 1973 Maruo Yoshiaki, a garage mechanic, had emerged as a key local figure in the Buraku Liberation League, and in February 1974 he set up a league district headquarters for southern Tajima. According to Maruo, some 80 percent of the 1,200 burakumin households in the area were at least nominally league members at that time.[22] The large turnouts during the Yōka protest of burakumin carrying signs and banners associating them with district headquarters attest to the organization's great local influence then.

In the period preceding the Yōka High School incident, the local league, led by Maruo, had turned its full efforts toward the question of burakumin education in the public schools. Maruo's recruitment tactics, according to his critics, involved a combination of persuasion, coercion, and personal magnetism; his focus on the young was fully in keeping with the league's view that liberation for burakumin begins with a change in consciousness through education. As the league states it, the aim has been to force a transition from "education for democracy with little attention to *bu* [*buraku*] and *sa* [*sabetsu*; discrimination], to the democratization of education through the perspectives of the most oppressed."[23] Over the year or so prior to the Yōka incident, then, burakumin students in both Yōka High and surrounding schools had been recruited through an extensive campaign to win them to the league cause. By the time a core group of eight burakumin students within Yōka began to demand recognition for their study group in May 1974, the burakumin youth had developed a strong consciousness of themselves as a minority with a right to demand that the educational system meet their needs. Fully linked with the local

---

lasted all day and until almost 3:00 A.M., two league officials were arrested for unlawful imprisonment, finally to be acquitted by the Osaka District Court in June 1975. Although the Osaka High Court reversed the decision six years later, the case has been regarded as a major league victory, for both courts upheld the league's right to use denunciation as a protest tactic, disagreeing only on the level of violence that was acceptable in its application. See Upham, *Law and Social Change*, 78–103.

22. Maruo Yoshiaki, interview with author, Tajima regional headquarters, Buraku Liberation League, August 1978.

23. Yasumasa Hirasawa, "Buraku Liberation Movement and Its Implications for Dōwa Education: A Critical Analysis of the Literature," Harvard University, Graduate School of Education, March 1984 (photocopy).

chapter of the league and led by Maruo, these students saw their own struggle within Yōka as part of the larger burakumin struggle in Tajima and nationwide.

The struggle at Yōka can be fully understood only in the light of the league-JCP conflict over which approach to burakumin problems was to prevail. For a number of years Yōka High School had had a social science study group devoted to burakumin-related issues; in 1970–1971 it was re-named the Buraku Problem Study Group and was effectively reorganized to continue under JCP guidance; by 1973 all but one of the burakumin student members had dropped out. The burakumin secession and their sub-sequent moves in early 1974 to form a new group of their own unquestion-ably were part of the overall league strategy in the southern Tajima region. Yōka High School was singled out by the league as a special target because it was considered a stronghold of JCP control, particularly so since the leader of the local branch of the high school teachers' union, itself a JCP center of power, taught there. The goal of the league was thus to break the JCP's control over burakumin education at the senior high school level, and it targeted Yōka High School as a test case. The league's right to orga-nize study groups in the schools, it may be noted, had already been estab-lished at the elementary and junior high school levels, where teachers be-longed to union branches not linked with the JCP. To focus on the senior high schools, then, was the logical next step in the league's campaign.

Even if we grant that the Yōka students' campaign to gain approval for their study group was part of an overall league plan, it is a mistake to un-derestimate their own personal commitment to the struggle. The "group of eight" (as indicated above in the comment of one of its members) stated that they had become deeply committed to the league and fully convinced that JCP-directed education for burakumin was fundamentally wrong in its approach. As in the case involving women workers, the process of dis-tancing, or what Murray Edelman calls "myth-making," can be seen to have already occurred before the actual protest began[24]—in the Yōka in-stance, almost certainly long before the group of eight, with the league in the wings, tried to place its demands before the school authorities.

If all Japanese, by virtue of being women or junior to others, may occa-sionally find themselves treated unsatisfactorily or oppressively because of attributes that are beyond their power to change, burakumin experience a far more extreme form of status-based discrimination. Historically, preju-dice toward burakumin often denied their humanity entirely; nevertheless,

24. Murray Edelman, *Politics as Symbolic Action: Mass Arousal and Quiescence* (New York: Academic Press, 1971), 53–54.

it is important to note that such discriminatory treatment, while extreme, was on a scale that encompassed all deference behavior—for example, whereas in Tokugawa times all status inferiors were expected to bow deeply to their superiors, for a burakumin this meant prostrating oneself before any majority Japanese. The difference, in other words, was in degree, not kind. In a hierarchically oriented society with the emperor at the apex, some group had to occupy the lowest tier and, in the logic of hierarchy, display the extremes of deference behavior. Likewise, whereas historically women were excluded from many spheres, such as politics or—in the case of the upper classes in prewar Japan—the leisure world of their husbands, burakumin were excluded from most spheres of majority Japanese social life. Exclusion, like various kinds of deference behavior, was designed to preserve hierarchy based on relations between unequals.

Of the three groups whose protest activity this book studies, burakumin are by far the most militant in their rejection of deference and other status-based behavior. But then, the material and especially the affective rewards of deference and quiescence that juniors and women in well-functioning superior-inferior relations reap do not accrue to burakumin today. It is also true that burakumin have had particular advantages in reaching a collective consciousness of the dissatisfactions of status inequality and in organizing to protest. One factor, as noted, is that the discrimination against them has been so extreme. But, as resource mobilization theory establishes so well, the extent of deprivation is far less significant to a group's capacity to successfully mount a protest than are other factors having to do with resource availability. Ironically, the greatest advantage for burakumin, as compared to other status groups, has probably been their isolation and exclusion from the rest of society, for, as noted earlier (and in a way that is consonant with the writings of Coleman, Simmel, Coser, and other theorists), the web of close affiliation in junior-senior and men-women relations in daily life not only constrains overt expressions of conflict but also presses status inferiors to find other solutions to unsatisfactory situations, including self-sacrifice and endurance in the name of preserving harmony, maintaining the long-term relationship, and winning the approval of others.[25] For burakumin, who in many cases have but limited interaction with majority Japanese, no such constraints or pressures operate. Little distancing need occur because distance has been in place all along.

25. Coleman, *Community Conflict*; Lewis A. Coser, *Continuities in the Study of Social Conflict* (New York: Free Press, 1967) and *The Functions of Social Conflict* (New York: Free Press, 1956).

For all status groups in postwar Japan who engage in protest, however, the greatest resource has been ideological change. Democratization, which carries forward a process that was under way on a lesser scale earlier in the century, supports their efforts at many levels. Their exposure to the "official" democratic ideology of postwar Japan, even with simultaneous socialization in behavior based on hierarchy and deference to superiors taking place, contributes to necessary consciousness-raising as they consider how to respond to unsatisfactory treatment due both to their status and to their consequent exclusion. Furthermore, the broader force of democratic ideology in the culture at large—as reflected in media treatment of intergenerational issues in politics, for instance, and in public awareness of ideological contradictions in the treatment of women—becomes an external resource to the status-deprived, supporting changes in their own consciousness and in the worldview of other potential allies. The next chapter will explore how status inferiors, having reached a point at which they are prepared to wage a protest, begin to take action.

6

The View from Below:
Mobilizing a Protest

The path is treacherous, but being fully aware of its dangers we
want to move steadily forward, step by step.

Kōno Yōhei, August 1976

The process by which people experiencing dissatisfaction over status issues
prepare for action may be lengthy. As the previous chapters showed, central to the process are those key individuals who initially experience a
transformation of consciousness regarding status issues and then, through
leadership and organization, draw others to the cause. That individuals become such agents of change is no surprise in terms of Western theory on
social movements. But to find individuals leading the way flies directly in
the face of a collectivity model thought to operate in Japan, in which the
group, not the individual, is the main locus of decision making and action.
Conflicts quickly gain momentum as these leaders, often joined by a close
circle of supporters, initiate a consciousness-raising process through which
a group comes to a common understanding of its objective situation. The
steps along the way are manifold: the leader's own transformation of consciousness; the recognition by a small group of supporters of that person's
leadership and the spread of consciousness to this inner circle; conversion
of other followers to the leader's analysis and interpretation of the objective situation; and the growth of the collective consciousness of the group.[1]

Protests can be thought of as arising from a particular mix of interest
and opportunity.[2] As we have seen, interests may be shaped by various factors that both impede and spur status-based protest; then, as changes occur
in the reward structure, the status-deprived come to see it as in their inter-

---

1. For a discussion of the process by which conflicts emerge, see Louis Kriesberg, *The Sociology of Social Conflict* (Englewood Cliffs, N.J.: Prentice-Hall, 1973);
Coser, *Continuities in the Study of Social Conflict*; and Coleman, *Community Conflict*.
2. Tilly, *From Mobilization to Revolution*, 7.

est to engage in active protest. In terms of opportunity, we have discussed how ideological change in Japan over the issues of status and equality has created an opening that makes status-based protest more possible.

Mobilizing a protest—moving from the domain of perception to that of action—involves numerous new hurdles, however. Two major tasks loom, the first internal: achieving a level of group solidarity sufficient for launching and sustaining a protest; the second external: winning credibility and support for the protest outside the group. This second task is multidimensional, for not only does a group contemplating a protest typically hope to gain additional adherents, but it also seeks the approval and support of the watching public as well as credibility in its negotiations with the targets of the protest. Although this dual challenge confronts all potential protest groups, whatever the national setting, in Japan there are special difficulties, stemming from the strong cultural aversion to protest and conflict. Furthermore, as this chapter will show, status-based protests encounter obstacles on every side as they seek to consolidate support, both internally and externally; a large part of their task, then, is given over to devising and implementing strategies aimed at overcoming those obstacles.

Achieving Solidarity

In status-based conflicts, as in other types of protest, groups form and become the basis for collective action. Since Japan is a group-oriented society, the effort of assembling a group and setting it toward purposeful activity would seem at first glance to be easier there than in many other countries. Western conflict theory holds that protest groups achieve solidarity in two major ways, both of which would appear to apply to status-based groups undergoing mobilization. First, solidarity is spurred if potential members share some major characteristic[3]—which status groups certainly do, being drawn together by a common ascriptive attribute. Second, the presence of internal networks—extensive links among group members through interpersonal bonds, friendship, and patterns of spending time together both in and outside the group—is thought to promote solidarity.[4] A related measure is "inclusiveness"—the amount of time, energy, and total social interaction that is absorbed in, or arises out of ties

3. Ibid., 62–63.

4. Harrison White refers to this combination of shared characteristics (or category) and networks as "catnet"—a shorthand term for key factors that promote solidarity; see White, "Notes on the Constituents of Social Structure," unpublished paper, Harvard University, cited in ibid., 63.

with, the organization.[5] Again, the cultural tendency in Japan to organize social life around groups and to devote much of one's time to activities in a primary group, with little attempt to maintain a sharp boundary between work life and "personal" life, would seem to encourage extraordinary levels of inclusiveness within groups of all types.

How these two factors work is especially well illustrated in the case of the Buraku Liberation League. The very reality of caste-based discrimination has meant that a vast number of burakumin, even today, live in a world made up almost wholly of burakumin. Not only did the burakumin participants in the Yōka struggle live in segregated communities, but the league itself was the major social organization in virtually all of those hamlets as well, enjoying an 80 percent membership rate among burakumin families.[6] League publications note that many burakumin have their first personal contact with majority Japanese only when they leave the public schools of their own segregated communities and go to senior high schools like Yōka that draw students from the entire region. Contact in this case is far more limited than it is for many segregated ethnic minorities in other countries, who frequently move in the world of the dominant majority as domestic servants, gardeners, and so on; because of pollution fears associated with "untouchability," such intimate personal contact between majority Japanese and burakumin is minimal. Burakumin who work outside the community may likewise have only very limited social contact with majority employers and co-workers. If they make their identity as burakumin known, majority Japanese may socially spurn them; and if, as many do, they "pass" (conceal their identity as burakumin), they will often avoid extensive informal contact for fear of discovery. For all these reasons, then, solidarity within individual burakumin communities and among burakumin in general is extraordinarily high. The league, as the major activist burakumin organization in the Tajima region, reflected this solidarity and, indeed, could capitalize on it for mobilization. For the burakumin participants in the Yōka struggle, students and adults alike, the league represented their single major organizational attachment, and shared membership in the league was a feature of most of their social relationships.

The groups formed by women and by juniors in our other case studies hardly had the same basis for solidarity as the burakumin in degree; still, the same factors operated, if to a lesser extent. By virtue of being brought together by a common attribute, the group members shared a common

5. Tilly, *From Mobilization to Revolution*, 64.
6. Figures provided by the Tajima regional headquarters of the Buraku Liberation League, August 1978.

identity. Moreover, they were linked by the interpersonal bonds that grow among people who occupy similar ranks in large organizations. Like the members of the union locals in the United States described by Seymour Lipset, Martin Trow, and James Coleman, members of status-based groups tend to have "distinct, compelling identities" and "extensive, absorbing interpersonal networks."[7] Since organizational solidarity is the key to mobilization, status-based groups, once formed, are, from the standpoint of internal characteristics, well positioned to act.

Capitalizing on shared bonds that are already in place owing to the members' low status, status groups can further enhance the members' "inclusiveness" in numerous ways. Groups in general, for example, may increase their value to members by offering solutions to personal problems; in the case of status-based groups this task is quite readily accomplished, since the daily problems that the members, as status inferiors, share are the specific focus of group efforts. Groups may also make it difficult for members to leave. In Japan, a diminished exit option is a natural consequence of group formation because of the close identification of members with their group and also because the stigma of engaging in conflict is so great that members are forced together even more by the protest—in effect, the damage has already been done, so there is little point in leaving.

Despite these seeming strengths, groups made up of status inferiors confront numerous obstacles when they attempt to gear up for action. First of all, there is the obstacle posed by the norms that govern inferior-superior relationships, which include an acceptable protocol for handling grievances. As discussed in chapter 2, the burden of addressing the problems of status inferiors is thought to rest with status superiors. Ideally, a superior is sensitive to the needs and interests of those below and heads off problems before they arise. For status inferiors to make open demands of their superiors or to seek redress for their grievances publicly, through collective action, flagrantly violates the code of the relationship.

The second obstacle is structural and arises out of organizational norms. In Japan, the dominant organizational forms link individuals in vertical relationships, rather than in the horizontal relationships characteristic of groups brought together by their shared status or interests. One of the most obvious expressions of this cultural pattern in Japanese society is the predominance of vertically organized enterprise unions, made up of the members of a single business organization, over horizontally organized trade unions. Membership in horizontally organized groups in Japan

7. Seymour Lipset, Martin Trow, and James S. Coleman, *Union Democracy* (Glencoe, Ill.: Free Press, 1956).

tends to be less salient for their members, even when solidarity, by obvious measures, might be thought to be high. Horizontally organized groups, of course, exist in Japan in numerous forms, from the village young men's group to the "company gang" to various women's groups, but these have more often been organized for leisure, study, or recreation than for purposeful action. Exceptions certainly exist: Japan does have some trade unions, and citizens' movements, as a major social and political development in the 1970s, have been much heralded as horizontally organized protest movements in a vertical society.[8] But status-based groups uniting individuals with shared attributes have the same problems on this score that citizens' groups do, for they too represent an organizational form that is less familiar, with a less ready cultural "fit," than older, vertical forms.

A third obstacle arises out of the risks inherent in directly challenging persons who, by their very role as status superiors, exercise power in an immediate and obvious way over the protesters. These risks can be quite high, since to challenge a pattern of authority relations is to go against the existing mechanism of reward distribution and those who control it. The three status-based protests studied here, for instance, involved groups of individuals with relatively little to lose from engaging in a protest. But even so, the risks were not inconsiderable. For Kōno's group, even if these men were less reliant on the rewards of LDP membership than many other junior representatives, nevertheless, political careers were at stake. The tea pourers, for their part, risked potential social exclusion in the small world of a Japanese office, in which smooth working relations are highly valued. Unmarried women faced the particular danger that if they came to be viewed as "troublemakers" their marriage chances would be damaged, a consideration that is still quite significant in a country where many young men (and their parents) seek a wife who is *yasashii*, a term that may be roughly translated as gentle, tender, and meek—qualities that are not well displayed in conflict behavior.[9] Only in the burakumin protest were the risks—at least to the Buraku Liberation League—of a mobilization effort not direct and personal; for the student members enrolled at Yōka High School and therefore challenging the authority of their own teachers, however, the personal risks were quite high.

The difficulties posed by these many obstacles differ, of course, according to the status group involved. In clearing the hurdle posed by the norms of status relations, for example, women are at the greatest disadvantage,

8. See McKean, *Environmental Protest and Citizen Politics.*
9. See Pharr, *Political Women,* 157–169, for a discussion of the risks to women of political activism.

being in general the most culturally constrained group in terms of conflict behavior. Burakumin, on this obstacle, represent the opposite extreme: for those associated with the movement, and among burakumin more generally, the process of consciousness-raising, the diffusion of a new perspective, and the growth of solidarity have all occurred over a long period of time, and the barriers against engaging in conflict behavior on behalf of agreed-upon objectives are thus minimal. Protest over the terms of senior-junior relations lies between these two extremes. Although juniors generally need to undergo a change of perspective in order to challenge the inferior-superior relationships of which they are a part, that process, and protest itself, are nonetheless less difficult for them than for women, since support in the culture for protest behavior is far greater with regard to male youth, and males in general, than women.

Cumulatively, these various obstacles mean that status inferiors may feel extraordinarily constrained when launching a protest. The horizontal ties that bind them together in their common plight render them—in a society where, as a rule, goals are set collectively in vertically organized groups led by high-status persons—leaderless and unsure of how to proceed. The strong sanctions against active questioning of authority leave status inferiors doubtful about their right to protest in the first place, and the highly visible risks of challenging persons with such direct say over their fortunes are powerful deterrents to action. The need, in effect, is to create one's own sources of legitimacy for a protest, when the culture is so niggardly in handing them out.

Three major resources can be brought to bear in overcoming the numerous constraints to action-taking. The first, ironically, is status itself—the legitimation of protest through the intervention, leadership, or participation of higher-status individuals or organizations.[10] Each case study reveals incidences of such a factor at work. Mr. Kawata, the union organizer who singled out a leader for the tea pourers' rebellion, is a good illustration, as are Makino, the college-educated woman leader of the same struggle, and Kōno, the son of one of Japan's most famous LDP politicians who led the mobilization effort that culminated in the New Liberal Club breakaway. Yet another illustration is the role played by the Japan Socialist party in the Yōka High School incident, in which the party, speaking through non-burakumin high-status officials in the community and the school, actively

10. See Morton Deutsch, *The Resolution of Conflict: Constructive and Destructive Processes* (New Haven: Yale University Press, 1973), 68–70, for a discussion of the importance of status differentiation for structuring the nature of the conflict.

supported the efforts of burakumin students to win the study group they sought. In each case, higher-status individuals inside or outside the group served to legitimate the efforts of persons who otherwise might have been doubtful about their right to protest.

It is not only in Japan, of course, that the participation of higher-status individuals or organizations has validated a protest attempt. The involvement of white liberals in the civil rights movement in the United States and of men in suffrage and feminist movements in the United States, Britain, and Japan suggests that the role of high-status third parties in legitimizing protest may be a cross-culturally significant feature of all status-based conflicts. Gaston Rimlinger, for instance, found that in the early history of the German labor movement, employees who doubted their right to protest looked to individuals of higher status to forge a protest ideology and to lead them; as he notes, in such a status-conscious society, workers could not accept someone of their own low status as a leader. Indeed, he attributes German miners' gains after 1850 in part to this very pattern of reliance.[11] In each case, representatives of the superior status group do what they normally do in interactions with status inferiors: they use their authority—but this time they use it to legitimize the substitution of a new, democratically based ideology of interstatus relations for an old one based on traditional values. For the status inferiors, this act of legitimation not only lends authority to their own emerging view of the objective conflict situation, but it also helps relieve the fears linked to the contemplation of hostile actions against status superiors. In sum, then, the intercession or show of support by a status superior functions to quiet anxiety, as well as to reassure inferiors that their new view of reality is comprehensible to at least some of their seniors.

A second resource in mounting a protest derives from the power of ideology. Naturally, numerous resources exist on which to base action, ranging from coercive (weapons, technology) to utilitarian (information, money, labor) to normative (loyalties, commitments).[12] Various types of protest movements in Japan have drawn on different mixes of these resources for mobilization. Right-wing nationalist protest in the 1930s, for example, which often involved assassination attempts, used both coercive and normative resources. Citizens' movements, in contrast, have been largely utilitarian, for in them mobilization has often required the harnessing of

11. Rimlinger, "Legitimation of Protest," 363–376, esp. 373. For other aspects of the role of status in the German labor movement, see chapter 10.
12. Amitai Etzioni, *The Active Society* (New York: Free Press, 1968), 388–389.

scientific resources (involving labor, money, and research) to amass information on such issues as the adverse environmental consequences of development or pollution by existing industries in order to convince their
membership that their cause was just.[13] All protest groups, by challenging
the status quo and those authority figures in charge, are resource-poor
relative to their opponents. But low-status groups, which often lack the
power to command coercive and utilitarian resources, are especially so.
Their key resource in building group solidarity, then, is normative.

In this task, ideology plays a key role. For one thing, official support for
democratic values and egalitarianism in the constitution and laws and in
the set of values transmitted through education constitutes a major normative resource in any status-based struggle in Japan. The knowledge that
they are in the right binds protesters together, setting them against those
who refuse to act according to the "official" ideology. Ideology may figure
in a second way as well, as seen in the burakumin protest. Because the Buraku Liberation League has had close ties throughout much of the postwar
period with the Japan Socialist party, many members of the movement see
socialist ideology as providing powerful normative support for democratic
principles; this affirmation in turn strengthens resolve and solidarity in the
mounting of a protest.

Research on the growth of the labor movement in Germany, another
society characterized by hierarchical social relations, confirms the importance of both these factors. Totalist ideologies, as offered by the Social
Democratic party and the Christian Social movement, provided a systematic critique and vision of society that supported nineteenth-century
protest efforts. As Rimlinger shows, German miners, who were enjoined
traditionally to show "esteem, obedience, and respect for their superiors," ultimately escaped dependency through ideological indoctrination:
industrial protest in Germany thus became entwined with broad programs of social and political reform.[14] It is noteworthy that, like the Buraku
Liberation League, numerous status-based protest movements in Japan
both today and historically have had ties with left-wing parties that provided such a program and vision.[15] In these cases, as in the German miners'

13. See Krauss and Simcock, "Citizens' Movements."
14. Rimlinger, "Legitimation of Protest," 371; see 371–376.
15. For a discussion of such ties in the prewar women's movement, see Pharr,
Political Women, chap. 2. On the links between student protest and the left, see
Henry Dewitt Smith II, *Japan's First Student Radicals* (Cambridge, Mass.: Harvard
University Press, 1972). On the connections among a variety of protest groups and

case, totalist ideology offers direction and purpose to individuals locked into positions of dependency and powerlessness, helping them to overcome their fear of defying authority through protest.

A third resource for building solidarity is anger—at least to the extent that it results in distancing. As discussed earlier, in the process of consciousness-raising status inferiors compare the objective terms of their situation with the promises held out to them under the terms of the "official" ideology of status relations in Japan. As this occurs, "gnawing uncertainty" is gradually replaced by myth—a new construction of characters and meaning—and the protesters' interior world becomes divided into friends and enemies.[16] The fuel for change is anger, which of course provides a powerful resource for building solidarity in all protests; but to the extent that anger in fact spurs distancing from an "enemy," it serves the particular function in status-based protests of enabling low-status persons to challenge the looming authority figures in their lives. In all three of our case studies, a clear sense of "us versus them" was firmly in place prior to action-taking.

Students of Japanese groups have long noted their inclusiveness and exclusiveness, epitomized in the Japanese notion of "we-ness" relative to outsiders or foreigners (*gaijin*). The same tendency is expressed more extremely in the behavior of protest groups. David Apter and Nagayo Sawa, for example, record the utter animosity with which protesters at Narita Airport came to see the Liberal Democratic party, bureaucrats, riot police, and others who supported construction of the airport.[17] Indeed, in the struggle it became common for the protesters to sling human excrement at the police from long-handled bamboo dippers—a stark statement of the loathing they must have felt. Their hostility toward the authorities was so great that many were prepared to give over some twenty years of their lives, and some even to die, for the cause.

The same alienation from the opposing side marks status-based protest, but there it is especially vital for action-taking. Even protesters who, as in the case of Kōno and his group, may be closely bound to and dependent

---

their ties to the left, see John F. Howes and Nobuya Bamba, eds., *Pacificism in Japan: The Christian and Socialist Tradition* (Vancouver: University of British Columbia Press, 1978). For the connections between burakumin protest and left-wing movements, see DeVos and Wagatsuma, *Japan's Invisible Race.*

16. See Edelman, *Politics as Symbolic Action*, 53–64.

17. David E. Apter and Nagayo Sawa, *Against the State: Politics and Social Protest in Japan* (Cambridge, Mass.: Harvard University Press, 1984).

Table 4. Two Worlds: The New Liberal Club Breakaway as Seen by
Inferiors and Superiors

Inferiors' View	Superiors' View
Role of Younger-Generation Diet Members in the Party	
All members should participate fully and actively in the life of the party	Members should participate on the basis of seniority
Specific Issues	
Party decision-making process should include junior members	Party decision-making process is best left to seniors, who will take junior members' interests into account
Motivation of Protest	
To force change in party for selves and other juniors; to seek alternative avenue for utilizing abilities	Self-aggrandizement to embarrass the party
Protesters' Commitment	
Strong	Weak
Protesters' Attitudes	
Reasonable, committed, unselfish	Unreasonable, immature, "spoiled," selfish
Superiors' Attitudes	
Arrogant, unsympathetic, disdainful of inferiors	Reasonable, sympathetic, understanding toward inferiors

on the authority figures against whom the protest is directed, express considerable hostility in their comments, reflecting the extraordinary amount of distancing that has occurred. Indeed, by the time a protest is under way, perceptions of the issues at stake have altered so much that protesters and those they oppose have developed wholly distinct views of reality, in a way reminiscent of the great Japanese film *Rashomon*. (See tables 4, 5, and 6.) To study a status-based conflict is an extraordinary experience, for it means moving back and forth between camps with wholly different perspectives on the way things are—and ought to be. Superiors who see themselves as sincere, sympathetic, reasonable, and unselfish (see table 5) are viewed by protesters as arrogant, unsympathetic, unreasonable, and selfish. Entirely different perspectives on the specific issues in the struggle have emerged, and the motivations of the opposing side have become suspect, even despicable. Once lines harden in this way and distinct myths take shape, the challenge of finding a resolution to the conflict is formidable indeed.

Table 5. Two Worlds: The Tea Pourers' Rebellion as Seen by
         Inferiors and Superiors

Inferiors' View	*Superiors' View*
Role of Women in Office Setting	
Men and women hired on an equal basis should be assigned similar work	Despite job descriptions, men and women are suited to performing different jobs
Specific Issues	
Tea pouring is not the natural duty of women, at least in the office; tea should be available on a "serve yourself" basis	Tea pouring is the natural duty of women
Since women are expected to pour tea, it is a job requirement and one that interferes with other duties	Women should pour tea, but it is not an "official" job requirement, and thus it should not interfere with other duties
Motivation of Protest	
To rationalize tea-pouring routines in the office	To make trouble; to humiliate superiors by asking them to perform a demeaning task
Protesters' Commitment	
Strong	Weak
Protesters' Attitudes	
Patient, reasonable, determined, serious, unselfish	Impatient, demanding, lacking seriousness, ridiculing of others, selfish
Superiors' Attitudes	
Arrogant, unsympathetic, unreasonable, selfish	Sincere, sympathetic, reasonable, unselfish

Winning Support for an Offensive Mobilization

The second major task of protesters is to marshal support and gain credibility, not only from potential participants but also from the public or that portion of it whose eyes and ears are trained on the protest. Mobilizing support is a central challenge in any protest, but it is all the more onerous in Japan in the case of status-based protests because of the type of mobilization that is involved.

Charles Tilly distinguishes among defensive, preparatory, and offensive

Table 6. Two Worlds: The Yōka High School Incident as Seen by
Inferiors and Superiors

Inferiors' View	Superiors' View
Situation of Burakumin Students in School Setting	
Burakumin students experience discrimination	Burakumin students are treated like majority students in school
Specific Issues	
Burakumin students need a special support and study group in school to address their specific problems; the existing group fails to do this, so it should be replaced	All students should have an opportunity to study the problems of burakumin in a broad historical context; a group for this purpose already exists and no other is needed
Motivation of Protest	
To bring an end to educational discrimination against burakumin; to support burakumin students in coping with majority Japanese in school; to advance the Buraku Liberation League as the only group qualified to represent burakumin interests	To promote the Buraku Liberation League, whatever the cost; to disrupt the normal educational process
Protesters' Commitment	
Strong, in the case of both burakumin students and league members	Weak in the case of students; strong in the case of league members
Protesters' Attitudes	
Reasonable, committed, self-assertive	Unreasonable, fanatical, demanding, violent
Superiors' Attitudes	
Arrogant, unreasonable, unsympathetic	Sincere, reasonable, sympathetic

mobilization, depending on the goals sought.[18] Overwhelmingly, status politics requires "offensive mobilization"—that is, an effort aimed at staking new claims rather than defending old ones. In Japan, a great many protests are defensive, aimed at guarding the status quo or preventing further erosion of it. Material and acquisitive protests, for example, are normally defensive, with people adversely affected by various measures rallying together around their cause—the peasant uprisings against taxation,

18. Tilly, *From Mobilization to Revolution*, 73–78.

corvée, and other state policies in the Tokugawa era and farmers' and workers' protests in prewar Japan being cases in point. Quality-of-life issues today also lend themselves to defensive mobilization, as when a community threatened with environmental pollution organizes to protest; the Narita Airport struggle, led by farmers seeking to keep their land and way of life, is a classic example. Many protests involving moral or value issues have likewise been staged defensively. Right-wing nationalist activism, for instance, has generally been justified as a defense of "true" Japanese values and of the emperor against people (such as party politicians in the 1930s) who sought to "sully" traditional beliefs and symbols. In a country with historically strong sanctions against dissent, it is no wonder that Japanese protest has been largely defensive in nature: when the state or other authority figures take new initiatives, those adversely affected protest. The cultural acceptability of defensive mobilization also creates powerful incentives for claiming that a protest is being waged in defense of some value, even when it is not—the Meiji Restoration being a compelling historical example.[19]

Almost inevitably, however, status-based conflicts run up against the cultural preferences surrounding protest. Defensive mobilization is essentially an effort to preserve what one has, whether it is a minimum standard of life now threatened by oppressive taxation or a belief in the emperor's divinity and spiritual purity now tarnished by party politicians. Status-based protests, in contrast, represent an attempt to break with the past, to alter traditional patterns of social relations and of role expectations. They call for a new way of doing things and, drawing on democratic ideology, assert new rights. Even when they have certain defensive elements, status-based protests are overwhelmingly offensive in character; they are thus exceptionally difficult to "package" in defensive wrappings.

Among our three cases, the clearest example of offensive mobilization—in which "a group pools resources in response to opportunities to realize its interests"[20]—may be seen in the Buraku Liberation League's efforts preceding the Yōka High School incident. At the time, the Tajima region had a socialist administration. Given its alliance with the Japan Socialist party, the league was therefore presented with an opportunity to advance its goals and interests by means of an initiative. In a sense, of course,

19. The Meiji Restoration, which widely touted the goal of restoring imperial rule, is in many ways a startlingly successful example of an effort to repackage as "defensive" a protest whose aim was to alter profoundly the status quo—and thus was offensive in its basic nature.

20. Tilly, *From Mobilization to Revolution*, 74.

this mobilization was defensive and competitive, for the league was deeply concerned about the encroachment on its turf by the Japan Communist party and the communists' hold over teachers locally through the teachers' union. But in no way was the league interested simply in protecting its territory or minimizing its losses. The educational campaign it launched represented a major new effort to extend the league's reach and to win acceptance for a program of reform.

In the case of the tea pourers' rebellion, the motive for mobilization was not protection of old rights and prerogatives but the assertion of new ones, encompassed in a new view that sees traditional female tasks as troublesome and demeaning. The erosion of rewards in the Housing Division for performing such duties well undoubtedly helped create a sense of urgency in these mobilizing efforts, and in that sense the moves were partly defensive. But overall, the women's initiative was overwhelmingly offensive.

The New Liberal Club's situation is more complex, because it had elements of all three major types of mobilization effort. As with the tea pourers, the strategy was in part defensive, in the sense that juniors were concerned about the possible erosion of future rewards because of the Liberal Democratic party's declining popularity in the mid 1970s and its uncertain ability to stay in power. It was also preparatory, in that it involved a pooling of resources "in anticipation of future opportunities and threats"[21]—as Kōno's founding in 1972, four years before the breakaway, of the Political Engineering Institute with primarily junior men demonstrates, for at that time it was still unclear whether the members' best interests lay in staying with the party and pressing for change or in taking the more dramatic step of a breakaway. In the end, however, the mobilization effort was decidedly offensive in character, focusing as it did on party reform and on achieving new gains—new posts, new political networks—for junior Diet members. And, like all status-based protests, Kōno and his group's breakaway asserted new rights.

In the light of the ideal model of protest set out in chapter 2, the problem inherent in offensive mobilization is readily visible. Whereas ideally protest arises from situations of grave injustice or deprivation in which a loss has been threatened or suffered, offensive protests are directed unambiguously at seeking new gains. Unlike "ideal" protests, they lack a selfless higher purpose; indeed, they openly assert the self and hold that making personal claims is worthy, proper, and legitimate. Rather than demon-

21. Ibid.

strate the self-sacrificing behavior that wins approval in Japan, protesters in conflicts over status celebrate the self and seek rewards for it.

Just as certain resources are useful for addressing the internal challenges of achieving group solidarity, some of the same resources are valuable in gaining legitimacy for the struggle among outsiders. The formation of alliances with higher-status third parties is a classic example, something that status groups, of course, do for many reasons. As Morton Deutsch notes, powerless groups must make up in numbers what they lack in other resources—power, influence, money, prestige, and so on.[22] Increasing power through alliances has particular importance in status-based struggles, however, for not only must protesters attract followers, but they must jockey for advantage in status terms as well. By becoming linked to individuals or organizations of higher status, then, the group both builds internal solidarity and increases its own political leverage.

Nowhere is this alliance-building strategy clearer than in the Yōka High School struggle. The Buraku Liberation League has a long tradition of forging partnerships, going back to the successful efforts of the Levelers' Association (Suiheisha) in the 1920s to ally with labor and proletarian parties, including both socialist and communist groups. Today, league literature links the organization with all the major labor union federations; opposition parties; other minority organizations such as those representing women, the handicapped, Ainu, and Koreans; religious groups; and many others. Similarly, league newsletters are filled with accounts of visits and exchanges with the Chinese, with groups representing the scheduled castes of India, with American blacks, and so on. Alliance politics has many functions for the league. Not only do alliances increase the league's clout as discussed by Deutsch, but they also create a bridge to the majority population in Japan and, at the same time, help to legitimize the league in the eyes of the public.

In the Yōka struggle, the league's ability to launch its ambitious educational campaign in the Tajima region was the direct result of its previous success with alliance politics. Ties with the Japan Socialist party at the national level made the campaign possible in the first place, for they allowed the league both to capitalize on the fact that a socialist mayor would support the initiative and to bring pressure on the principal of Yōka High School to cooperate with the league. Once the conflict began to escalate, these ties helped the local league chapter to build a network of alliances within Tajima itself.

22. Deutsch, *Resolution of Conflict*, 395–396.

The PTA was a more immediate target of the league's alliance-building efforts. In July, four months before the physical clash between league members and the teachers, the PTA (whose leadership was in the JSP camp) called a general meeting to question teachers about burakumin policies at Yōka. Soon after, leaders of the PTA urged the teachers to meet with the league-affiliated students and their parents regarding the study group. They also put pressure on the principal, already squeezed because of his links (through the Board of Education) to a socialist administration at the prefectural level. By the end of July he had yielded and, over faculty objections, used his veto power to override the teachers' earlier decision to forbid the formation of the study group. Throughout the struggle, the league's alliances with majority-culture organizations played a critical role in enhancing their standing and increasing their support in the community.

Similarly, in the protest waged by Kōno and his group a key tactic involved the attempted formation of an alliance with a man of higher status from among the middle generation of LDP leadership. Their aim was to find a candidate for party president in 1974 who was far enough from senior elite status to be sympathetic to the juniors' cause but still near enough to be a serious contender for the position. Kōno and his group approached three such men in turn in the fall of 1974. The first was Miyazawa Kiichi of the Ōhira faction, then age fifty-five, who had already established his credentials with junior party members through his leadership of the Hirakawa Society, one of the LDP's many study groups made up of junior members. Miyazawa, however, anticipating that he might be called on to support his own faction head, Ōhira, if a party election were held, declined the younger men's offer of support for his candidacy.[23] The group then approached Ishida Hirohide, age fifty-nine, a leader in the Miki faction, of which Nishioka and Yamaguchi were both members. Ishida also declined. A final approach was made to Fujiyama Aiichirō. Although this seventy-seven-year-old senior party statesman was hardly a part of the middle generation, in some ways he was the functional equivalent. For one thing, as a man who had been passed over in the contest for

23. Waiting paid off in some ways for Miyazawa, who in 1986 finally took over the faction once headed by Ōhira. But the costs of waiting are also quite evident in his career, for by the time he took the factional reins from Suzuki and became the most senior of three contenders for party president, his age (sixty-six) was considered a factor to be weighed against him, and he was not selected. (Since then he suffered yet another setback: criticized for his involvement in the Recruit Cosmos scandal, he was forced in December 1988 to resign from the post of finance minister and to devote himself to rebuilding his badly demoralized faction. See *Nihon Keizai Shinbun*, 23 December 1988, 2; and *Yomiuri Shinbun*, 29 December 1988, 2.)

prime minister and whose faction had drifted away, he had nothing to lose from running for the post. Ostensibly, the Kōno group hoped that he would be attracted to the idea of a final try for the presidency. Moreover, since he had followed the "career politician" route into the Diet rather than the bureaucratic avenue, he, among the various seniors in the party, was thought to be potentially more sympathetic to the cause of ambitious juniors. This view was based on a widespread LDP belief that the most meticulous observers of the rules of seniority, and the ones most critical of upstarts who attempt to push ahead of others in line, have been the ex-bureaucrats (including Satō, Ōhira, and Fukuda); pure politicians, in contrast, are thought to be most receptive to those ambitious young men who wish to maneuver to a position of greater advantage. In any event, Fujiyama also declined.

Of the three, according to Kōno, Ishida offered the most encouragement regarding the group's desire to open up the party decision-making process, even suggesting that "someone from among themselves" consider running for the party presidency.[24] It was only after Miyazawa and Ishida had turned them down that the group began to contemplate putting Kōno forward as a candidate. More important, the blessing of these higher-status leaders now gave Kōno's own claims to power added legitimacy. Thus, even when alliance politics failed, support could be won.

In the tea pourers' rebellion, alliance politics with higher-status individuals was crucial. The ties with the younger men in the office through the Youth and Women's Bureau of the union not only firmed the women's resolve, but they also gave the protest and the protesters credibility. Because the bureau was the only official forum in the division where the two sexes were, in an institutional sense, on an equal footing, once the protest plan took shape, the women went to these younger men for support. First Makino met with Kawata, as head of the bureau, and won approval for the plan; then the group sent a written notice to the male bureau members announcing the new arrangements for the serving of tea in the office. As was their normal practice, the leadership corps of the women's group attended the next bureau meeting, although they left the formal announcement of the plan to Kawata. According to all the available reports, no discussion followed the announcement: Kawata had already sought and secured the members' support. The next day, when the women put the plan into effect by making tea at the appropriate times but leaving it for the men to serve themselves, the role of the younger men was crucial, for by demonstrating that they considered it fully acceptable for a man to

24. Mainichi Shinbunsha Seijibu, *Seihen*, 194.

pour his own tea, they lent legitimacy to the protest. How faithfully these younger men performed their role beyond the first days, once the rebellion was under way, is disputed, but it is clear that for the women the alliance was a crucial legitimizing force.

Another major strategy that low-status, horizontally organized groups use to win legitimacy and gain broad support is to seek a more legitimate form for the group itself—a strategy that is hardly unique to Japan. Organizing a group of some kind is, of course, basic for taking action, regardless of the specific goals. It is striking, however, that in status-based protest the securing of official recognition for the group—for its very right to exist in the first place—is an important part of conflict strategy. In the burakumin protest, for example, the central goal involved approval for a study group as a legitimate organizational base for the league within the school. In the tea pourers' rebellion, no action of any kind was contemplated until the small group of women had been approved officially as a women's bureau within the union. And in the New Liberal Club breakaway, a basic step required the constitution of a group structurally acceptable to the Liberal Democratic party. Indeed, Kōno's group was hardly a loose collection of persons who met together on an informal basis; rather, it was established in 1972 as a "Political Engineering Institute" (Seiji Kōgaku Kenkyūjo), with an office in the Akasaka district of Tokyo near LDP headquarters. By so formalizing the group, Kōno could set his organization alongside numerous other "study groups" initiated by Young Turks in the LDP (see chapter 3). Formal organization, in short, offers protesters a way to increase their own authority. In effect, they "raise themselves up" from their position of inferiority, thereby broadening their appeal and enhancing their credibility in the eyes of both onlookers and superiors.

These strategies offer major ways for protesters in status-based conflicts to overcome the reluctance of others—both people who share the protesters' own low status and the public—to view the grievances of status inferiors as legitimate and worthy of being remedied. Seeking organizational forms that have already been acknowledged as legitimate and building alliances with higher-status groups thus represent important ways of overcoming the stigma associated with offensive (as opposed to defensive) mobilization efforts. The next chapter explores status-based protest from another perspective: in terms of the tactics, or repertoire of collective action, that protesters use.

7

The Japanese Repertoire of
Collective Action

Each culture at any particular time has a "repertoire of collective action"—that is, an "array of collective actions that people employ" which are both "well defined" and "quite limited in comparison to the range of actions theoretically available to them." That repertoire, moreover, is shaped by various factors: the historical legacy of protest for that particular population, the "pattern of repression" in the culture, "the daily routines and internal organization of the population," and the "standards of rights and justice" prevailing in that particular country.[1] Indeed, as Charles Tilly shows, strategies of protest are determined far more by these crucial historical, cultural, and normative factors than by how angry people are or how deprived the population is. The repertoire of collective action used in status-based conflicts thus offers considerable insight into both the obstacles and possibilities that confront those who decide to challenge the terms of traditional authority relations in Japan and the nature of protest in Japan, together with its chances for success.

The framework in which social conflicts unfold has been much analyzed.[2] Once a conflict becomes manifest, a group has formed, and that group is prepared to mobilize for action, various choices must be made, including what the arena for protest will be, what forms of protest the group will select from the culture's repertoire of collective action, and at what stage it will use which strategy.[3] Once the conflict is under way numer-

1. Tilly, "Repertoires of Contention," 134.
2. See Coleman, *Community Conflict*; Kriesberg, *Sociology of Social Conflicts*; and Coser, *Continuities*.
3. Kriesberg, *Sociology of Social Conflicts*, 110; Coleman, *Community Conflict*, 11–15.

ous factors affect whether the protest is likely to escalate or de-escalate.[4] Almost certainly, though, resistance will lead the protesters to reconsider the strategies available from their arsenal, and if they go forward with the protest, escalation will be forced upon them.[5]

A partial inventory of the repertoire of collective action used in status-based protests in Japan is found in the following list, which I have compiled from an analysis of the three case studies discussed here and from other cases explored in the literature.[6] The tactics are arranged roughly according to the level of conflict they represent and the degree to which they challenge authority. Certainly many of the tactics appear in accounts of other types of protest in Japan, both historically and today, as well as in at least some other geographic settings. Although other methods could be added to the list, many that appear in other countries' inventories—obscene gesturing, shoot-outs, "citizens' justice"–type lynchings, breaking windows and looting, bra-burning, and self-immolation, to cite but a few—are not a part of the contemporary Japanese repertoire of collective action. This list, then, represents a beginning step in assembling an inventory of key methods available to protesters, methods that fit well with the Japanese "ideal model of protest."

4. Kriesberg, *Sociology of Social Conflicts*, 155–161.

5. For a discussion of the complexities and choices associated with the termination stage, see Coser, *Continuities*, 37–39; Thomas Schelling, *The Strategy of Conflict* (Cambridge, Mass.: Harvard University Press, 1963), chaps. 2–3; and Kriesberg, *Sociology of Social Conflicts*, 204.

6. For discussion of the historical practice of "going through channels," for example by petitioning, see Kelly, *Deference and Defiance*; on the use of sit-ins by protesters opposing the extension of the bullet train, see David E. Groth, "Biting the Bullet: The Politics of Grass-Roots Protest in Contemporary Japan," Ph.D. diss., Stanford University, 1986, 311–318; on denunciation sessions and similar tactics, see Upham, *Law and Social Change*, 78–100; Takie Sugiyama Lebra and William P. Lebra, eds., *Japanese Culture and Behavior: Selected Readings* (Honolulu: University of Hawaii Press, 1974), 450–457; and Patricia G. Steinhoff, "Student Conflict," in *Conflict in Japan*, ed. Ellis S. Krauss, Thomas P. Rohlen, and Patricia G. Steinhoff (Honolulu: University of Hawaii Press, 1984), 176–186. Examples of the use of hostile verbal and nonverbal forms of protest behavior appear in Apter and Sawa, *Against the State*. Most of these methods are used in protests over issues other than status, suggesting that the repertoire set out in the list on page 111 has broad relevance and applicability, though it obviously is not meant to be comprehensive; indeed, its main intent is to show the richness of the relationship between protest on the one hand and conditions set by history, law, and culture on the other, and how that relationship shapes conflict strategies.

Early Stages

- requests for permission through existing channels (officially through bureaucratic channels or by petition)
- challenges mounted through existing channels (e.g., standing for election as a protest candidate)
- minor failures to engage in expected role behavior (ceasing to perform optional, but expected, duties)
- perfunctory performance of courtesy behavior
- low-level, nonverbal protest behavior (mildly challenging looks, minor displays of resentfulness, wounded expressions)

Later Stages

- major failures to engage in expected role behavior (ceasing to perform major role duties—e.g., failure to attend class in the case of students, failure to meet formal or informal job responsibilities in the case of workers)
- failure to engage in courtesy behavior (ceasing to use respect language, to bow as called for)
- supplication (demonstrative requests outside of existing channels using moral imperatives—"have mercy," "be fair," "take care of us")
- sit-ins
- hunger strikes
- denunciation sessions (*kyūdan*)
- hostile nonverbal behavior (angry looks, stomping around, slamming doors, blowing cigarette smoke in another's face)
- verbal abuse (using "status reversal" language)
- physical confrontation without body contact (e.g., blocking a superior's passage)
- physical confrontation with less-than-violent body contact (pushing or dragging another)
- physical confrontation with violent body contact (hitting, slapping, punching)

The Early Stages

In status-based protests in Japan, the action-taking phase tends to begin with an effort to press for reform through whatever existing channels for conflict resolution are available: bureaucratic avenues, elections, and so on. When the protesters cease to work within the rules—that is, cease to meet the full set of role expectations in dealing with the authorities who are the targets of their protest—but begin instead to challenge those rules (often simply by failing to meet role expectations), that is when the level of conflict increases.

Official Requests

The preference for "going through channels" in the preliminary stages of a protest is well illustrated by the LDP breakaway and Kōno's early activities. One of the first protests in which Kōno took part arose over the key issue of the LDP's stance in 1971 on admission of the People's Republic of China to the United Nations.[7] At the time, the party—under Prime Minister Satō, with Fukuda Takeo as minister of foreign affairs—opposed admission, a position with which Nakasone, Kōno's faction head, concurred. Kōno, however, favored admission. According to the terms of factional arrangements, major policy decisions on highly controversial issues such as this are arrived at consensually by the party's senior leadership; faction leaders then announce their collective decision, and members are expected to vote with the party when the issue comes before the Diet. Because party discipline is exceedingly strong in Japan, the pressure on juniors to go along with the decision is powerful. How, then, was Kōno to register his dissent with Nakasone and the party position?

The strategy that Kōno adopted is a commentary both on the nature of power relations within the LDP and on the Japanese approach to conflict. As Kōno tells it, at no time did he consider raising policy objections within the faction itself, either in a personal exchange with Nakasone or in an assembled meeting, or within the party as a whole.[8] Because Kōno was of junior status, there was no institutionalized means in either the faction or the party by which his views were sought. Therefore, he chose the Diet as the forum for voicing his opposition, and in so doing resorted to ideology to affirm his position in a status struggle. For whereas the faction and the party operate according to traditional norms that affirm the authority of status superiors, thus providing status inferiors with no meaningful avenue for dissent, the Diet operates according to the democratic ideology of par-

7. Kōno Yōhei, interview with author, Tokyo, June 1978. For a brief account of Kōno's various clashes within the party, see Ronald J. Hrebenar, *The Japanese Party System: From One-Party Rule to Coalition Government* (Boulder, Colo.: Westview Press, 1986), 212.

8. Kōno Yōhei and Suzuki Tsuneo, interviews with author, Tokyo, May and June, 1978.

ticipation in decision making: one person, one vote. In addition, by choosing the Diet as his forum, Kōno could oppose those who held authority over him, while still technically operating within his rights.

The conflict strategy that Kōno selected can be seen as a response to the limited possibilities open to him. Coercion and reward—strategies to which parties engaging in conflicts may resort—are not generally available to status inferiors, since status superiors monopolize both. Furthermore, the usual method employed in policy controversies—persuasion or "politicking"—is not appropriate for party juniors, at least insofar as major national policy issues on which the party's senior leadership has already taken a position are concerned.[9] The only real option, then, was to embark on the single legitimate route for protest: abstention from voting. Thus, when the issue in question came before the Diet, Kōno and the other protesters were significantly absent, in what the media, the Diet, the party, and the factions all interpreted as an act of silent protest.

Another protest move, this one in the fall of 1974 on the eve of Prime Minister Tanaka Kakuei's resignation over charges of corruption, demonstrates the persistence of this strategy of working through existing channels to try to effect change. By that time, the Political Engineering Institute had been established, offering Kōno and his followers a base for protest activities. Within the LDP, the inner circle of party elders, led by Shiina Etsusaburō, then age seventy-six, was considering who Tanaka's successor would be. The then-current process for choosing the party president was precisely what Kōno's group objected to most strongly in party decision-making, since it wholly excluded junior members and, indeed, all but the party elders and faction heads. To register their objections, Kōno's group once again went through the only legitimate channel open to them: they tried to put forward a candidate of their own. According to party rules at the time, if there was more than one candidate for party president, and if the candidate was endorsed by a prescribed number of LDP members, the party had to hold an election in which all LDP Diet members voted. After exhaustive attempts at alliance politics in which

9. Inside the LDP junior members can, of course, air their views in the "study clubs" attended by junior Diet members or in the context of positions they hold in the party, Diet, or government, and leadership certainly takes the party mood into account. During Nakasone's last year in office (1986), for example, he was ultimately forced to table his tax reform proposal because of opposition both within and outside the LDP. Leadership's attentiveness to the collective mood does not, however, answer the problem of how junior members who stand outside the consensus on certain issues should make themselves heard.

Kōno and his group tried unsuccessfully to persuade several middle-generation politicians to vie for the party presidency, the junior men ultimately decided to put their own leader forward as a candidate.[10]

As it turned out, their undertaking failed. Attempts to win the backing of junior party members met with only modest success, and in the end Kōno had only about forty votes. Nevertheless, he was fully prepared to make good his bid for the office—until, that is, he was suddenly preempted. In November 1974, shortly after Tanaka announced his intention to resign, the party elders—after first exerting pressure on Kōno's group through the members' various faction heads—undercut the group's plans by announcing the so-called Shiina decision to put forward Miki as the party's choice for party president and, hence, prime minister.[11] This move asserted the seniors' prerogative to decide such matters themselves and stilled all talk of an open election within the party.

The tea pourers' rebellion, too, was marked by an initial strategy of going through channels. Following the formation of a women's section of the union, the women were confronted with an agenda of issues for which they wanted remedies. Although they might have assembled the issues into one big request list or program for change and sought action on the entire list, instead they apparently ordered the issues according to two criteria: the availability of a channel for protest and the level of resistance they were likely to meet. The first request was for the changing room that would become the center of the group's organizational life. The petition was hardly "routine," since group requests from women workers were uncommon; yet by the very creation of a women's section in the division, status superiors were no doubt alerted to the likelihood that reforms were going to be sought. And in any case, the request itself was legitimate.

The next motion, made once again by Makino flanked by her lieutenants, was that the women not be required to explain in writing that they were taking a menstrual leave. This issue was thornier than the first for several reasons. For one thing, the problem was by its very nature embarrassing for the women to raise with their male bureaucratic superior. Moreover, since women at that time were entitled under provisions in Japanese labor law to several days of menstrual leave each month, this request—unlike the one for a changing room—carried the slight implication that division authorities were, however informally, preventing the

10. Mainichi Shinbunsha Seijibu, *Seihen*, 194. The account states: "The Kōno group ran about collecting votes and the endorsements of the ten Diet members who [formally] recommended him, and Kōno signed and sealed his application form."

11. "Jimintō no 150 nichi," *Sekai*, no. 369 (August 1976): 196–208.

women from exercising their due rights. Perhaps most significantly, the "request" was not really a request: it was a statement that, henceforth, the women would no longer indicate on the publicly displayed leave sheet the actual reason for their taking time off. The statement, in effect, put authorities on notice that certain procedures and expectations affecting women in the organization were unacceptable and could be challenged. In this sense, the request was a single drumbeat warning superiors of the cacophony ahead. As the women tell it, their petition was met first by a strangled silence and then by a confused, but generally positive, reply from the official responsible for sick leaves, who was apparently struck dumb with embarrassment. The women interpreted the response as a victory, and thereafter took their menstrual leave without stating the reason.

The Yōka High School incident provides an even better example of the Japanese proclivity for going through channels, even when doing so amounts to a largely pro forma gesture. With the Burakumin Liberation League, which had no official relation to Yōka High School, standing in the wings, its eight student members presented themselves to the school officials, stating that they wanted to form a new study group on burakumin problems. There can be no doubt that the league knew the request would be resisted; given the educational campaign then being waged throughout the region, the teachers, with their links to a JCP-supported teachers' union, would surely see the request for a study group as the opening sally in what was likely to become a protracted struggle. From the league's point of view, however, the gesture was most likely an effort to exhaust all legitimate avenues for bringing about change before moving to less sanctioned forms of collective action—a prudent step in a country where protests are held to high standards of acceptability.

Study of the various attempts to go through channels reveals several characteristics of early action-taking in status-based protests. Using these three cases as a guide, we can say that protesters tend to take up issues sequentially, rather than as a list of demands or a broad-based call for reform. In addition, the order in which issues are addressed reflects a scale of difficulty, with low-stake issues taken up first. In the tea pourers' rebellion, for instance, the request for a changing room—the easiest demand—was followed by what amounted to steadily increasing challenges to the authorities. Similarly, Kōno's pattern of protest moved from relatively mild forms such as abstaining from voting, to stronger acts, as when he thrust himself on the party as a candidate to force a public election.

With that said, it is also noteworthy that in each case, the existing channels for articulating status-based grievances or calling for specific changes were few and far between. The major modes for pursuing a conflict, as noted earlier, are persuasion, reward, and coercion, but neither persuasion nor reward—the noncoercive alternatives—is readily available for status inferiors to use. Rather, it is status superiors who normally do the persuading and give the rewards.

Withholding Deference Behavior

Protesters in status conflicts do, however, have other tactics available to them, one of which is failure to engage in expected behavior. Status-based grievances, after all, arise out of the very nature of the obligations, responsibilities, and behaviors that give definition to inferior-superior relationships. Failure to perform all or some of these incumbencies, then, can represent a significant statement of dissent. Naturally, this strategy offers a variety of possibilities: "optional" courtesy behavior or role duties may be withheld from superiors (through a perfunctory bow, lack of warmth in a greeting, averting the eyes when speaking with a superior, or, in terms of role duties, failure to pour tea); likewise, officially required role duties may be deliberately ceased (as in a work stoppage, strike, or boycott of school classes).[12]

The implications of such actions for the level of conflict, however, are not obvious. In status-based conflicts that unfold in the context of interpersonal relations, less "extreme" but more personally antagonistic forms of protest may evoke a more negative response on the part of authorities than more extreme but less personal forms. From the standpoint of a superior in the workplace, for example, displays of surliness that violate expectations for courtesy behavior in inferiors may render a situation more conflictual than if the worker were to goof off on the job. Indeed, in status relations the formal role duties of inferiors may be less important than the optional behavior and accompanying courtesies, with their important psychological and sociological benefits. For example, a husband may find it far more acceptable for a wife to fail to get dinner on the table than for her to produce the dinner with an air of martyrdom or of anger and resentment. In the same way, for women workers to fail to perform official duties that are undervalued anyway is apparently far less provocative and disturbing (at least in the short term) to authorities than is their failure to pour tea. What this suggests is that the tea pourers' strategy of simply failing to pour tea—a seemingly low-level conflict strategy at first glance—actually represents a major escalation of the conflict over their earlier strategies.

12. See Goffman, *Interaction Ritual,* 47–76, for a discussion of the subtle gradations of deference behavior.

How else are we to account for the anger on the faces of city officials when, nine years later, they responded to questions about the office workers' protest?

When Conflicts Escalate

Status-based protests can escalate from either failure or success. The tea pourers' rebellion seemingly escalated as a result of the women's initial success in gaining modest concessions and in encountering no overt opposition to their proposals. In contrast, the other two conflicts escalated when the protesters failed to realize their preliminary goals: in the case of the burakumin protest, to secure permission for the study group (a goal that was almost certain to be unachievable), and in the case of the LDP juniors' protest, to bring about changes in the party's authority structure or win increased rewards for group members. In none of the three cases, however, were authorities so responsive to the protesters' demands as to make definitive concessions or to initiate a dialogue aimed at solving the broader problems that status inferiors were raising. Instead, authorities responded with avoidance behavior, attempting to limit or contain the protest rather than actively work on the issues being broached (see chapter 8 for a detailed exploration of this response). Thus, the conflicts escalated.

On the protest side, escalation occurs on two fronts: with internal changes within the group itself and with external changes, that is, between the group and the outside world. Internal changes may include increases in the frequency of meetings, in the time members devote to group activities, in the intensity of discussion at meetings, and in membership solicitation efforts. In the case of the tea pourers' rebellion, for example, meetings grew dramatically more frequent as the women moved from demand to demand. Before the women constituted themselves as a separate section within the union, the group met on a monthly basis over dinner, in a generally relaxed and informal atmosphere. Get-togethers in between meetings were still more casual, with several group members having lunch or stopping at a coffeehouse after work. Once the group mobilized for action, however, and began to issue its series of demands, each one more assertive than the preceding one, the entire group met much more often. After they succeeded in securing a changing room, the leadership core would meet there weekly, and additional meetings of the leaders and, occasionally, of the whole group were held whenever necessary. As the group's demands intensified, the leaders took to holding several meetings a week. Indeed, the real escalation can be traced from the spring, when the women's request for a changing room was granted. As the women began to use the room as a base, their meetings increased in number and seriousness, culminating that summer in their second "demand" or declaration: that henceforth they would be taking their menstrual leave without stating the reason. The crescendo in the escalation process came in the fall when the women launched the tea pourers' rebellion. Even nine years after the rebellion, participants still vividly recalled the nervousness and tension that preceded this final action, a strong reflection of the growth in intensity over that half-year period.

The LDP breakaway similarly was preceded by an escalation that may be dated from Kōno's founding of the Political Engineering Institute in 1972, along with Yamaguchi and Nishioka. In an atmosphere of mounting crisis as the government of Tanaka Kakuei struggled to stay in power, some fifty LDP members from various factions attended the first meetings in 1973 and 1974. Following the prime minister's resignation, Kōno's moves in the fall of 1974 to affect the outcome of the election for party president represented a major challenge to authority, and thereafter the group moved steadily toward a possible break with the LDP. Although numerous members drifted away during this period, the activities of the group that remained accelerated as they worked to keep members in line, explore their options, and secure their financial base, until finally, after an all-night session, they announced their decision to leave the party at a press conference on 14 June 1976.[13]

In the Yōka struggle, the escalation process occurred over six months; once school authorities refused the burakumin students' request for a study group in early May, the conflict grew rapidly. By June the protesters were launching regular initiatives to change the teachers' position, an effort that required extensive planning and meeting time. By 30 July the protesters, backed by several newly formed alliances, had managed to bring pressure on Yōka's principal, who then yielded and authorized the league-organized study group. The following week, however—when both the principal and deputy principal were away—the faculty, stating that the principal had exceeded his authority, voted to forbid the use of a school club room by the study group, incidentally agreeing that none of them would serve as an adviser to the group. Thus the high school leadership had to produce an adviser, and in the end the deputy principal was obliged to take the job. By August, then, the league had managed to achieve its objective, at least nominally; nevertheless, the status of the study group remained ambiguous. After a summertime respite, the conflict escalated rapidly in the fall as the protesters pressed for a meeting with the school official responsible for burakumin education, to ask that the club activities

13. Mainichi Shinbunsha Seijibu, *Seihen.*

of the new study group be "normalized." By early November, when this request was finally made, the protest had become a full-time pursuit for key league activists and the student protesters. By the middle of the month, before the actual confrontation on 22 November, the burakumin students had stopped attending class and, along with league activists and even their parents, were in the halls of the school every day. The movement was in a state of total mobilization.

The Later Stages

As conflicts escalate, the strategies selected display the full range to be found in the repertoire of collective action. Early strategies aimed at finding routine solutions to conflicts (such as going through bureaucratic channels) would appear to be fairly common across nations, although particular preferences are clearly affected by the specific cultural, legal, and political setting. As conflicts escalate, however, the repertoire of collective action increasingly reflects the cultural and subcultural variables that are at work as individuals and groups select from among protest strategies that are not only familiar but also acceptable to them.[14]

In the tea pourers' rebellion, after a six-month escalation during which meetings were held with ever greater frequency and the group's plans were broached with the union bureau, the women were at last at their thorniest issue, that of tea pouring itself. Their goal at this stage was to "rationalize" tea-making activities; despite many discussions, however, no agreement on a precise formula for what that meant could be reached. In one section, for instance, the women were prepared to make the tea as usual, but they wished to end their responsibility for serving it; in another section they wanted to stop all but the morning preparation. In the end, the actual formula was left up to each of the four sections to decide.

Two guidelines in particular governed the group's choice of a conflict strategy. First, in a manner consonant with general cultural predispositions (as discussed in chapter 2), they wanted to keep conflict at the lowest possible level. Second, given the small world of a Japanese office with close, face-to-face relations, they wanted to avoid confrontational methods. The selection of a strategy that would meet these criteria, however, was difficult. Their preference was for finding a bureaucratic channel through which to deal with the issue—but this was no easy task.

The main problem was that there was no obvious authority figure with

14. See Tilly, "Repertoires of Contention," for the importance of cultural and subcultural factors in determining what protest strategies will be chosen.

whom to raise the issue, as there had been in the previous conflict episodes: because tea pouring did not exist as an official activity, no one was in
charge. One bureaucratic alternative, of course, would have been to approach the division head (*buchō*) or another appropriate high official. Yet
such a strategy, although within bureaucratic channels, would actually
have raised the level of conflict, in that such a meeting could no longer be
considered routine. In any event, what would the women say? The menstrual leave issue had been straightforward: because a bureaucratic rule
was at stake, they had no option but to challenge the rule's appropriateness
and announce their intent to ignore it. In the case of tea pouring, however,
since it was not an official part of their job responsibilities, no rules governed it. To ask a senior bureaucrat to permit women to cease to perform a
duty that did not officially exist would have been to extend the superiors'
authority over the women still further and to give tea pouring a semi-
official status that it previously had lacked. In other words, this strategy
would have been costly even if it had a chance of working, which by all
accounts it did not, since senior men in the division uniformly believed
that the women should be willing to pour tea. Thus the women eschewed
the bureaucratic route and simply ceased to perform the task. On a given
day, with advance notice transmitted to superiors through the union bureau's younger men, they put their plan into effect: they made the morning
tea and served themselves, leaving it to the men to decide whether or not
to follow suit.

Viewed in relation to the full array of conflict strategies available to
status-based protesters, the strategy the women adopted is one of the least
aggressive methods. Two factors appear to contrain protest of the kind
represented here. The first is the nature of the setting—the "daily routines and internal organization of the population in question,"[15] including
both structural features and values. The chief feature of the internal organization of the workplace is that superiors exercise immediate authority
over workers and their livelihood, thus allowing relatively little acceptable
opposition.

The second constraint on protest is the reality of the social structural
variables of gender role and class. In Japan and elsewhere, women, at least
in the middle- and lower-middle-class white-collar populations from which
our protesters were drawn, are socialized into a narrow range of acceptable
conflict behavior relative to men. Although it is conceivable that the tea
pourers, once the protest escalated, might engage in a shoving match or
other physical confrontation, the threshold for them, as women, to engage

15. Ibid., 134.

in such conduct would be quite high. Overall, then, the bureaucratic context and the effects of gender role socialization acted powerfully to constrain the tea pourers' protest behavior.

These findings have major implications for status-based protest—for both the options available and the chances for success. In an important sense the tea pourers' rebellion was a "vertical" conflict, for it brought inferiors and superiors into opposition in a setting in which authorities had the monopoly on power. The women's position was weak for the same reason that labor protests in enterprise unions are weak: structurally, such conflicts are more constrained than horizontal ones, where allies outside the organizational context are relied on to countervail the power exercised by the dissidents' superiors. Organizational checks set limits on what portion of a repertoire of collective action given subgroups consider viable, as does gender role. Since most women, owing to such factors as class and geographic locality, are socialized into a relatively narrow range of conflict behavior compared to men of the same background, their options for redress through collective action in status-based grievances are likewise more limited.

By the time Kōno's group locked horns with the LDP senior leadership in the fall of 1974 over the election for party president, both sides had chosen their weapons. As with the tea pourers, the primary mode of protest here involved failing to engage in expected behavior. Kōno's early lack of enthusiasm for the activities of the Nakasone faction was followed by his gradual withdrawal from the faction, culminating in a failure to participate at all.[16] Although he did not formally resign from the faction, his behavior between the fall of 1974 and the actual breakaway in 1976 ceased to be that expected of party juniors. How tenuous the relation between faction head and subordinate was even very early on in this interlude is revealed in an account (in a book sympathetic to Kōno) of a supposed exchange between Kōno and Nakasone during the time when the younger man was planning to run for party president. Consonant with his status position, it was Nakasone who summoned Kōno, and Kōno came. But strains in the relationship showed:

NAKASONE: There's talk of your running for office. I expect you to behave prudently and to cooperate. . . . If you have some thoughts to pass along to me, I expect you to say what you have on your mind. . . . You have a great future as a statesman.

16. Suzuki Tsuneo, interview with author, Tokyo, June 1978. See also Mainichi Shinbun Seijibu, *Seihen*, 183–194, esp. 185–186.

KŌNO: I'm grateful to you for your advice. I haven't decided yet if
            I'll run in the election or not. I'll consult with friends about
            it. I don't have enough time, [but] I have a sense of great
            crisis. It is something that I'm discussing seriously with
            friends.

NAKASONE: Do you have any ideas about what I should do?

KŌNO: I guess that you'd better not come forward as a candidate. I
            suppose that all the "strong men" are responsible for this
            crisis.

NAKASONE: Anyway, you ought to take care of yourself.

KŌNO: I'll consult with friends.[17]

Here Nakasone sets the terms of the discussion, using his prerogatives as a
status superior to confront Kōno regarding his intentions and chiding him
to "behave prudently." By instructing Kōno to "cooperate," Nakasone was
in effect pressing him to drop his plan to run for party president. Kōno was
still at a point in the relationship where he displayed the expected deference behavior—for example, by thanking Nakasone for advice that he did
not want. Following the behavioral requisites for a subordinate, Kōno did
not initiate criticism of Nakasone or the party, but when given an opening
he did register his objections to the decision-making style of the party's
senior leadership. By linking Nakasone with the seniors, Kōno in effect
placed the faction leader—to whom he was expected to show personal allegiance, whatever else he might think of the party—squarely in the ranks
of the enemy, and in so doing clearly renounced the allegiance. He also let
it be understood that he had traded in a vertical allegiance to Nakasone for
horizontal ties with his "friends" or peers. As he made clear, it was to them
that he would thenceforth look for the advice, support, and care that
ideally are thought to be in the domain of superiors in junior-senior
relationships.

The breakaway itself was essentially an extreme failure to engage in expected behavior, this time in relation not merely to Kōno's faction head
but to the party seniors at large. To a certain extent, the breakaway may be
seen as an instance of conflict avoidance. With relations between Kōno
and the party seniors maximally strained, Kōno's options if he stayed in
the party were so diminished as to be negligible. Meanwhile, the base of
support he needed to gain leverage within the party had eroded: his effort
at horizontal alliance-building with other junior Diet men had met with
little success (as seen in the fact that in 1972 when the Political Engineering Institute came into being he claimed some fifty supporters, but he took

17. Ibid., 186.

only five men with him in the breakaway in 1976), and he had failed in his attempt to bring his group under the aegis of a middle-generation LDP politician. Even when the New Liberal Club became official and sought to recruit members, only twenty-five conservatives, most of them candidates for office rather than incumbent Diet members, joined the NLC cause. Like sailors who jump ship rather than mutiny, Kōno and his core of supporters chose an option fraught with uncertainties. But by doing so he bypassed an even less attractive course, one that promised increased isolation in the party and declining prospects for political rewards from leaders to whom he was becoming anathema.

Failure to engage in expected behavior and nonconfrontational collective action-taking are both strategies of protest that, like the tea pourers' methods, bear the imprint of organizational constraints. A political party, of course, is quite different from a work organization: members have an independent base in their constituency, and their political survival depends ultimately not on the decisions of their organizational superiors but on votes. Party authorities, however, have the power to distribute many types of rewards (money, endorsements, posts) that affect a member's public standing and determine career mobility. Thus, the organizational context itself does narrow the range of strategic options available to those within it.

In contrast to the two cases just examined, the Yōka High School burakumin protest encountered no organizational constraints. The Buraku Liberation League members who embarked on the protest had very little to lose; only the student protesters ran personal risks, and these were relatively minimal given that burakumin already experience social isolation owing to their status. The long-term political effects of allowing the conflict to escalate to extreme levels were not obvious at the time the strategies were selected. Indeed, until the actual physical confrontation between league members and teachers outside the school, the league's local leadership core evidently saw the methods they were using as quite appropriate. Study of this struggle following its escalation, then, allows us to explore the cultural meanings of a rather full set of Japanese measures for collective action.

Failure to Engage in Expected Behavior: Dramatic Forms

Failure to engage in expected behavior occurred fairly early in the Yōka High School protest. The first appearance of this strategy was in meetings between school officials and students requesting authorization for a league-organized study group. If the canons of behavior in student-teacher interactions involve elaborate displays of respect and dutifulness by students, the league's student members were soon pressing their case more forcefully than is the norm, questioning why their request for a study group was being refused and repeatedly asking for reconsideration. The degree to which relations eventually broke down may be seen in a league account of an exchange that took place shortly before the actual confrontation between league members and teachers. The study group, now approved by the principal, had been officially denied use of a meeting room by the faculty, although the group was holding meetings anyway. The league's student members requested a meeting with the faculty to discuss "normalizing" the group's status. Finally three students encountered the teacher responsible for burakumin education, Mr. Takamoto,

> and talked with him in the hall in front of the faculty office; but Mr. Takamoto would only say that the reply [to the students' request for a meeting] would come from the deputy principal, as faculty supervisor of the Liberation Group.
>
> We asked: "If you can give your answer to the deputy principal, why can't you give it to us? If you can inform the deputy principal, we want you to give your answer in front of us."
>
> He [Takamoto] apologized: "I can't reply, since the deputy principal isn't here."
>
> We said: "We will be in the principal's office, so please bring us your reply."
>
> Then the bell for the next class rang. Mr. Takamoto said to us: "Lessons are starting, so return to your classroom!"
>
> We said: "We won't leave here until we hear your answer."
>
> [Takamoto reiterated]: "All this is making such trouble for me. I have to ask you to leave here."[18]

This league account meant to put the students and the struggle itself in the most favorable light possible; nevertheless, it reveals clearly the breakdown that had occurred in normal inferior-superior relations. Although their language is marked by polite expressions of request and routine courtesy language, by persistently challenging the teacher, questioning his behavior, and attempting to direct his actions, the students are in effect defying the very terms of those relations. The students attempted to take charge by demanding that the teacher do their bidding and on their terms; when he resisted, they pushed the strategy of failing to conform to expected behavior to its limits: they announced that they would no longer attend class, the ultimate renunciation of their superiors' authority.

As the conflict entered its final phase, the exchanges between league-

18. *Yōka Kōkō sabetsu kyōiku kyūdan tōsō*, 40–41.

affiliated students and teachers became vitriolic, with mutual verbal abuse running rampant and the teachers struggling to reassert control. Upon hearing that the teachers had met and refused a meeting with the students to discuss normalization, the students accosted Mr. Takamoto in a faculty room. The league offers the following account of what occurred:

> We continued to ask Mr. Takamoto the reason why he couldn't have a meeting, but he couldn't give us any clear answer. Mr. Takamoto asked that we change the discussion place to [another] faculty room. We followed him and entered the room.
>
> [Another] teacher [who was present in the room] said: "This is not the proper place to argue—there are too many papers [such as exams and records that students shouldn't see] here. Go someplace else."
>
> Students: "What [*Nandae*]? You asshole [*Ahotare*]! Shut up [*Damattare*]!"
>
> Teacher: "How can you say 'asshole' to a teacher? Mr. Takamoto says that he doesn't want to talk to ignoramuses [*bakamono*]."
>
> Then the deputy principal tried to restrain us and the teacher.[19]

From verbal abuse the exchange was moving toward physical confrontation, and bids to the students to hold themselves to acceptable canons of behavior had lost all force.

Status Reversal Rituals as Conflict Strategies

These exchanges exhibit yet another strategy that is important to collective action in status-based conflicts: as events escalate, status inferiors go beyond nonconformity to expected behavior and, in effect, turn the tables on superiors by laying claim to their very language and prerogatives.

This phenomenon is similar to what Victor Turner, describing rites in which the status-deprived use superiors' language and manner against those same superiors, calls "status reversal rituals."[20] Turner notes two models that operate in any society: according to one, society is made up of individuals who are located and treated on the basis of their "jural, political, and economic positions, offices, statuses, and roles," and the "individual is only ambiguously grasped behind the social persona"; according to the other, society is "a communitas of concrete idiosyncratic individuals who, though differing in physical or mental endowment, are nevertheless regarded as equal in terms of shared humanity."[21] In status-based protests,

19. Ibid., 43.
20. V. Turner, *Ritual Process*, 172–203.
21. Ibid., 171, 177.

status-reversal behavior allows inferiors to strip away the overlay of role and status expectations in dealing with those who claim ostensible superiority and to confront the individual unmasked.

Numerous rituals in Japanese daily life reduce social distance or involve an element of status reversal. Drinking rituals, for example, present a way to reduce distance and strain in junior-senior relations in the workplace. The superior takes the office gang drinking periodically, and they all get "drunk" together in a club or bar. Although status differences hardly disappear, the move is toward equalization. While in their cups inferiors may (within limits) needle the superior or "mouth off" about their grievances; the superior, for his part, assumes a chastised or sympathetic demeanor, it being tacitly understood that everything that is said will be "forgotten" the next day. When in progress, these exchanges do have some of the leveling effect that Turner describes, but as rituals they function to maintain the status quo, ending in reunification of all, inferiors and superior alike.[22] In the rituals explored by Turner, the opportunity for status reversal is approved and orchestrated by those in power as a method that ultimately serves their own interests. In status-based protests, however, status-reversal rituals become a device initiated by the weak to alter the terms of social relations, thus offering the possibility of serving a different end: changing the terms of status relations to bring about a new consciousness.

The Radical Tactic of *Kyūdan*

Failure to engage in expected behavior, use of status reversal behavior or physical confrontation, and similar methods are all combined in a particular conflict strategy that is perhaps the chief form of action-taking used by Buraku Liberation League activists today and, indeed, by the movement as a whole since the early 1920s. That strategy is the "denunciation session," or *kyūdan*, the root verb being translated variously as "to denounce, censure" or "to bend or twist back to the correct position." According to a leading intellectual of the league, *kyūdan* is "a direct form of opposition. If someone steps on your toes, you strike back. People have a right to resist. Burakumin are oppressed. They shouldn't remain quiet about being oppressed."[23]

In a typical denunciation session, a group of burakumin (the number

---

22. Ibid., 178–181.

23. Oga Masayuki, interview with author, Osaka headquarters of the Buraku Liberation League, August 1978. See also Yagi Kōsuke, *Sabetsu kyūdan: Sono shisō to rekishi* (Tokyo: Hihyōsha, 1976).

varies from a few to many) confront the person who is accused of discriminatory behavior and publicly charge him or her with having behaved unacceptably. In some cases an actual list of charges is read out; in others the criticism is delivered more informally by the burakumin present. The methods used in a session vary greatly according to the seriousness of the discrimination and the degree of resistance offered by the accused. It is common for burakumin to shout, stamp the floor, use insulting language, make angry gestures, and dance and chant around the accused, creating a sense of chaos. The object of these tactics is manifold: first, they create a sense of solidarity among the burakumin themselves; second, they constitute, in effect, a shock treatment aimed at awakening the accused to the gravity of his or her actions and of trying to induce a fundamental transformation of consciousness, or conversion; and third, they make a public example of the accused so that neither that person nor others who have heard about such sessions will engage in further discriminatory behavior. Indeed, the league has been remarkably successful in achieving this third aim. Fear of becoming the target of a denunciation session is widespread among public officials, newspaper reporters, and others in visible public positions whose work brings them in contact with burakumin-related issues.

The precise goal of a denunciation session, however, is a matter over which league members do not fully agree. Certainly a primary aim is that discriminators should understand exactly what about their behavior was discriminatory. League sources agree that, because the discrimination against them is so subtle, this educational and consciousness-raising task is essential. Moreover, the discriminator should show contrition (sometimes with a deep bow) and promise not to discriminate in the future. The disagreement is over which of these last two goals should be more emphasized: whereas older-generation league members apparently favor the formal apology and show of contrition, younger members would rather emphasize corrected behavior, caring less about the spirit in which concessions are made.[24]

In a denunciation session, the accused is in effect isolated from mainstream society and held accountable for purported violations of the "official" Japanese ideology that outlaws discrimination. There is no out; release comes only when the respondent capitulates and admits wrongdoing. In the *kyūdan*, majority Japanese are stripped of all resources. The accused is cut off from the support of family, colleagues, and others

24. Interviews with officials at the Buraku Liberation League headquarters and branch offices, Osaka, Kyoto, and Tajima, June–August 1978.

who could affirm that the accused's behavior was reasonable and justified, given dominant societal norms—norms that are at variance with official ideology. In the particular reality created in a denunciation session, the world is turned topsy-turvy. It is now the burakumin who monopolize information and coercive power, and who dominate in numbers. Thus the *kyūdan* represents an institutionalized instance of status reversal, one developed as a major conflict strategy by burakumin. Virtually all the characteristics described by Turner with regard to status-reversal rituals are found in *kyūdan* sessions: public accusation by inferiors, leveling, mutual honesty, airing of grievances, "plain speaking," "humility and passivity" on the part of the accused, and displays of "aggressive strength" by the accusers.[25]

Conflict strategies involving systematic denunciation of persons accused of wrongdoing have been used in other types of protest in Japan and elsewhere. More generally, *gekokujō* (inferiors' assertion of control over superiors) has been historically fairly common in political life. The takeover of the Tokugawa government by younger samurai and military actions overseas initiated by middle-ranking field officers over the objections of their superiors during the 1930s represent major episodes in which younger men have renounced the control of those above them and acted without authorization.[26] Other protest methods, however, bear even greater similarity to *kyūdan*, for example the self-criticism sessions used by villages and cells in communist countries as a way of effecting changes in attitude and behavior. Indeed, experimentation with denunciation sessions in the early 1920s by the emerging burakumin liberation movement was spurred in part by Russian revolutionaries' accounts of the method's effectiveness.[27]

Among leftist groups in Japan, sessions aimed at creating unity or synthesis (*sōkatsu*) have often been used to examine a group's past acts, set new policy directions, and bring wayward members in line.[28] *Sōkatsu* is akin to *kyūdan*, for both involve the creation of a setting in which the individual is helpless to escape and is ultimately pressured into accepting a collective point of view. *Sōkatsu* sessions, however, are conducted by peers as a device for securing in-group solidarity, whereas denunciation sessions of the kind used by burakumin focus on an outsider brought into the group's midst.

25. V. Turner, *Ritual Process*, 179–180, 185.
26. On *gekokujō*, see Satake Akihiro, *Gekokujō no bungaku* (Tokyo: Chikuma Shobō, 1970); and Ohnuki-Tierney, *The Monkey as Mirror*, chap. 3.
27. See DeVos and Wagatsuma, *Japan's Invisible Race*, 42–52.
28. See Steinhoff, "Student Conflict," 180–181.

Key writers and activists of the Buraku Liberation League hold that although the burakumin learned many methods from other protest movements, such as those of farmers and labor in the 1920s, they themselves refined the technique and used the term *kyūdan* for the first time. One league activist viewed the influence of movements abroad as having been minimal: the early Levelers' Association (Suiheisha), he stated, was originally drawn to the idea of denunciation sessions because "they did not see discrimination as a social problem, but as an individual problem"; in that sense, he argued, the method reflected a "feudalistic" and "old-fashioned" conception of social ills and the means for addressing them.[29] It is no surprise, then, that the *kyūdan* method forged by burakumin bears distinct similarities to the confrontational, accusatory approach used by peasant groups in some of the *ikki* (uprisings) of the Tokugawa era.[30]

The primary use of denunciation sessions recently, other than by burakumin, has been in intergenerational conflicts between students and university authorities, especially in the late 1960s. Typically, students would abduct a professor or dean, or confine him to his office, and then, in what is called *taishūdankō* (literally, "mass negotiations"), collectively bring pressure "to induce the 'confession' or repentance" of the accused.[31] Consonant with the status reversals of burakumin *kyūdan* meetings, the language of superiors and inferiors was often turned upside down as students adopted the expressions used to dress down or wield authority over inferiors, while professors and administrators spoke in honorifics.[32] Indeed, in such exchanges superiors typically became exceedingly polite in order to highlight the students' "rudeness" and to establish their transcendence of the situation (an "undercutting" strategy that will be discussed in the next chapter)—an attempt, actually, to reassert authority and control.

Given our present concern, we must ask why the denunciation session has become perhaps the most central tactic used by one dissident group, the burakumin. The answer seems to lie in the unique functions of *kyūdan*

29. Oga Masayuki, interview with author, Osaka headquarters of the Buraku Liberation League, August 1978.

30. William Kelly (*Deference and Defiance*, 112–113), for example, describes protests in 1844 in Ōyama in which villagers formed a human wall around the shogunal office to force negotiations in a dispute over jurisdictional transfer.

31. T. Lebra, *Japanese Patterns of Behavior*, 76. The *taishūdankō* phenomenon is also discussed in Takeo Doi, "*Higaisha-ishiki*: The Psychology of Revolting Youth in Japan," in *Japanese Culture and Behavior: Selected Readings*, ed. Takie Sugiyama Lebra and William P. Lebra, 450–457 (Honolulu: University of Hawaii Press, 1974).

32. T. Lebra, *Japanese Patterns of Behavior*, 72.

relative to other available collective action strategies, for it alone represents a radical attempt to achieve a dialogue between status inferiors and status superiors where before none existed. The burakumin, as outcastes, were traditionally cut off by majority Japanese and relegated to separate villages outside the normal channels of communication; indeed, their social isolation still remains extreme today. Thus it is acutely difficult for them to find a forum in which conditions affecting them can be discussed or negotiated with representatives of the majority culture. With other key conflict methods, such as demonstrations or picketing, protesters are outsiders who may or may not be listened to by a watching audience; no channels for dialogue are guaranteed. With *kyūdan*, in contrast, a forum is perforce created with the charged party becoming a captive within it. Superiors and inferiors are brought into communication whether those accused like it or not.

One final question about *kyūdan* concerns its effectiveness—whether it works and why. *Kyūdan* has been a burakumin protest tactic since the 1920s, and today most people associated with the movement, whether its socialist or communist wing, appear to accept the method itself. (Where disagreement arises is over what form it should take as well as what tactics should be employed in the course of a session.) Likewise, the Japan Socialist party and many labor unions have supported the burakumin use of *kyūdan;* indeed, activists in Tajima claimed that before the Yōka struggle some 280 groups backed its employment in the league's educational campaign.[33] Nevertheless, there has been much litigation in Japan over the issue of *kyūdanken* (the right to *kyūdan*). In a decision of 3 June 1975 concerning the Yata case, in which league members subjected high school teachers accused of discriminatory behavior to a *kyūdan* session, the Osaka District Court ruled that "use of *kyūdan* by burakumin should be socially admitted as long as the means are permissible"[34] and found the two defendants not guilty. On appeal, the Osaka High Court six years later reversed the decision; however, it sentenced the now-guilty party (the other having died in the meantime) to the minimum sentence of three months in jail, suspended, and upheld the right of *kyūdan*, stating that "legal redress for discrimination is in reality limited" and that "direct demands by victims of

33. Interviews with former hunger strikers and league officers, Tajima regional headquarters, Buraku Liberation League, August 1978. Representatives of the Tajima office said that after the Yōka struggle only Sōhyō, Japan's major labor organization, which is affiliated with the Japan Socialist party, backed the league's *kyūdan* efforts in the region.

34. Yasumasa Hirasawa, "Review and Analysis of the Yata Case," Harvard University, 1982 (photocopy).

discrimination for explanation and self-criticism are to be permitted."[35] The league continues to use the method, and to hold that it is highly effective for bringing about change in discriminatory attitudes and behavior.

Over the years, the major change in *kyūdan* practices has concerned the targets for the sessions. In the 1920s, the accused were generally individual discriminators—for example, a father who refused to allow his son or daughter to marry a burakumin. In the postwar era, however, the focus turned to administrators—persons in positions of responsibility—in organizations that, through their policies and practices, discriminate against burakumin. Indeed, the method has been used for so long that it is now thoroughly routine, with league newspapers listing the times, places, and objects of upcoming *kyūdan* sessions so that interested members can participate if they wish.

League activists maintain that in the ideal outcome of a *kyūdan* session (1) a change in consciousness induces the accused to admit (*mitomesase*) his or her mistake, (2) the accused ceases to engage in discriminatory behavior, and (3) the repentant wrongdoer joins the league in working to keep others from discriminating. But as one activist noted, even if the first and third objects are not attained, the second always is, and the public is made aware that discrimination will not be tolerated. Even the severest critics of the league admit that the threat of *kyūdan* is a major deterrent to open discrimination—or, as they put it, the league "gets its way" because of people's fear of its methods, especially "violent *kyūdan*" (*kagekina kyūdan*).

In the case of the Yōka struggle, denunciation sessions that occurred in other schools before the league's educational campaign reached Yōka contributed significantly to the conflict's rapid escalation. Tajima teachers, newspaper reporters, police, and public officials all indicated their fear and dread of being singled out as a target of denunciation. And in fact, many of the tactics used as the conflict mounted did resemble *kyūdan*, such as the students' waylaying of teachers in the halls or in their offices and attempting to press them into meetings to discuss the issues. Yet the best examples of violent *kyūdan* are to be seen in the events that followed the confrontation between league members and teachers outside the school gates on 22 November 1974.

At 9:30 that morning, the teachers, after days of rising tension and disorder inside the school, attempted to leave the campus in a group, only to be blocked by waiting league members who had gathered outside the school gates. During the hour or so that followed, league members con-

35. Cited in Upham, *Law and Social Change*, 100. Upham has a lengthy and excellent discussion of the legal disputes over *kyūdan* as a tactic, pp. 78–123.

ducted the teachers back into the school compound (in most cases by carrying them, since most, adopting the methods of passive resistance, had gone limp) and to a school gymnasium, where the league conducted a marathon *kyūdan* session that lasted approximately twelve hours, or until 10:30 P.M. In the gymnasium, according to the league account, activists "attempted to persuade the teachers individually." As soon as a teacher agreed to talk with the parents of the league-affiliated students (who then were engaged in a hunger strike), the teachers were taken to other rooms where parents and league activists attempted to persuade them to confess to discriminatory behavior. The league admits to no unwarranted violence in the exchanges that occurred, only that certain league activists "stamped on the ground around the teachers, who kept silent and looked at the parents cold-heartedly in spite of the parents' fearful appeals."[36] Given the length of the *kyūdan* session, it is obvious that many teachers strongly resisted admitting any wrongdoing. The existence of a "resting room" for the teachers, presumably for use between rounds, suggests the intensity of the sessions. After all the teachers had "confessed" they were conducted en masse to another gymnasium for a "reconciliation ceremony" in which, witnessed by numerous league members, they affixed their seals to statements of confession and apology.

Accounts of the violence that accompanied the *kyūdan* session obviously vary. Although both sides agree on the basic events, they disagree vigorously as to the level of violence involved as well as to who was responsible for whatever violence did occur. According to the teachers, the JCP newspaper account in *Akahata*, and virtually all other accounts published by JCP-connected unions and groups, the violence was extraordinary and provoked. The league members, said one account, "were like bloodthirsty wild beasts"—a charge, it may be noted, that recalls the deepest type of prejudice toward burakumin, arising from their traditional associations with blood, filth, and bestiality. The same JCP account held that league members tortured the teachers in the denunciation sessions: "The deadly weapons they used were flour sacks; iron bars; tacked rainshoes; sticks; cigarettes to burn [the teachers'] faces; pails of water poured into noses and mouths; wooden chairs, which were kicked out from under the teachers so that they would fall; milk bottles; and padlocks with which to uppercut."[37]

Whereas the various JCP sources uniformly portray the teachers as victims—indeed, martyrs—league sources maintain that accounts of the vio-

36. *Yōka Kōkō sabetsu kyōiku kyūdan tōsō*, 52.
37. *Ima . . . Tajima de okotte iru koto: Bōryoku shūdan—Asada ippa no kyōikuhakai* (Kobe: Nihon Kyōsantō Hyōgoiinkai, 1974), 7.

lence were exaggerated and that the teachers' injuries consisted mostly of minor bruises and scrapes that resulted from their resistance to and provocative behavior in denunciation sessions. Nevertheless, the teachers, under directions from the JCP, went to the hospital and stayed there as long as possible to dramatize the struggle and discredit the league. Moreover, league members maintain that although their own side sustained similar injuries, because burakumin are poor and must work for a living it would have been unthinkable to stay in the hospital with such minor injuries. Ever since 22 November 1974, when the conflict terminated, up to the present, both sides have been engaged in a prolonged struggle to win support for their side of the story—a struggle that continues in court.

The Contest to Be the Victim

As the conflict was escalating, the league moved from relatively moderate strategies of protest—failure to engage in expected behavior, status-reversal techniques, nonaggressive *kyūdan*—to successively more intense and disruptive methods, ranging from a sit-in and hunger strike to confrontation followed by violent *kyūdan*. Yet why did the league switch tactics? After all, by August 1974 the league had managed to secure its objective, at least nominally; the Liberation Study Group had begun to meet at the school, with the deputy principal as its adviser, even if the teachers were formally on record as opposing the move.

Three factors appear to have brought about the league's change in tactics. First, the ambiguity surrounding the "unblessed study group," as a league publication calls it, made de facto existence unacceptable as a long-term solution to the problem of inadequate burakumin education at Yōka High School.[38] Second, the teachers' failure to acknowledge the study group signaled the continued power of a rival group at the school, a situation that was unacceptable. Finally—and this point is especially important—the league was carried forward by the momentum of its past successes at Yōka. Solidarity was growing within league ranks, alliances with outside groups were holding firm, and now—thanks to the league's ties with the Japan Socialist party—the mayor's office, the Board of Education, the PTA, and numerous other groups were lined up behind the league.

Solidarity was also building among the teachers, but their response to league initiatives was largely defensive: in fact, the teachers came increasingly to view themselves as a minority.[39] They had their own source of sup-

38. *Yōka Kōkō sabetsu kyōiku kyūdan tōsō*, 3.
39. Interviews with five Yōka Senior High School teachers who were involved in the conflict, Yōka Town, August 1978.

port, however, in the local Japan Communist party–organized teachers' union, as well as in the party itself. Even though relatively few of the teachers were active JCP members, their loyalty to the party line on burakumin issues was fairly steadfast, and the backing of the JCP was a major resource in the struggle. In early November, after the league's demand for a meeting to discuss normalization of the new study group, the teachers moved to extend their own base of support. A Diet member representing the Japan Communist party, along with leaders from the prefectural office of the teachers' union, arrived in Tajima to lend moral support and give advice on strategy. The league, convinced of its strength and seeking to counter the opposition, switched tactics. Following weeks of increasingly antagonistic exchanges between the league's student members and the stonewalling teachers, the students on 18 November initiated a sit-in outside the office for faculty.

It can well be imagined how disruptive to the normal life of the high school this act was. The authority structure, the ordered relationships between students and teachers, the controlled pattern of student movements regulated by bells, the hushed stillness in the halls as each new period began—all were disrupted, and there could be no pretense on either side of business as usual. The teachers responded to the sit-in by continuing with their lectures and instructing the protesters to return to class. They attempted, in other words, to restore order, but, as a league account neutrally notes, "Things did not change at all."[40]

Between 18 and 22 November the conflict escalated dramatically. By 18 November the original group of 8 burakumin students demanding a study group had grown to 21; after the sit-in began, however, their ranks were swelled by some 130 additional students, many of them majority Japanese. The teachers meanwhile continued in their attempt to carry on normally, despite the chaos around them; by some accounts, they gave their lectures even when virtually no students were in attendance. The league now had the support of some 110 organizations, and representatives of these groups began to appear in the area of the school. On 20 November the league, backed by these groups, began to deal with the teachers using methods similar to its denunciation tactics: cross-examining them on their motives for refusing a meeting, attempting to force a meeting through confrontations, urging them to proceed to a meeting place for a lengthy face-to-face exchange, and so on. Then on the following day, a Thursday, the core group of 21 burakumin students who had begun the sit-in initiated a hunger strike as well. The result was high drama. Parents of the

40. *Yōka Kōkō sabetsu kyōiku kyūdan tōsō.*

strikers appeared at the school to plead with teachers to grant the students' demands and hold a meeting. Executives of the Student Association joined in with similar appeals. In the meantime, as the other students milled about confusedly in the corridors, the teachers carried on their instruction in near-empty classrooms.[41]

The success of the sit-in and hunger strike, in terms of rallying support for the league's position, was striking—and readily comprehensible in light of the Japanese ideal of protest (see chapter 2). Protest in Japan gains approval to the extent that, among other things, it has a high moral purpose and those committed to it are prepared to exercise self-sacrifice in the name of the cause, two features that were well displayed in both the sit-in and the hunger strike. At the same time, the hunger strike cast the teachers as arrogant, disdainful superiors who, by refusing to do something as simple as meeting with the students, were willing to place the protesters' physical well-being in jeopardy. Thus, the strategy forced the teachers—through nothing more than their stance on the issue of a meeting—to appear to be violating the norms of behavior for superiors. Rather than seeming to demonstrate a spirit of caring and concern for the dependents presumably under their protection, they came across as callously indifferent. The students themselves came off as martyrs, a distinct advantage in any conflict.[42] As Orrin Klapp has noted, "from the standpoint of casting martyrs . . . it is partly a matter of finding a suitable villain—one who will accept his part and play it with vindictive glee, showing no remorse and not spoiling the scene by being human."[43] In this case, the teachers had the part of villain thrust on them. Though they hardly played it with "vindictive glee," by default they ended up as the heavies who, disdainful of a student tactic that they saw as orchestrated by militant league activists to win sympathy, gave the appearance of refusing to treat the protesters with humanity.

Dragging, Shoving, and Coming to Blows

From that stage of the conflict the progress of events, at least to one studying them retrospectively, takes on a ritual quality as both sides—the hun-

---

41. This account is reconstructed from a variety of sources (including *Akahata*, league publications, and *Mainichi Shinbun*) describing the developments that led up to the clash outside the school. See, e.g., *Mainichi Shinbun*, 24 November 1974 and 18 March 1975.

42. The best evidence that the students were successful on this score may be seen in the support their fellow students gave them at this stage, as reported in the school newspaper.

43. Orrin E. Klapp, "Dramatic Encounters," in *Protest, Reform, and Revolt*, ed. Joseph R. Gusfield (New York: John Wiley, 1970), 387.

ger strikers and their league supporters on the one hand, the teachers on the other—give the appearance of preparing for battle. On the evening of 21 November the league began to park sound trucks next to the school compound and to train huge lights on the grounds, an action whose specific meaning, in the context of the league's educational campaign then in progress in the region, was fully understood by all concerned. It announced that preparations were under way for a protracted denunciation session; indeed, if necessary the activists would, as they had in a number of other schools, continue the session all night, and possibly for days, until a favorable outcome was reached. With the league gearing up for their part, the teachers proceeded en masse to a hot-springs resort hotel to stay overnight, with the clear intent of resting up for the next day and discussing strategy. The Japan Communist party–led teachers' union provided them with a bus for their safe transport, and it was by that bus that they arrived at the school on the morning of Friday, 22 November.

Upon their arrival the teachers proceeded to their classrooms and announced the cancellation of the day's classes. Then they went to the school library to meet. During that period, four representatives of student organizations begged (reportedly in tears) the teachers to negotiate with the league so that the students on hunger strike would not be forced to continue. Their appeal was marked by urgency because it was a Friday and a vacation was scheduled to begin: if the hunger strike continued, the students would have to go for eleven days without food before classes reconvened. The teachers, however, were steadfast. By their account, there could be no outcome to a meeting with the league other than violence. As an account sympathetic to their view states, "It was common sense in this region that a meeting with the Liberation Study Group would involve anticommunist and violent elements of the [league], and that it would turn out to be a violent *kyūdan* session in which [the teachers] would be forced to swear to obey [the league]."[44]

Operating from this position, and believing that a violent *kyūdan* session was imminent, some seventy teachers left the school together. According to a league account, they moved in scrimmage formation—that is, briskly and shoulder to shoulder. Outside the main school gate they encountered the waiting protesters. Just who "provoked" the incident is a subject of continuing dispute: the teachers maintain that they felt violence was likely and thought it best to leave the school,[45] whereas the league holds that the teachers deliberately inflamed the situation by leaving at a

44. *Ima . . . Tajima*, 5.
45. See note 39.

time when league-affiliated students were on hunger strike and a school vacation was about to begin, in effect saying, "Let them starve."[46] In any case, certain facts stand out. It does seem clear that by leaving the school before a holiday, the teachers were dissociating themselves from any responsibility for the outcome of the hunger strike; their hard line on the question of the meeting is indisputable. By the same token, the league had obviously engaged in substantial preparation to conduct a *kyūdan* session, and probably a lengthy one, at the school. Therefore, both sides contributed to the conditions leading to the confrontation of 22 November.

Numerous theories attempt to explain why violence occurs in conflicts. One view sees violence as a method of last resort, used only when a group is frustrated, weak, or desperate. By contrast, Gamson, in his study of U.S. social protest movements, found that violence occurs when a group is marked by "confidence and strength" and with "attendant impatience at the pace of change"[47]—a finding with clear applicability to the Yōka struggle. For six months the teachers at Yōka had resisted pressures to approve the league's study group, which would have meant in effect turning over authority for burakumin education to the league and so taking it out of the hands of the Japan Communist party. Moreover, the league had during this same period amassed substantial backing in its struggle and appeared to have authority (the mayor's office and the police, the Board of Education, the PTA) on its side. Student support for the hunger strikers was likewise strong.

Riding high on the crest of the movement's success, then, the league was suddenly confronted by the collective departure from the school of teachers who evidently would rather see burakumin children starve than yield. While the league could have allowed the teachers to leave the school grounds and so scored a major moral victory, it would then have been left with the problem of how to deal with the hunger strike. Presumably few parents were prepared to see their children go without food for the eleven days until school was once again in session—assuming, of course, that the teachers would return after vacation, which was doubtful. The alternative would have been to call off the hunger strike, but this would have meant incurring a moral defeat just when the league was at the peak of its strength. Faced with these unattractive alternatives, the league clearly could not allow the teachers to leave. Meanwhile, the very fact that the teachers had shown up for school on that last Friday before a vacation,

46. See note 33; also, *Yōka Kōkō sabetsu kyōiku kyūdan tōsō.*
47. William A. Gamson, *The Strategy of Social Protest* (Homewood, Ill.: Dorsey Press, 1975), 82.

only to leave the grounds as a group thirty minutes later—thus passing through the school gate into a large crowd of assembled league members—constituted a virtual challenge for some sort of response. The league's local leader, Maruo, who figured prominently at every stage of the struggle, gave the following explanation almost four years later when asked why the league attacked the teachers:

> The situation has to be seen from both sides. The students had appealed to the teachers. Those involved were emotionally angry. From the standpoint of strategy, it was bad strategy. When you think about our objectives, well, we should have suppressed the anger. Things took the direction they did because we're not on friendly terms with the JCP. But from our standpoint, it was clear that the teachers didn't care about the students.[48]

The league's position is that although league members were the aggressors, the teachers, orchestrated by the Japan Communist party, actually provoked the confrontation; moreover, they say, the number and seriousness of injuries were exaggerated by the communists. The teachers, in contrast, describe the episode as an unprovoked attack by an inherently violent group. In general, in abundant publications circulated by the JCP, they have portrayed themselves as martyrs who were dragged back into the school compound and beaten, in a confrontation in which they were vastly outnumbered.

Klapp has held that "in any dramatic encounter, . . . the single most important factor . . . is the apparent ratio of forces. This ratio has much to do not only with how the event will actually turn out but with who will be hero, villain, fool, or victim and where audience sympathy will turn."[49] His comments accurately predict the overall outcome of the Yōka confrontation. The teachers "lost," in that they were driven back through the school gate and forced, in the marathon denunciation session that followed, to confess that they had behaved wrongly toward burakumin. But because they were greatly outnumbered, the teachers' claim that they, not league members, were the true victims was compelling. The arrest of key league activists, including Maruo, in the wake of the confrontation and *kyūdan* session and the subsequent defeat of the town's Socialist administration in an election three months later, in which the incumbent's handling of the Yōka struggle was the main issue, are testimony to the teachers' ultimate victory in the contest to be the victim.

48. Maruo Yoshiaki, interview with author, Tajima regional headquarters, Buraku Liberation League, 17 August 1978.
49. Klapp, "Dramatic Encounters," 390–391.

What occurred in the confrontation was, strategically speaking, a dramatic role reversal. With the hunger strike, the league seized the role of victim and cast the teachers and their JCP backers as powerful villains who, merely by agreeing to a meeting, could have brought an end to the hunger strike and the controversy. The confrontation recast the opponents. In a single day, victims became villains, and villains, victims.

Conclusions

The weapons in the Japanese arsenal for collective action are in many ways quite limited. Perhaps the single most potent method of protest in status-based conflicts, failure to engage in expected behavior, arises directly out of the nature of relationships based on inequalities. As chapters 2 and 3 showed, hierarchical relations between inferiors and superiors in Japan have highly elaborated rituals of courtesy behavior, accompanied by formal and informal expectations for both parties. Thus, not only is status behavior affected by conflict, but expectations themselves also become a resource for inferiors to use in challenging authority. Our three case studies offer numerous examples of strategic violations of these expectations, from subtle defiance in the early exchanges between the tea pourers and their male bureaucratic superiors to the outright violation of virtually all norms and expectations of status inferiority in the later stages of the Yōka High School struggle.

Challenges to deference behavior have long been a part of status-based protest movements. The opening declaration of the Levelers' Association included a pledge that "we must never again insult our ancestors and profane our humanity by slavish words and cowardly acts."[50] Another famous example is the rejection by the first burakumin elected to the Diet, Matsumoto Jiichirō—regarded as the father of the burakumin liberation movement—of an audience with the emperor at the Diet's opening ceremonies in 1948 because he refused to bow obsequiously or adopt the crablike, sideways walk that was then still expected of persons coming forward to meet the emperor.[51] This chapter has shown, however, that ex-

50. DeVos and Wagatsuma, *Japan's Invisible Race*, 44.
51. Buraku Kaihō Kenkyūsho, ed., *Long-suffering Brothers and Sisters, Unite!* (Osaka: Kaihō Shuppansha, 1981), 273. Matsumoto ran as a Socialist and was elected to the upper house in April 1947. The audience with the emperor was a normal part of the opening ceremonies, in which he was to participate in his capacity as vice chairman of the House of Councillors. It may be noted that he was purged from public office along with several other burakumin activists during the Allied Occupation; he was restored to good standing in August 1951. League activists

pected behavior offers a rich array of possibilities for forging strategies of protest in status-based conflicts. Not only is the behavior expected of inferiors a valuable resource, but that expected of superiors in the ideal junior-senior relationship offers inferiors abundant material with which to work as well. Thus, the hunger strike was particularly effective in the Yōka struggle because it cast the teachers as disinterested spectators to the sufferings of their student charges—a violation of every norm of benevolent paternalism.

Other protest strategies also derive from the terms of superior-inferior relationships, with status-reversal behavior being an especially compelling example. By the last stages of the Yōka struggle, considerable role-switching was taking place as burakumin students attempted to lay down terms for future exchanges, challenged the teachers' authority, and forsook the language of inferiority and deference for that of superiority and control. In general, denunciation sessions represent an institutionalized forum for status-reversal behavior, a way of forcing a change of consciousness on the part of status superiors. Through cajoling and behaving condescendingly toward majority Japanese, as well as pressuring them to see the error of their ways, burakumin not only assert their power in a "new order" which they create in the sessions but also open up a channel of communication where few existed before.

Status inequality—its sources and accompanying behavioral expectations—functions in myriad subtle ways in status-based protests. The tea pourers' success with their request regarding menstrual leave, for example, was due in part to their capitalization on a biological difference that contributes to gender-based inequality: in short, by raising a taboo topic they embarrassed their superiors into compliance. Burakumin may achieve a similar effect by using their stereotypical attributes of violence and aggressiveness to their benefit. Whenever intent to conduct a *kyūdan* session is publicly stated, the threat of violence that inheres in the burakumin mystique lends the announcement far greater impact than might otherwise be the case; neither the person accused nor potential discriminators dismissive of burakumin concerns take such proclamations lightly. Thus, although the stereotype of violence can work against burakumin, it may also be turned to advantage in drawing attention to their cause.

Many factors besides those discussed thus far can work in inferiors'

---

held that his purging was instigated by conservative Diet members who were offended by his refusal to display traditional courtesy behavior; as a result of his protest, however, the special protocol in the Diet for behavior toward the emperor was dropped. See Yoshino and Murakoshi, *The Invisible Visible Minority*, 56–57.

favor as they go about staging a protest. One is the power, in a larger sense, of their cause. Average Japanese, especially younger people, are conscious of inequality as a social issue and sympathize with the plight of the status-deprived, at least in principle. The favorable public and media response to the NLC breakaway and the accompanying media condemnations of "party gerontocracy" indicate the potential support that exists for inferiors who attempt to improve their situation, as does the success of the Buraku Liberation League in drawing the PTA and majority students to their cause at Yōka High School. Many people, especially the postwar educated who have had maximum exposure to the ideology of egalitarianism, are deeply conscious of the gap that endures between the way things are and the way things ought to be. This public awareness in turn provides status inferiors with important ideological leverage, whether they are trying to reach the watching public and potential allies or to deal with their superiors. Even male bureaucrats who declare that "it is women's duty to pour tea" are likely to do so aggressively or defensively rather than matter-of-factly—a situation quite at odds with the social order before the war.

A second positive factor at work in protest movements is, curiously enough, the particular tradition in Japan of rule from above, which can put authorities—especially those with coercive means at their disposal—at a certain disadvantage in conflicts, especially vis-à-vis groups that are obviously weak. This problem is revealed in many ways. For example, Japan currently has no antiespionage law, despite concern in government and business circles about national security and industrial spying. Prospects for such a law, however, are not promising; strong memories of the coercive methods and constant surveillance of the prewar police arouse fear that such a law would be an excuse for the state once again to abuse its authority.[52]

Similarly, the police often go to great lengths to display restraint when dealing with student protesters and other conflict groups lest they be seen as overbearing or authoritarian. In the early confrontations at the Narita Airport site, for example, the police, despite their superior numbers, sustained greater damage than the protesting farmers and students.[53] Klapp's dictum seems to apply: Almost the only way a party with superior forces can come out ahead is through the use of restraint.[54]

Another example of caution on the part of the police may be seen in the

52. *Washington Post*, 17 August 1984.
53. Apter and Sawa, *Against the State.*
54. Klapp, "Dramatic Encounters," 391.

Yōka struggle. Here a key question was why the police did not intervene until after a lengthy denunciation session in the school had concluded, despite the violence that same morning outside the school gate. The answer they gave their critics later on was that in repeated phone calls school officials assured them that the situation was under control. The same school offficials, of course, were linked to the Socialist town administration, which, because of the cooperative relation between the league and the Japan Socialist party, supported the league's educational initiative and the tactic of *kyūdan*.[55] An additional factor, however, according to a veteran newspaper reporter who followed the developments at Yōka closely, was police concern over "stirring up an image of the interventionist prewar police. They [the police] were worried, but they waited outside and didn't act."[56] This reluctance to use coercive power when a conflict escalates affords movements committed to affecting social change considerable opportunity both to grow in size and strength and to elaborate effective radical tactics.

A third factor working for protesters is the Japanese protest tradition itself, together with the ideal model of protest that emerges from it. This legacy provides valuable material for the construction of effective strategies, particularly in conflicts that pit the weak against the powerful. As noted earlier, status-based protesters typically mobilize offensively rather than defensively, which proves to be a disadvantage, since defensive behavior is more consistent with tradition. Nevertheless, the ideal model of protest offers a rich reservoir of symbols and cultural associations that protesters can use in shaping their demands and in forging culturally effective conflict strategies—for example, as a means of convincing authorities, potential allies, and the public that the protest has a high moral purpose. Status-based protests are easily characterized as moral in nature, since protesters themselves see discrimination and poor, inegalitarian treatment as ethical issues. When asked why the burakumin movement has commonly eschewed legal channels for ending discrimination and instead has relied on *kyūdan*, for example, league activists were apt to respond by focusing mainly on the moral aspects of the problem. Indeed, when viewed closely, the mistreatment suffered by the status-deprived does often seem to represent moral failings on the part of superiors.

The question of moral purpose, in fact, proved to be one of the most

55. See Rohlen, "Violence at Yoka High School," 693–694.

56. Hirano Takeo, reporter for the *Mainichi Shinbun*, interview with author, Amagasaki City branch, 11 August 1978.

heated points of dispute following the Yōka struggle as people debated whether the league-affiliated burakumin students and other league members had really been "serious" about the hunger strike. According to the league, the strike had begun at 4:00 P.M. on the Thursday before the confrontation. But Japan Communist party–associated groups, eager to portray the protesters as lacking high purpose, disputed the starting time and even published a picture of the remains of a substantial lunch that, they held, the protesters had eaten after the hunger strike had allegedly started.[57] The fervor and detail with which this debate was pursued is testimony to the importance of establishing (or alternatively, of discrediting) the moral resolve of protesters.

Similarly, the honored protest stances in Japan of martyrdom and self-sacrifice can be used to great advantage in forging conflict strategies. The Buraku Liberation League, for example, uses martyrdom symbolism in its flag, which displays a crown of thorns, and the language of martyrdom is strong in Suiheisha's 1922 declaration of resistance. In prewar protests, burakumin on at least one occasion formed a "resolved-to-die" group in a protest against ultranationalists over an incident of discrimination.[58] The use of sit-ins and hunger strikes today as devices of passive resistance in the face of authority likewise strongly evokes the positive image of self-sacrifice. It should not be surprising, then, that the league's peak of success in the Yōka struggle came when it chose these methods, with all their rich symbolic associations.

The Japanese protest tradition has another side, however, which proves a handicap for both inferiors and superiors in status-based struggles, and that is the hard reality that, when there is a conflict, nobody really "wins." No matter who started it or who is in the right, ultimately both sides lose because of the high value placed on social harmony and the strong cultural dislike of conflict. By many measures, the Buraku Liberation League "lost" in the Yōka struggle, but relatively few observers were prepared to say that the teachers "won," despite their emergence as martyrs. Parents, members of the public and press, local officials, and others—even those sympathetic to the communist stance of the teachers' union—commented in interviews that teachers should have done more to solve the problem in the school and that the conflict itself had brought shame on the school and all those associated with it. The teachers themselves would be the last to claim that they had "won." Despite their injuries and seeming victory in

57. Sugio Toshiaki, ed., *Shiryō: Yōka Kōkō no dōwa kyōiku* (Kobe: Buraku Mondai Kenkyūjo, 1975).

58. DeVos and Wagatsuma, *Japan's Invisible Race*, 47.

the confrontation, four years later they were still trying to justify their own behavior. Similarly, even though the tea pourers' rebellion failed to bring widespread change in office tea-pouring rituals, it is hard to conclude that the male bureaucrats "won" in the dispute, and certainly they did not claim victory.

If the Japanese distaste for conflict has negative consequences for all parties to a protest, it offers certain final advantages to protesters. Individuals who have overcome their own powerful inner unwillingness to engage in conflict behavior and have organized and mobilized a protest effort have the psychological edge. Because the opposing party typically responds to a dispute, at the start at least, with conflict-avoidance behavior, protesters who are ready to escalate the level of conflict have the initial advantage; authorities may prefer to make certain minor concessions (in essence, to buy off the troublemakers) in the interest of ending the conflict and avoiding the stigma associated with it.[59] This factor may explain in part the male bureaucrats' early acquiescence to requests of women office workers for a changing room and a revised menstrual leave policy. Similarly, in cases of Burakumin Liberation League initiatives, in some cases authorities have evidently acceded to the league demands for funds for various projects mainly to avoid conflict. In this context, there is little question that the league has used radical, and occasionally violent, tactics with considerable effectiveness for bringing about reform; as even an account sympathetic to the league notes, "mass activities of burakumin have so frightened local mayors and other authorities that they have agreed to whatever the burakumin demanded."[60] This evidence of success from radical protest techniques should come as no surprise. Gamson, in his study of social protest in the United States, found that "unruly groups," including those that used violence, had a better-than-average chance of success compared with groups that relied on less conflictual methods.[61] In Japan, where cultural abhorrence of conflict is so strong, similar outcomes under certain circumstances would seem likely.

59. Apter and Sawa, in *Against the State*, 85–93, for example, indicate that in the struggle over the siting of Narita Airport, farmers who threatened violence succeeded in exacting better prices for their land from the authorities.

60. Setsurei Tsurushima, "Minority Protests: The Burakumin," paper presented at the Conference on Contemporary Social Problems: Institutions for Change in Japanese Society, University of California, Berkeley, 17–18 November 1982.

61. Gamson, *Strategy of Social Protest*, 87.

8

The Authorities Respond

A protest by its very nature forces a response, even if initially that response is, in effect, a nonresponse. If despite the authorities' best first efforts the protest escalates, the pressure builds for them to reach into their own "bag of tricks"—the collected methods, shaped by history and culture, that are available in any particular setting to counter a protest groups' repertoire of collective action. To talk of authorities "choosing" or "devising" strategies, of course, ignores the complexity of people's motives and means for doing what they do. Machiavelli emerges from his work of long ago as the ultimate strategist, concocting schemes (now considered timeless) for turning situations to the advantage of his Prince—in short, for staying on top. Yet as Charles Tilly and others have shown, and as Machiavelli would undoubtedly have agreed, the arsenal of methods available to protesters is culturally bounded.[1] The same holds with respect to the authorities: they have room to choose, to maneuver, but the range of responses is not open-ended. Indeed, much conflict behavior is "unconscious," the impulse behind it coming to the individual spontaneously as the situation warrants. The driver whose way is suddenly blocked at an intersection, for example, may direct an obscene gesture at the obstacle "without thinking." But this seemingly "natural" response is culturally shaped—Italians might make one gesture, Americans another, whereas Japanese, who are not culturally cued to respond to that particular situation in that way, simply will not

1. Tilly, "Repertoires of Contention"; K. M. Jamieson, "Generic Constraints and the Rhetorical Situation," *Philosophy and Rhetoric* 6 (1973): 162–170; and K. M. Jamieson, "Antecedent Genre as Rhetorical Constraint," *Quarterly Journal of Speech* 61 (1975): 406–415.

think of gesturing at all. In Japan, then, authorities faced with a conflict choose methods of social control, whether consciously or unconsciously, from a circumscribed array of available resources.

The methods themselves may be spontaneous or studied, direct or indirect, formal or informal, "soft" or "hard."[2] Responses to a conflict range from the flicker of an eyebrow to a declaration of war, depending on who is mounting the challenge, who the responding authority is, and the circumstances. David H. Bayley, writing about India, holds that the "role of protest, and by extension its effects, must be understood in terms of the requirements, structures, and habits of particular systems." The same may be said of the methods of social control used by authorities. Bayley argues that in India, where at the time of his research three-fifths of the police were armed and living in barracks rather than mingling among the public as civil constables, coercion is a major mechanism for maintaining social order.[3] In this regard, however, postwar Japan has seen a dramatic reversal, for today coercive methods are used infrequently as compared to the past and, in fact, as compared to many other industrial democracies. For our purposes, coercive control may be defined as the opposite of social control. Whereas coercive control—the legitimate use of which resides largely with formal authority figures (public officials, the police, the military)—involves the threat or use of force, social control consists of all noncoercive methods, from subtle persuasion and manipulation to the use of legal mechanisms, and is used routinely by authorities at all levels, from public officials to superiors in social relations.[4]

The chief determinants of the particular mechanisms of social control available in a given culture are to be found in established patterns of social relations, whether between individuals, within groups and organizations, between organizations, or in larger contexts such as structured socioeconomic relations between class or status groups.[5] Likewise, the methods used vary from situation to situation. An adult male, for example, may use one method to dissuade his adored aging mother from pursuing what he

2. On the concept of "soft" methods of social control in the Japanese context, see Jeffrey Broadbent, "Environmental Movements in Japan: Citizen Versus State Mobilization," paper presented at the annual meeting of the American Sociological Association, 1983.

3. David H. Bayley, "Public Protest and the Political Process in India," in *Protest, Reform, and Revolt*, ed. Joseph R. Gusfield (New York: John Wiley, 1970), 306–308; quote p. 308.

4. Janowitz, "Sociological Theory and Social Control," esp. 84–87.

5. Zald and McCarthy, *Dynamics of Social Movements*, 238–241.

Table 7. Method of Social Control Used, by Density of Social Relations
        Linking Authorities to Protesters

	High-Density Social Relations	Medium-Density Social Relations	Low-Density Social Relations
	("Soft" control ————————→ "Hard" control)		
	New Liberal Club break-away	Tea pourers' rebellion	Yōka High School struggle
Relation of protesters to authorities	In-group	Out-group	Out-group
Relative status	Closest	More distant	Most distant
Organizational control	Tight	Tight	Tight to none

sees as an undesirable course of action, and quite another to rein in a whining and rebellious child. In both cases he is exercising power, but the social structural nature of the relationship itself finally dictates which methods from a range of acceptable options will be used.

In status-based protests in Japan, the exercise of social control appears to be guided by three central factors (see table 7). First is the social rank of the protesters relative to the authorities in question, ranging from similar to distant. The second factor, one crucial in considering conflicts in daily life, is the degree of intimacy that obtains between the two sides. In Japanese bureaucratic or organizational contexts this may be judged by the protesters' standing as "in-group" (*uchi*) or "out-group" (*soto*)—that is, by their relations with the primary face-to-face groups (the faction, the work group) to which the authorities belong.[6] The third factor is the extent of organizational, bureaucratic, or other structural control that the authorities exercise over the protesters, which can range from strong to none. In general, if social relations are "dense" (the protesters and authorities are close in rank, the protesters are in-group, and organizational control is

6. See Takeshi Ishida, "Conflict and Its Accommodation: *Omote-Ura* and *Uchi-Soto* Relations," in *Conflict in Japan*, ed. Ellis S. Krauss, Thomas P. Rohlen, and Patricia G. Steinhoff, 16–38 (Honolulu: University of Hawaii Press, 1984).

strong), the full range of methods of social control may be brought into play; nevertheless, "soft" backstage methods (such as persuasion and psychological pressure), which traditionally prove quite effective in such relationships, are likely to figure prominently.[7] Conversely, if social relations are not dense, authorities will tend to select "harder" rather than softer methods of social control.[8]

These factors allow our three cases of status-based conflict to be lined up along a continuum. The densest social relations between the dissidents and the authority figures can be found in the case of the New Liberal Club breakaway, where both groups belonged to a single political party—and the ruling party at that. The least dense relations were to be found in the Yōka High School incident, where no organizational context or bonds of affiliation bound the Buraku Liberation League members and the teachers together.[9] As for the tea pourers, as "permanent" office employees they were nominally in-group, but as women they were treated so differently from their male peers that, practically speaking, their status was marginal relative to the male-dominated core in-group.

When social relations are dense, the authority exercised by status superiors is more complete and initial constraints on the emergence of conflict more powerful. Once a conflict begins to surface, however, a full range of methods of social control present themselves, from subtle "soft" methods to overt pressure. Where social relationships are least dense, as in the Yōka case, the resources available to status superiors are fewer and the range of acceptable "hard" methods—stonewalling, direct verbal insults, physical confrontation, and so on—narrower. In an important way, dense social relations guarantee a bridge between the two parties in a conflict, over which may pass a wide array of weapons to be used in the struggle for social control. But where no pattern of social relations binds the two opposing sides, a great many forms of social control, especially those of the "soft" variety, simply will not work.

7. The existence of works such as Masaaki Imai, *Never Take Yes for an Answer: An Inside Look at Japanese Business for Foreign Businessmen* (Tokyo: Simul Press, 1975), suggest the extensiveness of the Japanese inventory of soft, indirect methods for registering negative reactions.

8. See Broadbent, "Environmental Movements"; and Ishida, "Conflict and Its Accommodation."

9. In the case of the Yōka struggle, league-affiliated students were, of course, tied to teachers by a social relationship, but the league itself, which the teachers saw as their real adversary in the conflict, was neither under the teachers' authority nor bound to them in a preexisting social relationship.

The Japanese Formula

The Japanese "formula" for handling status-based protest is suggested below:

Goals
- conflict containment
- isolation of protesters
- marginalization of the protest

Early Stages
- conflict avoidance
- making of minor concessions when avoidance fails
- use of soft, backstage methods of social control

Escalation
In the presence of dense social relations:
- use of soft, backstage methods of social control

When indirect methods fail, or in the absence of dense social relations:
- stonewalling
- undercutting
- baiting

Termination Stage
- delay
- preemptive concessions to head off future protests

In Japan, the first response of authorities is generally conflict avoidance behavior, which may be followed by minor concession-making. As the conflict progresses, especially when social relations between authorities and protesters are dense, soft, backstage methods centering on persuasion come into play. With particularly dense social relations, soft efforts will continue even after escalation has occurred, but often with increased reliance on go-betweens as relations between the two groups grow more strained. Because the countermobilization process tends naturally to distance authorities from protesters and to harden the lines of the struggle, however, if these tactics fail to produce the desired results, other "harder" methods may be used, such as stonewalling, undercutting, and baiting. The major goals underlying these hard strategies, if we are to judge by their effects, involve isolating the protesters from the resources that would increase their chances of success, thus marginalizing them, and containing the conflict, even if containment means assigning a lower priority to many other goals (such as appearing responsive) that authorities may value. Unless they are under time pressure of some kind, authorities may be quite prepared to wait out a conflict rather than force a termination that might involve major concessions. To the extent that they do address the social problems that gave rise to the protest, a pattern of preemptive concessions aimed at heading off future conflicts is the typical response.

While strategies that make up this "Japanese formula" for social conflict management are certainly not unique to Japan, they do seem to be heavily relied on and to work especially well in that country. In fact, an examination of a wide range of social, economic, and political disputes in Japan suggests that these strategies and tactics are not used only in status-based protests, or even just in social protests more generally. Rather, they crop up in numerous and diverse conflict situations, ranging from protests over environmental pollution to U.S.-Japanese trade negotiations. Obviously, if a conflict is easily contained early on or authorities are fully prepared to make concessions, there is no need to bring the full arsenal into play; but when a dispute proves intractable and steadily escalates, the combined strategies and tactics of the "Japanese formula" provide a rich array of possibilities for its resolution.

Protests over equality issues often place on view the full contents of Japanese authorities' "bag of tricks," for in these conflicts major concessions are generally granted only with the greatest reluctance. The reasons are many: the protesters' demands involve assertions of self and rights that fly in the face of the "ideal model of protest" and thus evoke little sympathy from social superiors; the ideology guiding the protests, despite its "official" status, involves "Western" democratic values that are not fully accepted; and, quite fundamentally, status-based protests constitute an outright challenge to the basic terms of social relationships in Japanese life. Thus, the uppermost objective is to contain these protests using all available means, a situation that causes a full battery of conflict management methods to be brought into play—ultimately with considerable success, if the cases of status-based protest examined here are any guide. Certainly, the authorities' score in handling even these "worst-case" protests helps to explain, at least in part, why the overall level of conflict in Japan has remained more manageable than in most other advanced industrial nations.

One point of clarification is in order. In discussing the "success" of the Japanese formula, the perspective in this chapter, as hinted at earlier, is Machiavellian. Judgment on moral rights and wrongs is suspended; instead, the analysis here looks simply at how elites deal with protest, with other perspectives on success being left for the chapters that follow. With that caveat, let us now explore each of the major strategies of conflict management.

The Early Stages
Avoidance Behavior

The most common Japanese response to an emerging conflict takes the form of avoidance behavior. Obviously, it is not unusual for a targeted group to engage in avoidance behavior, no matter where the protest is staged. Yet in Japan, from among the array of possible responses to early signs of trouble—which can range from admonition to active intervention to actual repression—avoidance is resorted to with great frequency. One book called *Never Take Yes for an Answer* posits at least sixteen ways of saying no without actually speaking the word—a telling reminder of how prevalent conflict avoidance behavior is in the general culture.[10] Indeed, the lengths to which Japanese will go to avoid facing or talking directly about an unpleasant situation can be extraordinary. Even when Japan's major cities lay in ruins at the end of a war in which three million Japanese died, the late Emperor Hirohito, in his famous radio broadcast that ended the war, would say only that the war had "developed not necessarily to Japan's advantage."[11] The dominance of this mode of response is readily comprehensible in light of the political culture surrounding protest, with its emphasis on social harmony. In essence, given the negative connotations attached to conflict, a status superior may lose face simply because a conflict surfaces. As Goffman has noted in his writings on "face-work," the "surest way for a person to prevent threats to his face is to avoid contacts in which these threats are likely to occur." Goffman's use of "face" corresponds to the Japanese use: "the positive social value a person effectively claims for himself . . . an image of self delineated in terms of approved social attributes."[12]

The earliest stages of both the tea pourers' rebellion and the New Liberal Club breakaway were characterized by long delays as status superiors avoided responding to the protesters. In the first case, because the women civil servants had been meeting for over a year to discuss their problems, their superiors were aware that something was wrong; and yet nothing was done to engage the women in a dialogue over their grievances. Similarly,

10. Imai, *Never Take Yes for an Answer*.
11. Cited in the *Washington Post*, 3 September 1984.
12. Goffman, *Interaction Ritual*, 15, 5.

in the case of Kōno and his group, the LDP party seniors evidently never attempted to address the junior men's concerns about party decision-making practices directly.

The case of the Yōka struggle is even clearer, because there the lines of conflict were apparent from the outset owing not only to the league's educational campaign regionally but also to its extensive use of denunciation sessions elsewhere. Administrators and faculty at Yōka High could have had little doubt that the school would be the target of the league's education campaign; nevertheless, they were totally unprepared and uncoordinated when in May 1974 a league-organized study group was requested. In this case conflict avoidance behavior extended beyond the immediate situation with the league to include relations within the school itself, for with teachers and administrators sitting on different sides of an ideological fence (because of respective ties to a JCP-affiliated union and a JSP-led local administration), any attempt to develop a school position would itself have been conflictual. Thus, when the request came, the principal and vice principal, without consulting the faculty, went ahead and approved the idea. When the teachers failed to back this decision, however, the administrators simply reversed their position and denied the request. Finally, after the initial period of vacillation, a long period of avoidance behavior followed: over the summer prior to the ultimate confrontation in November, the students repeatedly sought meetings with school representatives to discuss the matter, but their requests were met with excuses and evasions.

Minor Concessions

Together with avoidance behavior, however, may come modest concessions. Both strategies are seen as ways of keeping the level of conflict down, either by ignoring it and hoping it will go away or by attempting to head it off indirectly. Noticeably, the one strategy that is missing in all three of our cases is that of open discussion between the protesters and the targets of their protests in an attempt to dispel the mounting bad feeling. Whereas in American culture such expressions as "clearing the air," "laying the cards out on the table," and "seeing where we all stand" suggest a view of conflict in which open discussion has positive functions and an airing of differing views can provide a basis for moving forward, this is not the view of conflict in Japan. There, conflict is seen as painful, unpleasant, and almost invariably undesirable.

The concessions that are made, however, can be quite modest. In the early to mid 1970s, for example, the Liberal Democratic party was under regular attack from the media, the public, and many junior members over its handling of the Lockheed scandal and the tight control exercised by the senior leadership over internal party matters. At that stage (as evidenced by the "Shiina decision," by which a few party elders put Miki in power in 1974), the party's senior leaders were determined to keep tight control over how decisions were made. Their only major concession may have been to tolerate the emergence in the early 1970s of numerous intraparty clubs or study groups composed of junior men. These clubs offered juniors a way to distance themselves from a party coming under mounting criticism in the wake of the Lockheed scandal and, in the case of Kōno's group, to call for party reform. In effect, the study groups provided junior members an outlet for self-expression even while decision making regarding the corruption issue and other internal matters remained firmly under the control of senior men. In the case of the tea pourers' rebellion, agreeing to the women's first two requests (for a changing room and for revised leave requirements) may also be seen as minor concessions. In effect, neither response represented any attempt to deal with or initiate a dialogue on the broader issues underlying the women's requests or the party juniors' concerns.

In the Yōka struggle, because the lines between the protesters and the teachers were drawn from the outset, nothing would have been gained from concessions. Here, however, the "density" of social relations has a definite bearing on the hard line the teachers took. Where social relations are close and the authority exercised by seniors extensive, the full range of conflict behavior comes into play as seniors strive to preserve the existing relationship. The participants in the Yōka High School struggle, in contrast, had few ties with each other, other than through the small number of league-affiliated students involved in the protest. Thus, the incentives for concessions were few.

"Soft" Backstage Methods of Social Control

Authorities' final response in the early stages of conflict includes various "soft" backstage methods by which they seek either to persuade protesters to end the conflict or to explain their own position in it. These methods range from direct persuasion, both forceful and mild, to far more subtle verbal and nonverbal approaches that put psychological pressure on the protesters to desist. Such techniques play on the social power that authorities exercise over subordinates, reminding inferiors of their prerogatives; in that sense, they mirror the protesters' own strategy of failing to display expected behavior.

Direct persuasion appears most frequently in the case of the New Liberal Club breakaway—as would be expected, given the dense social relations of party politics. In interviews, both LDP and NLC members were quite open in saying that the factions had applied much informal pressure to the Kōno group in an attempt to deter the breakaway. When Kōno was launching his plan to run for party president, for example, although Nakasone's message (as reported by sources sympathetic to Kōno; see chapter 7) was complimentary and solicitous, it also bore pointed warnings: "I expect you to behave prudently and to cooperate. . . . You ought to take care of yourself." Whereas Nakasone's tone, remarks, and unsolicited advice assert his status as superior quite clearly, Kōno's response was in essence to renounce the older man's authority over him by stating that he would "consult with friends" about what to do.

The astonishing effectiveness of soft methods of social control may be seen clearly in the tea pourers' rebellion, even after the conflict had escalated and the protest was in full swing. According to Makino, when the women stopped pouring tea the men in the office "didn't say anything," "didn't do anything"—and yet before long several women were pouring and carrying tea to the men as before. What occurred was a type of psychological warfare in which the men, through nonverbal behavior embodied in expressions of anger and of pain and hurt, both made it clear that the women had failed to live up to expectations and communicated their sense of loss at being denied an expected service. Had the superiors acted overbearing and demanded that the women return to their duties, the conflict would likely have escalated yet further.

The response of university faculty to student activists in the 1960s provides another example. In mass negotiation sessions, as noted earlier, students often engaged in role-reversal behavior by adopting the manner of overbearing, arrogant superiors; the targeted faculty in turn responded with expressions of hurt, passivity, and resignation.[13] By using polite language in the face of insulting language they in effect maintained their authority, but by behaving passively as victims they—like angry parents who grow painfully quiet when met with criticism from their children—point up the tragically regrettable, inappropriate, and wrongful nature of the behavior to which they have been subjected. Such exchanges constitute yet another round in the battle over who is to be the victim (see chapter 7). The students assert their claim by expressing outrage at the way they, the weaker party, have been treated and call on seniors to feel "grossly guilty of complacency" for failing to meet their needs.[14] The professors reciprocate by turning the tables, charging the students with lack of respect and claiming the victim role for themselves.

13. T. Lebra, *Japanese Patterns of Behavior*, 76; and Doi, "Higaisha-ishiki," 450–457.

14. Doi, "Higaisha-ishiki," 452.

It is important to recognize the complexity of what, on the surface, might seem to be merely manipulative behavior on the part of status superiors. When protesters use conflict strategies that challenge the terms of status relations, many superiors probably do see themselves as victims, for by withholding deference behavior the dissenter denies a form of gratification that the senior has come to expect. As Goffman puts it, when "a putative recipient fails to receive anticipated acts of deference, or when an actor makes clear that he is giving homage with bad grace, the recipient may feel that the state of affairs which he has been taking for granted has become unstable." In Goffman's terms, such violations disturb "face," that "image of self delineated in terms of approved social attributes."[15] In other words, such strategies work.

Doi argues that in relationships based on *amae*, or dependency ties, the persons on the receiving end suffer when their dependency needs are not met. By the same token, however, the givers' egos may suffer when the terms of the relationship are in disrepair. The parental response in the face of a child's defiance or disobedience—"After all I've done for you!"—captures in kind, if not necessarily degree, the pain, bitterness, and anger that can result when the terms of a relationship based on hierarchy and dependency are violated by those at the bottom. Doi has gone so far as to argue that superiors may experience a feeling close to paranoia when something goes amiss in a dependency relationship.[16] Their self-perception as the victims of protests may arise as well from the fact that conflict in Japan tends to discredit all those it touches. Thus, even those superiors who do not suffer "ego chill" or other psychological whiplash as the targets of a status-based protest are likely to experience a certain threat to "face" because the protest, simply by embroiling them in a conflict, has led to humiliation in the eyes of their peers, their own superiors, and other observers.

Counterattack for the Conquest of Ideas and Symbols

When superiors assert their prerogatives through backstage maneuvering, they are also engaged in ideological warfare, for by reasserting the traditional ideology of status relations they are effectively challenging the protesters' use, whether explicitly or implicitly, of the ideology of equality and

15. Goffman, *Interaction Ritual*, 61, 5.

16. See Doi's discussion of the paranoid reaction as provoked by the frustration of dependency wishes, which, he makes clear, can occur in either the superior or inferior, depending on whose dependency needs are not being met; Doi, "Higaisha-ishiki," 454–455.

democracy. Yet superiors may use these same egalitarian and democratic principles in their own defense as well. In the earliest stages of the tea pourers' rebellion, it may be recalled, the women's complaints that tea-serving duties kept them from their "official" duties were met with the reminder that Japan was a democracy and that women must accept equal responsibilities in exchange for their rights; since tea-serving duties were not official, they should not interfere with women's taking up their fair share of the normal workload. Similarly, in the Yōka struggle it was not uncommon for teachers to use democratic ideology in an effort to strengthen their position vis-à-vis the league-affiliated students. For example, in one explanation for their denial of a burakumin study group the teachers stated that such a group, if approved, "would step outside the basic democratic rules" of the school—to which the league responded: "They [the teachers] have no right to talk about democracy, since they are fascists."[17] These uses on both sides of democratic principles as weapons suggest the great cultural power of this ideology, despite disagreement over how such principles should apply in practice in superior-inferior social relations.

Countermobilization

Faced with a conflict that will not go away, even with modest concessions and soft methods of social control being brought into play, authorities must mobilize their own resources if they are to be in a position to respond as the conflict escalates. In cases where the authority in question routinely deals with such challenges—such as those involving the police, local government in areas where social unrest is common, upper management in heavily unionized industries, and university administrations—this effort may involve no more than activating an existing structure to address a new round of conflict. In many contexts of daily life, however, the authority figures who become the targets of a protest may be relatively unprepared, both organizationally and strategically, to respond, and in these cases countermobilization often requires substantial effort.

In conflicts occurring in organizational contexts, however, even authorities who are caught by surprise operate from a position of strength, for they have an impressive range of resources at their disposal, including bu-

---

17. "Yōka Kōkō no konran no genkyō wa Nikkyō sabetsusha shūdan Miyamoto ippa da!" *Sayama Sabetsu Saiban* 14 (September 1974): 7, 8. By their statement the teachers meant that the proponents of the study group would not abide by school rules for putting up posters and so on. The handbill in which this explanation was printed represented a bid for the support of majority students in the school.

reaucratic authority over the protesters, command of organizational facilities and staff, access to information, and, in most cases, links to higher tiers of authority, both public and private. It is thus generally much easier for authorities to countermobilize than for protesters to mobilize. Nevertheless, the two endeavors use many of the same techniques, including solidarity building, alliance forging, and distancing.

Authorities' countermobilization efforts can be best seen in the Yōka struggle. The teachers routinely used faculty meetings to develop their response to the protest; likewise, the various faculty offices in the school served both as informal meeting places and as points of refuge when student protesters accosted teachers in the corridors to press their case. Faculty alliance efforts were directed at one of several command structures of which they were a part: the local and prefectural offices of the teachers' union, of which most were members, and the local, prefectural, and national offices of the Japan Communist party, to which the regional teachers' union was linked. If the teachers had been in accord with the school authorities on how to respond to the league, of course, the conflict would have been played out quite differently. Indeed, in the end the protest group's greatest resource proved to be the links between the league on the one hand and the town's Socialist administration (and through it, the principal and deputy principal) on the other.

Given the alliance possibilities available, the degree of solidarity that the teachers achieved is quite striking. Using facilities of both the school and the local branch of the teachers' union, they were able to distribute handbills to make their positions known. According to the league, the teachers maintained steady contact with the Hyōgo prefectural union office, which dispatched an official from a nearby town to meet regularly with the teachers. A delegation from Tokyo that included a representative from the national teachers' union office and JCP Diet member Yasutake Hiroko of the House of Councillors also came to the region at one juncture to provide moral support as the conflict mounted.[18]

Once the conflict began its rapid escalation in November, the teachers were in every sense a team. Although several teachers reportedly had some sympathy for the league's position, or at least seemed to prefer a more accommodationist solution to the problem, they played no open role in the conflict and rejected the league-affiliated students' efforts to enlist them as allies. By the time of the teachers' overnight stay at the hot springs hotel just prior to the confrontation outside the school gates, the teachers were moving as a unit, in a bus provided by the teachers' union. On the day of

18. Ibid., 12.

the actual clash, they left the school shoulder to shoulder; when confronted by league members gathered outside the gates, they sat down in the street en masse and maintained collective silence, even as the protesters began to try to carry them back into the school by force. Almost four years after the struggle, nine teachers from the school agreed to an interview; their accounts of the events of the Yōka incidents jibed completely. They continued, in other words, to stand as one, at least as far as the leadership core was concerned.

In the other two conflicts, countermobilization on the part of authorities is reflected in the results. Kōno's dissent, for example, elicited an orchestrated response from the party's leaders when they sought to persuade members of his group through their respective factions not to mount Kōno as a candidate for the party presidency in 1974 and not to leave the party. Similarly, in the tea pourers' rebellion, the *non*-response of the men in the division ("they didn't say anything, they didn't do anything") when the women failed to serve tea as usual suggests that some type of coordination had occurred, even if only informally.

One remaining feature of countermobilization stands out, and that is distancing. In status politics protests, the involved parties are linked in interactive, asymmetrical relationships involving dependency; thus each side needs somehow to back away as a basis for action. One means for establishing distance is negative labeling. While this device may be used by authorities to denigrate protesters and their motives in the eyes of potential allies and the public, it also serves an internal function in relation to solidarity building: by assigning negative labels to protesters or to their behavior, a relationship that may in the past have been infused with good feeling is drained of its affect and objectified; individual faces merge into a conception of a depersonalized "enemy" that, in the mind's eye of authorities, is charged with negative associations. Just as nineteenth-century European elites often used terms such as *mob* and *rabble* to refer to strikers or other protesters, all the targeted authorities in the conflicts discussed here referred to protesters using epithets, which operated in a distancing fashion.

Another method of achieving distance involves the creation of myths. As the Yōka conflict progressed, the teachers often portrayed league-affiliated burakumin students alternately as either hapless pawns of the league or initiates who had been so indoctrinated into the league's views that they were beyond human feeling. Whatever else it accomplishes, the objectification reflected in pejorative labeling and dehumanizing explanations of "the enemy's" behavior brings authorities close together and facilitates their ability to respond. Seemingly in the burakumin protest, it enabled teachers to walk out of school leaving behind their own hunger-striking students—just as a similar process among the protesters freed the dissident students to call their teachers "assholes" to their face.

One feature in particular of countermobilization in Japan stands out. Considering the strong consensus on basic values that most writers agree characterizes Japan, one would expect authorities to obtain the support of other elites with relative ease as countermobilization proceeded. Such is not necessarily the case, however. Because social harmony is so highly valued and because conflict itself, no matter who is responsible for it, is met generally with such aversion, authorities may find themselves quite isolated, particularly in a moral sense. Even if others in positions of power officially and publicly back status superiors who have been targeted by a protest movement, "backstage" displays of support may not be forthcoming. This is true largely because of the principle of verticality, which traditionally has held superiors responsible for maintaining harmony among those below them. For an authority figure to report dissatisfaction among inferiors to higher-ups is, in many cases, tantamount to admitting failure. Even if the superior is backed to the hilt materially speaking, he may incur various long-term costs by involving higher-ranking persons in the unpleasantness of a conflict.

The lack of support that the teachers received, even from officials in their own union, in the wake of the Yōka struggle—a conflict that they had ostensibly "won"—is one example of this phenomenon. Although the union stood behind them during the struggle itself, afterward leaders among the teachers reported feeling quite isolated and widely criticized within the local community, despite their status as "martyrs." This pattern is also evident in the aftermath of Japan's longest and most volatile postwar conflict, the anti–United States–Japan Mutual Security Treaty struggle of 1960. In the midst of this struggle, leadership circles within both the Liberal Democratic party and the business community gave their full backing to Prime Minister Kishi as he strove to resolve the conflict; yet when the treaty at last went into effect, over the objections of the protesters, and the "danger" (as the authorities viewed it) had passed, Kishi soon found himself ousted as party president, and hence as prime minister.[19]

Given the negative associations that attach to open conflict in Japan, and the intense pressure that is placed on authorities not only to contain protest actions but also to prevent future recurrences, an effective formula for response often proves elusive. The tentativeness or conditionality of

19. George R. Packard III, *Protest in Tokyo* (Princeton: Princeton University Press, 1966), 301–304.

moral support from other elites who are outsiders to the conflict helps explain why status superiors so frequently portray themselves as victims in status-based struggles and go on the defensive afterward, despite their seeming victory.

When Conflicts Escalate

Having mobilized their forces, authorities then launch their own conflict strategies, either in retaliation against the moves made by protesters or preemptively. Many of the same strategies that typify the earliest stages enter here as well, but they may be pursued in new ways as the conflict escalates. For one thing, the use of backstage methods of social control intensifies as superiors try to bring inferiors in line. In the LDP conflict, for example, pressure on Kōno and his group increased—yet now contact between the two groups was accomplished primarily by means of go-betweens.[20]

Similarly, with escalation the struggle to be the victim continues, even as the situation becomes more confrontational. In denunciation sessions, for example, the targeted authorities typically display humility and, in some cases, exaggerated politeness toward the complainants, since other responses, such as anger or, alternatively, silence, would merely escalate the conflict and thus be at cross-purposes with the goal of containment.[21] Once the conflict is in the open and cannot be denied or simply dismissed, both persuasion and the playing of the victim may be aimed less at the protesters themselves and more at their potential allies and the public: the steady application of pressure makes clear to potential joiners what will happen to them if they take up the protesters' cause. The influence of go-betweens on Kōno's group almost certainly had such a discouraging effect, as evidenced by the large number of original members who chose to stay within the ruling party.

At the same time that pressure is applied to the dissidents, moreover, selective rewards may be granted to vacillating potential allies of the protesters. The career success of Fujinami Takao, a close associate of Kōno who decided on the eve of the breakaway to remain in the LDP, suggests that backstage methods may have included overt incentives to stay, or at least indirect reassurances that protesters would not be negatively sanctioned if they chose not to defect.[22]

Finally, in all countries authorities' behavior in conflict situations (much

20. Tagawa Seiichi, *Dokyumento Jimin dattō* (Tokyo: Tokuma Shoten, 1983).

21. Doi, "Higaisha-ishiki."

22. Fujinami was appointed minister of labor in November 1979 when he was forty-six years old and in his fifth term. Since then he has served as deputy chief

as in meting out punishment for crimes) may be aimed at the public as much as at the protesters proper.[23] But this is especially true of Japan. There, the concern of authorities is not only with the deterrence of future opposition, but also with absolving themselves of any responsibility for the unpleasant state of affairs represented by a conflict.

Stonewalling

When conflicts escalate, the lines become more rigid. One important "hard" method of social control that appears at this juncture is stonewalling: avoidance behavior that persists after the conflict has become manifest and after the terms of the protesters' demands have become known—in short, an across-the-board refusal to yield. In the Yōka struggle, for example, early faculty rejection of a meeting to discuss a burakumin study group took the form of excuses and evasions; by the fall, however, equivocation had given way to point-blank refusals.

Stonewalling as a strategy has various consequences. Almost certainly it forecloses the possibility of opening a dialogue that might lead to resolution. In the Yōka struggle, by declining to negotiate the teachers signaled a point of no return, and from then on the conflict escalated. The teachers, of course, maintained that that point had been reached anyway, since a denunciation session, and probably a violent one at that, was in the cards from the beginning. To the extent that authorities feel the conflict cannot be contained anyway, stonewalling may appear to be a reasonable recourse. The strategy can, however, be risky, for it may at least temporarily discredit authorities in the eyes of onlookers, and it is likely to anger protesters. Yet it also offers a certain advantage, in that the very rage of status inferiors may lead the protesters to so escalate the conflict that they bring about their own defeat.

Undercutting

As a status-based conflict proceeds, authorities engage in various actions, both verbal and nonverbal, that work to demean or dismiss the protesters and that demonstrate disapproval of the protest itself. One such method is the display (sometimes directly to the protesters, sometimes indirectly to the media or other third parties) of open contempt; another is the "silent treatment," in which authorities act as though the protesters are unworthy of response. The silent treatment, of course, is akin to avoidance behavior

---

cabinet secretary (November 1982) and chief cabinet secretary (December 1983) and is considered to be a leading candidate to take over the Nakasone faction.

23. I am grateful to Ezra F. Vogel of Harvard University for this observation.

in form, but its specific meaning and effect are different: if at the onset of protest the goal is to escape the problem, the silent treatment once the protest is in progress undercuts the protesters by treating their behavior as illegitimate. In effect, undercutting strategies push status inferiors back into the terms of their original position of inferiority. By reminding the protesters of "their place," superiors reassert the traditional norms governing superior-inferior relations in Japan, according to which any adjustment is granted at the discretion and initiative of those above, not in response to demands from those below.

The typical working of these undercutting strategies may be seen in the tea pourers' rebellion, where, according to the women involved, the men both invoked the silent treatment and assumed various facial expressions that communicated disapproval. In the case of the Yōka High School protest, undercutting behavior surfaced at various stages of the conflict, particularly toward the end—as, for example, in the last week of the struggle, when teachers reportedly responded to demonstrative verbal pleas by students and parents for an end to the sit-in with cigarettes in their mouths or their backs partly turned on those addressing them, behavior that is extraordinarily degrading in the Japanese context.[24]

Authorities achieve a similar effect through the use of demeaning language. As already noted, negative labeling is apparently part of the distancing process that in turn makes action, particularly in close interstatus relations, possible. Yet it is in addition a conflict strategy, for it may affect not only the protesters and potential allies, but also the watching public.

Liberal Democratic party members, for example, frequently referred to Kōno Yōhei (in particular), as well as his two chief lieutenants, as *obotchan*, or "spoiled brat"—a pejorative reference to their independent financial bases as second-generation politicians, but also suggestive of the character failings of immaturity, selfishness, and egotism. Party elders in comments to the media also referred to Kōno and his key followers as "runaway girls" and "incubator babies."[25] An excerpt from a song purportedly written in 1979 by Kōno's uncle, Kōno Kenzō, a senior LDP member, poking fun at his nephew plays on the same theme:

24. Interviews with league officials who observed the conflict during the hunger strike, Kyoto branch office, Buraku Liberation League, July 1978.

25. Nakasone Yasuhiro, for example, was quoted in the press as having referred to the group as "runaway girls" (*iede musume*) when they left the LDP (*Shūkan Posuto*, 14 December 1979, 24). The term *obotchan* (spoiled baby or brat) was used by any number of LDP members in interviews conducted in 1978 for this study, as well as in comments to the press, to refer to the group's leader, Kōno Yōhei, and other New Liberal Club members.

When the LDP was in an ugly mess,
We heard of the birth of the NLC.
In less than a week Yōhei and his chums came up,
Up with a party platform—
"Down with plutocracy!"
"Rehaul the conservatives!"—
For his newborn party.
Though they frolicked about [*hashagi mawatta*],
Blowing their trumpets,
I, his uncle, wondered where it would all lead.[26]

Even opposition Diet members joined in the hazing of the junior men. When the NLC abruptly switched policies on the budget bill then before the Diet, one opposition member reportedly commented, "'Our Gang' ought to go to a playground [instead of the Diet building] to play."[27] The mood is light in much of this name-calling, as might be expected in a conflict involving dense social relations, but the tone is unmistakably derogatory; it trivializes both the protest and the protesters, drawing heavily on their junior status for source material.

In a similar vein, the women office workers' initiative to end tea pouring came generally to be called an "*ochakumi* struggle" among co-workers—in what must be considered another victory for the male bureaucrats. The term *ochakumi* refers to women (and the duties they perform) who pour tea for office guests and do other menial tasks. Because the status of these women is far below that of women bureaucrats, the term, when used for the protesters and their struggle, is one of denigration. Likewise, in the Yōka High School incident the teachers routinely referred to the league not by its official name, but as the "Asada group," after its leader, Asada Zennosuke. Use of the term thus not only denied the legitimacy of the organization's leadership but also rejected the league's claim that it spoke for burakumin generally. In this protest, moreover, demeaning language aimed at accentuating the group's inferiority took on a much harsher form—as, for example, in the description of the protesters as "bloodthirsty wild beasts."[28]

The effect of undercutting in Japan is quite specific. Within the traditional norms governing relations between persons of unequal status, status

26. From the "Black Joke" column by Shitō Kineo, *Shūkan Posuto*, 14 December 1979, 44.

27. From "Notes Around the Political World," *Yomiuri Shinbun*, 8 March 1979; reference is to the vintage U.S. movie series, popular in Japan, featuring a mischievous group of children.

28. *Ima . . . Tajima de okotte iru koto*, 7.

inferiors ideally do not complain directly about those relations or put demands to their superiors. Similarly, superiors in relations guided by benevolent paternalism are supposedly in tune with the unstated needs of their inferiors and grant unilaterally whatever concessions they deem appropriate.[29] By demeaning status inferiors, then, those in authority in effect invalidate the protest itself; they deny the legitimacy of the movement and reassert their authority over status inferiors, exposing the protesters to ridicule through use of labels evocative of the latter's junior and dependent status.

Undercutting is a particularly powerful strategy of the strong against the weak in Japan for the very reason that the legitimacy of status-based protests (as compared to the other major types of protest) is still not well established. Undercutting can stir strong feelings of self-doubt among the protesters, particularly when their cause is trivialized and they suffer ridicule. Those activists with weak resolve may drop away altogether, and even the more confident protesters may have to overcome pangs of doubt and uncertainty. The high dropout rate from Kōno's group and from the ranks of the tea pourers once they ceased pouring suggests how effective such methods are. Most essential of all, labeling serves to lessen the protesters in the eyes of potential supporters, isolating them still further.

Baiting

A related strategy is baiting, the essence of which is to make opponents look bad by forcing them to extremes. A cardinal rule in Japanese martial arts is to "stay cool" and thereby force an overreaction in one's opponent. Similarly, goading causes protesters to lose control and engage in behavior ultimately damaging to their cause; to succeed, the baiters must keep a tighter control over their own ranks than the opponents do over theirs.

A paramount example of this strategy may be seen in the burakumin protest case. On the eve of the confrontation between the teachers and the league, tension had reached an upper limit. Yet despite this highly charged atmosphere, the teachers left the school by bus and proceeded to a local resort to relax and prepare for the next day. From the standpoint of league

29. For a discussion of traditional expectations for attributes in a superior, see John Bennett and Iwao Ishino, *Paternalism in the Japanese Economy: Anthropological Studies of Oyabun-Kobun Patterns* (Minneapolis: University of Minnesota Press, 1963); and Austin, *Saints and Samurai*, 23–27. This point is also well made in Shigeki Nishihira, "Political Opinion Polling in Japan," in *Political Opinion Polling: An International Review*, ed. Robert M. Worcester (New York: St. Martin's Press, 1983), 166.

members, more inflammatory behavior on the part of authorities is hard to imagine. For the teachers to be off relaxing in the convivial setting of a hot springs inn while burakumin children went without food—and on the eve of an eleven-day school break that left the fate of the hunger strikers in doubt—added insult to injury. Thus, although many factors were already at work to speed the conflict toward its violent conclusion, the teachers' actions had the effect of pushing the protesters toward overreacting the next day.

The Final Stages

Making Termination Interminable

When it appears that, despite the use of all previous strategies, the protest will continue, authorities who are firm in their determination not to compromise are likely to wait out the protest, even to the point of allowing it to continue indefinitely. This strategy, if it can be judged by its results, plays on the assumption that eventually the participants may tire of the affair and the watching public will lose interest in the outcome. One example of this delay tactic occurred in the protest over tea pouring: rather than retaliating directly, superiors and male officials opposed to the women's stance merely waited for the leaders of the protest to marry and leave the office or to be transferred to other divisions. Long delays in the courts provide another, more formal example. Only in 1988, fourteen years after the fact, did the court case resulting from the Yōka incident reach a partial resolution when the Osaka High Court upheld the conviction of the league activists charged in the disturbance; with a Supreme Court appeal now being made, still more delay is inevitable.

Numerous examples of the use of this strategy may be cited for many protests in Japan other than the three set out here. For example, the famous Narita Airport struggle, in which farmers and their radical student allies protested the confiscation of land to build a major new airport serving Tokyo, persisted into the late 1980s as authorities continued to tolerate the existence of protester-occupied "fortresses" and huts near the airport. The fight against the airport—and, in a larger sense, against the state itself—has thus dragged on for some two decades.[30] The November 1975 railway strike provides another example. With much of the country paralyzed, the government allowed the strike to continue for several days as

30. For an account of the struggle, see Apter and Sawa, *Against the State.*

newspapers ran pictures of businessmen, briefcases in hand, walking the Yamanote track lines to work.

Consider also the authorities' response to the extended occupation by student radicals of university campuses in 1968–1969: after setting up operations around the perimeter of barricaded campuses, riot police then simply waited out the protest. Contrast this response with the authorities' actions in similar incidents in the United States—the almost immediate removal by police of student demonstrators from university administration buildings, for instance, or the bombing of two city blocks by Philadelphia police to flush out a handful of radicals in May 1985.

Violent confrontations between authorities and protesters have been relatively rare in postwar Japan. When they do occur, it is usually because the particular circumstances or the nature of the issue impose a deadline on resolution. Thus, during the 1960 treaty crisis, when opposition-party politicians and their staffs were engaging in sit-ins in the Diet to prevent passage of the Japan-U.S. Security Treaty, the government felt itself under a deadline because it wanted the treaty to be passed and in effect before President Eisenhower's scheduled visit to Japan. Some five hundred police were therefore called in to drag protesting Diet members off the floor so that a vote on the issue could be forced and the protest broken up. The treaty passed, but the government's action created public sympathy and support for those in opposition and added to the size and intensity of the mass demonstrations taking place outside the Diet.[31]

A great many social protests, of course, have no such deadlines. When a time limit is not at issue, Japanese authorities appear to prefer to wait out the conflict rather than bring about a resolution through sudden, forceful action.

Why the Japanese Formula Succeeds

In surveying the various strategies that the targets of a status-political struggle use, we might ask what their methods achieve. Three overarching and related results in particular stand out: isolation of the protesters, marginalization of the protest, and containment of the conflict.

Resource mobilization theory argues that the success of social protest activity depends as much on the protesters' efforts to mobilize resources, forge links with other groups, and win support from third parties as it does on such factors as the force of specific grievances, the nature of the social

31. Scalapino, *Parties and Politics*, 135–136.

structure, and the role of ideology.[32] Thus, if authorities can isolate the original group of protesters, they effectively cut off all access to resources and so significantly diminish the movement's chances of ultimate success. Baiting or undercutting opponents has precisely such an effect. In social action over equality issues, the pool of potential supporters of a cause may be vast, particularly in the case of protests by juniors or women. The way the protest is perceived by onlookers is thus very important. The strategy of demeaning status inferiors and trivializing their protest not only has the effect of potentially delegitimizing the protest in the eyes of all but the most committed activists, but it also raises questions about the appropriateness of the protest among both potential supporters and the public at large—a quite likely outcome, in fact, given that protest by status inferiors still enjoys only partial legitimacy in Japan. When authorities admonish or dismiss protesters, they in effect are reasserting traditional norms: onlookers may for this reason alone find themselves persuaded. Delay isolates protesters as well; as the less committed drop away, potential supporters lose interest and the protest fades from the public view.

The confrontation between Buraku Liberation League members and Yōka High School teachers illustrates vividly how isolation operates. Prior to the incident, the community had been divided on the issues involved in this heated controversy at the region's largest senior high school. Once the violence occurred, however, public support swung quickly away from the local branch of the Liberation League, leaving it cut off and incapable of mobilizing a broader circle of backers. Indeed, as noted earlier, the Socialist party, which had backed the league, was voted out of office the following February; and even other league chapters, though they officially defended the local chapter's actions, were privately critical. Thus, even though several years later participants continued to debate whether the teachers had deliberately provoked the confrontation, there is no question that waiting for the protesters to make the decisive move served the teachers' long-term interests.

As status-based conflicts unfold, numerous strategies may serve to isolate the opposition. It is striking, for example, that once the New Liberal Club announced its intention to leave the LDP party, elders began to treat the group as renegades. Rather than to withhold criticism, attempt to work out their differences, and concentrate on keeping the younger men in the party, the LDP effectively closed ranks on the seceders. The use of undercutting language to describe Kōno and his followers ("incubator

32. See Zald and McCarthy, *Dynamics of Social Movements.*

babies," "runaway girls") drove a further wedge between the breakaway group and junior members who had stayed in the party. As one younger man who remained behind put it, "Leaving the LDP was like leaving the mainland to go to an island"—a comment that captures the sense of exile associated with the dissident group.[33]

The larger goal of such strategies, seemingly, is to contain the conflict and to marginalize the protesters and their cause. Whereas in virtually all industrial societies authorities see the containment of social protest to be a critical concern, other objectives may be equally important, such as preserving a principle or demonstrating responsiveness to protesters. In Japan, however, containment appears to take precedence over other goals.

Privatizing Conflict

All industrial countries offer similar formal channels for the resolution of social, political, and economic conflicts, such as the courts, institutions for labor-management conflict resolution, and, in the case of political conflicts, elections, committee votes, and party caucuses. Yet while these channels are all available in Japan, and are certainly used, a great many conflicts nevertheless unfold, and stay, outside the formal venues of resolution. The strong preference in Japan, in short, is—wherever possible— to handle each conflict on a case-by-case basis. Even when disputes find their way into established channels, the tendency is to avoid resolutions that might have broad application to other situations. Ultimately, then, the Japanese tend to privatize conflict—and status-based conflicts provide excellent illustrations of this phenomenon.

In the case of the New Liberal Club breakaway, for example, the specific grievances of Kōno's group were at no time taken up by decision-making bodies within the party, nor were they (according to NLC members) ever discussed, either formally or informally, at faction meetings. As for the tea pourers' rebellion, the dispute never spread beyond one division of the public bureaucracy—even though one-quarter of the eight thousand employees in the municipal office where the protest occurred were women and complaints over tea-serving duties were reportedly widespread[34]—because leaders of the employees' union (all of whom are male bureaucrats) turned down the protesting women's request to take up the issue unionwide. In the case of the Yōka struggle, the conflict found its way into the courts only in the wake of a violent confrontation that re-

33. Fujinami Takao, interview with author, LDP headquarters, Tokyo, 31 May 1978.

34. Interviews with union officials of the Kyoto city office, June 1978.

sulted in numerous injuries; the courts' role in the dispute has been ultimately to punish the protesters for excesses, not to find a resolution for the issues raised.

Privatizing social conflict and keeping key social issues—such as equality—out of the various channels that would generate principles for their future resolution is the essence of the Japanese formula. Although such an approach involves numerous costs, both to protest itself and to Japan as a democracy, from the authorities' standpoint the formula does achieve certain useful ends. For one thing, by privatizing a status-based conflict authorities may be positively seen to be limiting its overall social impact. For another, containment serves to protect, at least in the short term, the legitimacy of status superiors' authority in social relationships from fundamental challenges.

Preemptive Concessions

If we step back from these specific episodes of conflict, what stands out is the fact that elites, independent of the protests themselves, often do finally address at least some of the particular grievances raised. The aftermath of each of our three cases will be explored in the next chapter; thus, a few examples here should suffice to illustrate this point. Within the LDP after the 1976 breakaway of the New Liberal Club, several reforms, directly or indirectly, responded to the criticisms leveled by disgruntled party juniors at senior party members. Restrictions on campaign funding introduced in 1976 answered their calls for a tough response to the Lockheed scandal. The introduction in 1977 of the party primary for narrowing the slate of candidates for party president was another notable reform; although the system has rarely been used since its institution, it at least provides a mechanism for broadening participation in party decision-making. In the aftermath of the tea pourers' struggle, tea-making equipment has been upgraded in the municipal office where the conflict occurred. And although it is hard to point to specific concessions granted to burakumin in Hyōgo Prefecture itself, the general government response to burakumin grievances in the postwar era has been to pass legislation aimed at improving their living conditions. In each case, although the concessions amount to less than what protesters have wanted, nevertheless they do constitute an active response to the issues raised (see chapter 9).

Authorities take such steps quite independently of a specific protest incident in a pattern of what might be called preemptive concession-making. This strategy, of course, is far from uniquely "Japanese." Gamson, in his 1975 study of social protest in the United States, concluded that preemptive concessions are but one of four possible outcomes to social conflicts; significantly, however, this solution characterized only 11 percent of his cases.[35] Close study of Japanese responses to social conflict, in contrast, suggests that reliance on preemptive concessions is particularly strong in that country.

Granting concessions independently of a protest serves a number of purposes at once in Japan. First and foremost, it represents an attempt to ward off future protests. Second, by making concessions unilaterally and without reference to the protest proper, authorities reaffirm the traditional patterns of status relations in which superiors magnanimously grant favors to inferiors based not on the articulated needs of inferiors but on their own sense of what is appropriate and deserved. Finally, preemptive unilateral concessions offer a way of addressing the issues raised by protesters while simultaneously denying the legitimacy of open protest itself.

In Machiavellian terms, the Japanese formula for dealing with social protest succeeds admirably. A "successful" outcome of a status-based conflict, from the authorities' perspective, is one in which (1) elites stay in power, (2) the basic pattern of status relations is not fundamentally altered, and (3) protest as a strategy is not legitimized. All three ends were met in the outcomes of the conflicts studied. In the LDP's case, even though the institution of a party primary system has opened up the decision-making process (at least nominally), seniors continue to make key party decisions; indeed, basic patterns of junior-senior relations within the party and the behavioral expectations associated with them are little changed. The fundamental division of work within the Kyoto city office that gave rise to the tea pourers' rebellion likewise, as of the mid 1980s, remained unchanged, despite sporadic outbreaks of similar protests: women bureaucrats still make and pour the tea. As for the burakumin protest, status relations between burakumin and majority Japanese at Yōka High School have undergone no fundamental improvement; in some respects, in fact, the situation of burakumin in that region worsened as a result of the conflict.

In a larger sense, strategies used by Japanese authorities to handle social conflict have two major advantages over other possible formulas. First, they achieve the authorities' ends without the use of force. Indeed, in the case of the burakumin protest the protesters essentially brought about their own defeat: their leader and twelve other league members ended up in jail, for reasons that the general public regarded as justifiable; and the alliance with the Japan Socialist party broke down, with the party most sympathetic to the Buraku Liberation League ultimately being voted out of power. Certainly coercion on the authorities' part (which in the

35. Gamson, *Strategy of Social Protest*, 37.

United States is used in so many conflicts involving comparable levels of disorder and provocation) could not have accomplished half as much.

Second, this formula allows the authorities to control the pace of social change. Undercutting, baiting, and persuasion undermine the protesters' will to dissent; at the same time, such methods make it difficult for protesters to mobilize broader support for their cause. Keeping the protest outside the established channels for resolving conflict also means that any particular incident of status-based conflict has little chance of affecting social change in a significant way. In a context where social protest still does not enjoy full legitimacy, the formula, in particular the component involving ameliorative concessions, enables authorities to avert future conflicts while maintaining a manageable threshold for social conflict in general.

9

Goals Reconsidered:
The Issue of Success

The previous chapter explored the outcome of social conflict from the perspective of authorities and their interests. This chapter rounds out the discussion by looking at the final stages of the same three conflicts from the protesters' vantage point, including their goals in organizing and mobilizing a movement for change in the first place and the extent to which those goals were met. A final section addresses the obstacles that stand in the way of more successful outcomes for protesters in Japan.

What Protesters Want

The goals of status-based protests are many and varied, being perhaps the most complex of any of the four main protest types described in chapter 2. Conflicts over material issues, for example, generally involve objectives—from higher wages to an end to class-specific oppression in taxation—that are fairly straightforward. The same is true for issue-based disputes over quality-of-life concerns, such as petrochemical pollution or new bullet train routes through congested urban areas, and for protests over value issues, such as those in the 1930s concerning party politicians who had allegedly deviated from an ideal of loyal and uncorrupt service to the emperor (here the solution was simply to end these politicians' role in government by whatever means necessary, including assassination). All of these conflict types, of course, become more complex when examined with care: moral outrage may demand that polluters not only shut down the plant but also apologize publicly, thus adding a symbolic-affective goal to a concrete one; likewise, noneconomic goals may loom alongside economic ones in struggles that are basically over material issues.

In the case of status-based protests, however, there is almost always a great multiplicity of ends sought. As Morton Deutsch notes, conflicts involving contests over principles or rights are far more difficult to resolve than those over more delimited issues.[1] By the same token, the goals of contests that seek a new state of reality are apt to be diffuse and multidimensional. Even a status politics protest with one principal goal, such as the sixty-year-old campaign in the United States for an equal rights amendment, while at one level symbolic, involves powerful affective and concrete dimensions as well: a desire on the part of many American women for full legal recognition as equals and for the elimination of legal barriers to employment and other material opportunities.

Status-based protests almost invariably involve all three types of goals: concrete, affective, and symbolic. This diversity of goals may be due in part to a combined vision of the way things should be, together with a questioning, rife with affect, of what is. The objective sought, at a minimum, is better treatment for the status group in question and a renegotiation of the terms of status relations. The precise formula for the changed state being pursued, however, may not be clear or even agreed on by all the protesters. These goals, then, deserve closer examination.

To begin with, each of our three protests involved certain concrete goals. Those in the burakumin protest were particularly clear cut. The Buraku Liberation League sought to win formal acceptance for a study group at Yōka High School that would address burakumin problems in a framework of interpretation developed by the league. At the same time, it sought abolition of the existing Japan Communist party–guided study group, as a means both of diminishing the JCP's influence on issues affecting burakumin and of enhancing the league's position as the single most important spokesman for burakumin in the school and the region. An additional, and broader, concrete goal was to end discrimination against burakumin in the schools and in society. Yet because this last goal involves movement to an altered state of affairs that members of the group concerned have never actually experienced, its real content is less clear than might be thought.

The tea pourers' rebellion, too, involved various straightforward concrete goals, such as a changing room, revised menstrual leave procedures, and a "rationalization" of tea-pouring duties. Lurking behind these goals, however, is the far broader objective of improving women's status in the workplace, and in fact the protest raised some of the most basic issues facing working women in Japan today: job content, particularly the assign-

1. Deutsch, *Resolution of Conflict*, 162.

ment of work tasks based on sex, including waitress and custodial duties; tracking, the channeling of women into jobs that limit their promotion and career prospects and effectively marginalize them in the male-dominated workplace; and on-the-job treatment.

In the case of the New Liberal Club breakaway, one set of goals centered on policy issues: the LDP's handling of internal problems, including corruption charges; its pro-Taiwan stance on the China issue up until 1972, which Kōno and many other junior members opposed; its choice of party presidents, including the party's decision to give a fourth term to Prime Minister Satō in 1970 and to put Miki in power (as a result of the "Shiina decision") in 1974. Related to these goals were concerns about party decision-making, which offered junior members few formal or informal channels to register objections or recommendations on issues of policy or personnel. In that sense, a status politics goal—that of instituting changes in the decision-making process so as to increase junior members' influence in party matters—was a necessary corollary to the dissidents' policy goals. A final goal centered on overcoming the limits of a reward structure based on seniority; the available route to power, with its demand for many years of displaying a "cooperative spirit" and deference to superiors and of avoiding contentious stands on issues—and all this with no guarantee of rewards beyond a bare minimum—held few attractions for the protesters. By trying to bring about these changes, the protesters were obviously hoping to maneuver for more rewards for themselves, either through the workings of a "reformed" decision-making system or, in the form of preemptive concessions from party elders, through the system as it was.

In addition to concrete goals, however, each conflict involved ample affective goals. Indeed, the very desire for better treatment itself reflects dissatisfaction with things as they are. The affective dimension can be particularly powerful in Japan, where status-based protests typically are fueled by moral outrage at the discrepancy between what the laws say and peoples' actual treatment of status inferiors. Indeed, the outrage can be so potent that it causes protesters to lose control, with high costs for the protest as a whole—as we saw in the case of the Yōka struggle, where, it may be recalled, the league's local leader, Maruo Yoshiaki, portrayed the final confrontation as having been partly the result of league members' intractable anger at the teachers' tactics. Similarly, the frustration and resentment of Kōno Yōhei, blocked in his own career by the terms of advancement in the Liberal Democratic party, are reflected in his comment that "basic doubts" about the party sat like "dregs in [his] heart."[2] The anger

2. Kōno Yōhei, "Jimintō yo saraba."

that many women feel about issues of job content and their treatment in the workplace likewise surfaced in interviews with both participants in the tea pourers' rebellion and other women bureaucrats of the city office; several informants broke down in tears as they described their frustration at being kept from more interesting job-related duties (involving tasks to be performed outside the office, for example) on the grounds that, as women, they had to be available to serve tea.

Affective goals take two forms. First, protesters seek an admission of responsibility for wrongdoing, to be followed by an apology to assuage the hurt and anger of the group—in short, emotional compensation. And second, they pursue more emotionally satisfactory treatment in the future. The demand for an acknowledgment of wrongdoing is perhaps most evident in burakumin protests, where denunciation sessions are used to force the accused parties to recognize and admit (*mitomesase*) their mistakes and offer an apology.[3] To be sure, the demand for an apology has long roots in the movement. In the 1920s, for example, the burakumin movement called on the Tokugawa family to apologize formally for the actions of their ancestors against burakumin.[4] Typically, what is sought in concrete terms is a low bow and a display of shame (*haji*) at wrongdoing (the latter being an important form of contrition in Japanese culture more generally).[5] In a major pollution controversy in the 1960s, in fact, the president of the company responsible ultimately attempted to assuage his accusers by kowtowing—bowing so low from a seated position on the tatami mat that his forehead touched the ground.[6] Abject displays of deference behavior by superiors toward wronged persons of lower status, it may be noted, is yet another form of status-reversal behavior of the kind discussed in chapter 5. Yet here such rituals are more than simply strategies of protest; they may constitute an explicit and important affective goal of the conflict overall.

The second affective goal of better treatment in the future appears in all three conflicts as well. The emotional importance of respectful behavior was seen in the early stages of the tea pourers' rebellion, for instance, when many women expressed a willingness to pour tea for men who acknowledged their act with warmth and appreciation. A major objective of buraku-

---

3. Interview with officials of the Buraku Liberation League, Osaka and Kyoto branch offices, 1978. On the tactic of *kyūdan*, see chapter 7.

4. DeVos and Wagatsuma, *Japan's Invisible Race*, 47.

5. Interview with Muraoka Sukeyuki (a noted intellectual connected with the league), Kyōto Buraku Kaihō Kenkyūkai, 12 July 1978.

6. Norie Huddle and Michael Reich, *Island of Dreams: Environmental Crisis in Japan* (New York: Autumn Press, 1975).

min movements, in turn, has been treatment on a par with that accorded majority Japanese. As would be expected, accusations of discriminatory treatment toward burakumin are common in such protests. For example, the Yōka High protesters held that on the fateful day of the confrontation some of the majority students were shouting derogatory epithets at them as the teachers left the school grounds. League members also found much at fault in the teachers' behavior toward burakumin students and parents, which was easily interpretable as deliberately condescending.[7] Being accorded genuine respect and courtesy is thus no minor goal in conflicts centering on issues of status.

The final dimension of hoped-for outcomes in status-based conflicts is symbolic: recognition on the part of the targeted authorities that the protesters' cause was just. Such recognition not only helps to redress past injustices and violations of official ideology, but it also serves to vindicate protesters for their disruptive activities—an important consideration in a country where status-based protest lacks full legitimacy and conflict is regarded so negatively. The meeting of symbolic goals is most clearly identifiable in the "reunification" phase following a *kyūdan* session, in which the person accused of discrimination toward burakumin signs a statement of confession and pledges not to behave intolerantly in the future. Typically this phase is treated as a ceremony and is conducted in a mood of celebration; as such, the confession may be seen as marking a symbolic victory for burakumin over the issue of discrimination. As for the tea pourers, in a presentation to union officials the following summer, Makino, the group's leader, reported victoriously of the women's challenge and the fact that most, if not all, of the original number were now dealing with the duty on an altered basis—another signal of symbolic triumph. And in the NLC breakaway, the mood of excitement and celebration among Kōno's small group suggests that successful defiance of the terms of status relations is itself an important symbolic victory in status-based protests.

Addressing Inequalities: Alternative Remedies

Although altering the terms of status relations is a common goal of all status politics actions, the nature of the changes sought may vary considerably, depending on the group. The case studies reveal the presence of two distinct value orientations at work, which in turn suggest the existence of a

---

7. Interview with former hunger strikers, Tajima regional headquarters, Buraku Liberation League, August 1978. See also chapter 8 for specific examples.

third to which the first two respond. Together they represent three alternative orientations to the problems of unequal treatment in Japanese society.

The first orientation is the traditional approach to discrimination and unsatisfactory treatment: that is, the terms of status relations are simply accepted. The aim here, in effect, is to elicit better treatment by exhorting superiors to meet their broader, tutelary responsibilities toward status inferiors. The cry—appropriately enough, in a system based on benevolent paternalism—is "take better care of us." At the same time, inferiors focus on living up to their side of the bargain by improving their own performance. In this traditional approach, there is no appeal to democracy as counterideology; the traditional ideology in which status relations are considered natural and legitimate is fully accepted.

Evidence of the traditional approach may be seen clearly in the early history of the burakumin liberation movement. In the Meiji period, long before an actual protest front had taken shape, certain burakumin reform groups, rather than calling superiors to task for discrimination, concentrated instead on "self-reform": trying to get burakumin communities to improve their own attitudes and behavior. The premise was that by raising moral standards, improving standards of cleanliness, and so on, burakumin would make themselves worthy of better treatment—a pattern of behavior that has parallels in many other cultural settings.[8] Of particular interest here is not just the group's acceptance of the negative stereotype projected onto it by the dominant group, but the full acceptance of inequality itself: indeed, this is the hallmark of the traditional approach.

Another version of the same approach appears in the early petitions of burakumin groups to the Meiji leaders and to the emperor for improved conditions.[9] These appeals, in which can be heard the call for greater paternalism, have, it may be noted, analogues in the early history of worker protest in Germany, where miners in the 1860s, for example, "often pleaded with state and king, through petitions and delegations, for protection from 'the capitalists.'" In both settings, significantly, the protests

---

8. On the burakumin strategy, see DeVos and Wagatsuma, *Japan's Invisible Race*, 39. With regard to other cultural examples of such behavior, note for example P. C. Lloyd's account of turn-of-the-century Liberia and Sierra Leone, where the indigenous populations in the capital cities adopted Victorian dress and furnishings, partly as a way of proving themselves according to European standards for "civilized" behavior (*Africa in Social Change* [Baltimore: Penguin Books, 1967], 128–129).

9. DeVos and Wagatsuma, *Japan's Invisible Race*.

were marked by overt acceptance of "dependence and subordination and prevailing social values emphasizing obedience and deference."[10] Barrington Moore argues that pleas to authority along these lines are based on a concept of reciprocity that underlines widespread conceptions of justice and fairness. As he notes, "in many different times and places popular criticism of authority has been to the effect that authority has not lived up to its obligation to take care of its subjects, that it has oppressed and plundered where it should have cherished and protected."[11] Such an approach to seeking remedies for unsatisfactory treatment predates other concepts (see below) based on the idea that boundaries, or basic rights, need to be defined in all relationships.

The burakumin abandoned this approach in the movement that took shape in the 1920s. The opening declaration of the Levelers' Association, in fact, called on burakumin never again to "profane [their] humanity by slavish words and cowardly acts," thus explicitly rejecting attempts to "earn" better treatment through self-improvement or to induce it through self-effacing entreaties to authorities.[12] Nevertheless, the general acceptance in the culture of the view that changes in one's own behavior offer the best hope of bringing about desired results in social relationships (as opposed, for example, to appeals on the basis of rights) has been demonstrated by numerous surveys in postwar Japan. In one such survey, for example, when asked to complete a sentence that began "In order to be respected by others . . . ," well over the majority of those questioned (63.5 percent of younger Japanese) invoked the appropriateness of making changes in oneself: "You must polish yourself" or "You should respect others first."[13]

The second orientation to the problem of inequality calls for what may be considered a renegotiation of the terms of interaction. Here again, hierarchy itself is accepted as the basis for social relations; the aim now is to "rationalize" and set limits on those relations. Indeed, when Japanese call for changes in the terms of status relations, it is precisely this approach that is normally meant: the aim is not "equality" in the sense of ending

10. Rimlinger, "Legitimation of Protest," 373, 372.

11. Barrington Moore, Jr., *Injustice: The Social Bases of Obedience and Revolt* (White Plains, N.Y.: M. E. Sharpe, 1978), 509.

12. DeVos and Wagatsuma, *Japan's Invisible Race*, 4.

13. Takie Sugiyama Lebra, "Intergenerational Continuity and Discontinuity in Moral Values Among Japanese," in *Japanese Culture and Behavior: Selected Readings*, ed. Takie S. Lebra and William P. Lebra (Honolulu: University of Hawaii Press, 1974), 111. The survey was conducted in 1970.

hierarchy based on ascription; instead the aim is to redefine the content of what is expected in relationships based on inequality. In effect, what is sought is a "rationalization" of the relationship through adjustments in the implicit social contract that exists between inferiors and superiors.

Actually goals may vary. In status-based conflicts, protesters often want to see their social roles redefined on the basis of their achieved status—as workers, as members of the Diet, as students, and so on. They object not to the displays of deference that go along with ascribed or achieved roles in Japan, but to the "extra" duties and behavior associated with their ascribed status as juniors, women, or burakumin—at least when such behavior is treated by their superiors as expected, rather than optional.

Juxtaposed against what is sought is a clear sense of what is rejected— that is, "feudalistic" behavior on the part of authorities, in which a wide range of demands having no clear boundaries are made of the inferior. Because the implicit social contract, based as it is on paternalism, puts the individual at the disposal of the superior in exchange for care, renegotiation necessarily means setting limits. This process is aided by numerous historical forces that have worked to undermine the terms of "feudalistic" relationships. Whereas in the Tokugawa era the relative rankings of loyalties and obligations were clearly understood in society (a retainer's relationship to his lord, for example, took clear precedence over other role obligations), in the modern age, with the diversification of social roles that accompanied social, political, and economic change, the situation has changed fundamentally. As Yamazaki Masakazu argues, exclusive attachments to a single group have been replaced by numerous attachments, and thus by the need "to make frequent choices regarding relationships of belonging"; the individual today exists "in a framework of multiple human relationships and will need to adjust the various obligations involved."[14]

What is involved in the actual "adjustments" may vary widely. In some cases the major objective appears to be a redefinition—which the superior overtly accepts—of what types of behavior will be "expected" of inferiors. The tea pourers' rebellion had such an aim, at least for those women who remained willing to pour tea for men who treated this service not as expected behavior but as optional behavior to be warmly rewarded. In other cases a certain amount of "leveling" is involved, the call here being for greater "respect" or, in essence, a reduction, however modest, in social distance. The values brought to bear in these negotiations are those associated with the ideologies of equality and democracy, such as respect for hu-

---

14. Yamazaki Masakazu, "Atarashii kojin shugi no yochō," *Chūō Kōron* 98 (August 1983): 70–71, 86.

man dignity; nevertheless, the appeal itself reflects a basic acceptance of hierarchy.

The third orientation, and the one most familiar to Western readers because of its role in so many "equal rights" movements in the United States and Europe, is that involving an appeal for fundamental rights. This third view rejects, at least in principle, the notion of ascriptively based hierarchy and calls for a fundamental reordering of human relationships along more egalitarian lines. In this, advocates in Japan as elsewhere accept a view of egalitarianism that is consistent with Samuel P. Huntington's: no person, they say, should have the right to control or to exercise power over another.[15]

Strikingly, however, this view, which Huntington sees as a central tenet in the American creed and which has underlain status politics struggles in many other countries, has relatively limited support in Japan. In a study of one hundred politically active, postwar-educated women, for example, I found that only 20 percent of a group of women that was unusual to begin with shared this belief, and most of this minority were activists either in new left student groups or in radical feminist collectives or other women's groups.[16] To counter social hierarchy as reflected in the Japanese language, for instance, these women often eschewed the polite forms of speech widely used by women in favor of plain forms, including expressions that are considered "men's language" in Japan; the use of nicknames within their political groups, too, was a direct effort to avoid the inherent inequality in the usual ways of addressing men and women in Japan.[17]

In the present study, the only protesters holding the radical egalitarian view were the Buraku Liberation League members who became involved in the Yōka High School struggle. This fact is reflected in the very language that the burakumin students used in questioning their teachers in the school; historically as well, the position taken by the league's founding father, Matsumoto Jiichirō, in refusing to display ritualized deference to the emperor suggests the radical egalitarianism of the league's basic protest stance (see chapter 7). As for juniors as a class, even if Kōno's coterie did not propound an egalitarian view, certain other groups do, including the student movement activists described in chapter 5; like radical feminists and Buraku Liberation League activists, these student pro-

15. Samuel P. Huntington, *American Politics: The Promise of Disharmony* (Cambridge, Mass.: Harvard University Press, 1981), 33.

16. Pharr, *Political Women*, 66–72.

17. In friendship relations, for example, whereas women may address men by their last name, with a polite suffix for "Mr.," men often address women using more familiar forms (ibid., 68).

testers were mounting a fundamental challenge to social arrangements founded on hierarchy at the same time that they pressed for specific concrete gains.

In Japan, while small minorities call broadly for equal rights, most people engaged in status politics struggles appear to want something far more modest. In other words, what they seek cannot be understood as "equal rights" in a Western sense, despite the fact that they do draw on democratic ideology and egalitarianism in their effort to "rationalize" hierarchical relationships.

Significantly, these two fundamentally different approaches to remedying inequality are found in Western society as well. Within marriage in the United States, for example, women can choose between calling for a reallocation of power based on a notion of equal rights on the one hand (e.g., through contract marriages) and simply accepting and maneuvering for advantage within the general terms of the relationship on the other (e.g., through persuading the husband to do more housework while continuing to acknowledge housework as primarily a woman's responsibility). In both cases, egalitarianism as a culturally current ideology is an important external resource to the wife in pressing her case, but the specific objectives and the methods of attaining those objectives differ markedly. Similarly, in the relationship between graduate students and their professors in U.S. universities, students with grievances about their treatment may opt for either active protest, in which they explicitly challenge the terms of the relation and demand their rights (by appealing to an outside authority, perhaps, or by forming a union, such as a teaching assistants' union), or, alternatively, renegotiation of the relationship within the established parameters. In a larger sense, much litigation and lobbying activity in the area of civil rights represents efforts on the part of unempowered groups in the United States to mitigate the effects of inequality with the aid of an outside agency. As Stuart A. Scheingold notes, by reaching a settlement on a case, external authoritative agencies function to redistribute power in the relationship in question.[18] Without this approach, radical egalitarian solutions are difficult to achieve.

Why Japanese, even in status-based conflicts, favor renegotiation over appeals to rights may lie in Japan's particular traditions. For as Scheingold points out for Western societies, "at the core of the myth of rights is the legal paradigm—a social perspective which perceives and explains human interaction largely in terms of rules and of the rights and obligations

---

18. Stuart A. Scheingold, *The Politics of Rights: Lawyers, Public Policy, and Political Change* (New Haven: Yale University Press, 1974), 6–7.

inherent in rules." This perspective extends back through centuries of rational-legal development, in which the notion of contract, evolving first in Western feudal relationships, came to apply to virtually all types of human interaction. In this view, rights are the key not only to properly functioning relationships, but also to the rectification of conflicts over grievances or inequalities. Americans, Scheingold argues, "break down social problems into the responsibilities and entitlements established under law in the same way that lawyers and judges deal with disputes among individuals."[19] It is mainly in close, very dependent relationships, such as between wife and husband or graduate student and major professor, that Americans may feel pulled between renegotiating the relationship within its own terms and resorting to rights.

In Japan, in contrast, calls for individual rights, along with demands for fundamental power realignments in relations based on status, run contrary to prevailing norms, even today. Although some status politics cases based on the assertion of rights have found their way into the courts since the war, the modest gains to date suggest how difficult it is in Japan to win acceptance for the "radical egalitarian" view. One litigation campaign mounted by women over inequalities in the workplace, for example, has been instrumental in bringing to an end certain blatantly discriminatory practices of Japanese employers, such as the forced early retirement of female workers.[20] But far more basic problems that figure centrally in affirmative action litigation in the United States, such as discrimination in hiring, promotion, and job content, have only lately begun to be addressed in Japanese courts, so far with little success.[21] On these larger issues, it seems, the courts, like society at large, have been reluctant to see the "official ideology" of egalitarianism carried into the workplace.

Outcomes: Alternative Measures of Success

The previous chapter adopted a Machiavellian perspective and assessed the success of a protest outcome from the standpoint of authorities. Obviously there are other ways to think about the outcome of social protest

19. Ibid., 13, 17.

20. See Upham, *Law and Social Change*, 124–165. In the famous Sumitomo Cement case, which was decided in favor of the plaintiff in 1966, at issue was the company's policy of forcing women employees to retire at marriage or by the age of thirty. Although such employer policies were "virtually universal" in the 1960s, by 1980 they had almost disappeared, largely as a result of this particular litigation campaign (p. 134).

21. Ibid., 138–144.

and to judge its success. One measure concerns the fate of the protest group itself: a protest is successful if, as a result of the protest, the group comes to be recognized by those it challenges as a "valid spokesman for a legitimate set of interests."[22] A second measure is the actual yield of the protest effort for the intended beneficiaries: if the effort is successful, then presumably the grievances or issues raised are in some way addressed—whether or not the gains realized result directly from the protest itself.[23]

From a broader standpoint, a third criterion of success is whether or not channels for the resolution of future similar conflicts open up as a result of the protest effort. Lewis Coser, for instance, holds that the prerequisites for conflict termination include both the availability of an institutionally prescribed endpoint and the presence of a "shared universe of discourse."[24] Clearly, if neither exists already, then one successful outcome of a protest movement would be to see them established. This may occur regardless of whether the original protesters are included in the new decision- or policymaking apparatus that comes into being. Dorothy Nelkin and Michael Pollak, for example, show that in the case of French protest movements over nuclear energy development, new policy structures emerged, even though the original demonstrators were excluded from the consultation process and the new structures did not necessarily respond to the protesters' specific demands.[25]

These three measures view success purely from the standpoint of the protesters. Giuseppe DiPalma's work suggests a fourth measure of success, this one from a societal perspective: the degree to which the conflict "maximizes outcomes satisfactory to all contestants, thus increasing their propensity to stay in or join the game."[26] We might then ask whether the protesters themselves are content with the outcome. It is quite possible that the group might be dissatisfied despite concrete gains—for example, if the gains fall short of the group's overall aims, or if the group's efforts are

22. Gamson, *Strategy of Social Protest*, 28–29.

23. Ibid., 31. Gamson, in his study of fifty-five "challenging groups" in the United States, sought to establish simply whether results were forthcoming, independent of who or what caused them.

24. Coser, *Continuities*, 37–38.

25. See Nelkin and Pollak, *The Atom Besieged*. As they showed, the antinuclear movement was not successful in terms of concrete goals, for the government continued its program of nuclear energy development despite the new policymaking apparatus. Getting the issue onto the public policy agenda, however, and thereby increasing public access to policymaking, appears to be a gain in its own right, for it provides a foothold where none existed before.

26. Giuseppe DiPalma, *The Study of Conflict in Western Society* (Morristown, N.J.: General Learning Press, 1973), 4.

felt to have made little difference in bringing about the changes. If so, the propensity of that group or of others in the future "to stay in or join the game" may be affected, with, according to DiPalma, negative consequences for society generally.

By these various measures, the three protests considered in this book could not be considered unqualified successes. But neither are they unqualified failures. The outcome of each may now be considered in turn.

The New Liberal Club breakaway case demonstrates the rather limited gains that characterize many status-based protests. The ideal outcome of the struggle, from the protesters' point of view, would have involved the group's seeing their grievances satisfactorily addressed while remaining in Japan's ruling party. Had the LDP been more responsive to their complaints, Kōno's group might conceivably have been able to express their opinion on policy issues or advance their aim of effecting a change in party decision-making, to the extent that staying in the party would have seemed preferable to leaving. Likewise, had the LDP elected a strategy of appeasement, then rewards in the form of desirable posts might have satisfied the junior men's goal of getting more sooner, with the same ultimate result. None of this happened, however; Kōno and his group thus felt compelled to leave the ruling party, with its minimal guaranteed rewards for junior members, for an uncertain future as a fledgling political group. According to DiPalma's criterion, then, the outcome was less than satisfactory.

By the same token, the group experienced but limited success in terms of being recognized as representing legitimate interests, especially as far as the LDP's senior leadership was concerned. Nonetheless, Kōno did succeed, at least initially, in winning public support for a new political group made up primarily of junior men, and this indeed amounted to recognition of the kind he sought. In an *Asahi Shinbun* survey conducted several months after the NLC was formed, 13 percent of those surveyed said they supported the new party—a most impressive showing.[27] The prominence given in the media to the intergenerational issues that underlay the breakaway, together with the generally favorable public reaction (particularly among younger, better-educated voters in metropolitan areas) to seeing a political group of younger men emerge, satisfied a number of goals. Certainly the NLC established a means for its members to have an independent voice in policy matters. It also provided a basis at last for negotiation with the LDP's senior leadership, at least following those elections in which the LDP was forced to turn to the group to gain a majority; following the LDP's poor showing in the 1983 lower house election, the NLC

27. *Asahi Shinbun*, 17 February 1977, 1.

officially became part of a coalition government and managed to secure a cabinet post in return.[28]

It is difficult to argue that NLC members were able to use their bargaining position with the LDP as a fast track to power, however. Tagawa Seiichi, the first of the three NLC members to serve in the cabinet as a result of the 1983 coalition, did so only in his ninth term; Kōno and Yamaguchi each joined during their seventh terms, and Nishioka not until his eighth term. Had they stayed within the LDP, they would have been virtually assured of a cabinet post during their sixth term (see chapter 3). Certainly Kōno and his co-leaders, Yamaguchi and Nishioka, were set back career-wise by the breakaway. When the NLC disbanded, Kōno returned to the LDP, where in January 1987 he joined the Miyazawa faction as a newcomer. Kōno, now in his eighth term in the Diet, noted in an interview that he would have to "work hard and learn from scratch" in his new faction—language consonant with the traditional terms of status relations in Japan.[29] Like Kōno, both Yamaguchi and Nishioka joined different factions from the ones they had left earlier, suggesting the strains associated with returning to the LDP.[30]

A final question concerns whether, the fate of the Kōno group aside, the goals of the protesters were realized as a consequence of their movement. Like Gamson, in other words, we must ask whether results were forthcoming, independent of who or what caused them. In that sense, it is quite striking just how much of what the Kōno group sought was actually effected, sooner or later, by the LDP. Recognition of the People's Republic of China and a cap on the number of terms the party president may serve, for instance, were adopted as party policy quite soon after Kōno's group pressed for them.[31] On the issue of party corruption, too, the NLC

28. In the 1979 struggle between Fukuda and Ōhira for party president, Ōhira turned to the NLC for the support that made his win over Fukuda possible. Kōno attempted to negotiate an arrangement in which the NLC would get the education ministry cabinet slot in exchange. Once public, however, the deal was poorly received by both the LDP and the other NLC members, and it fell through, with Kōno forced to resign as NLC president as a result. See Hrebenar, *Japanese Party System*, 217–218.

29. *Asahi Shinbun*, 15 January 1987, 2.

30. Both Yamaguchi and Nishioka had formerly belonged to the Miki faction (now the Kōmoto faction); Yamaguchi subsequently joined the Nakasone faction, and Nishioka (with Kōno) joined the Miyazawa faction. In summer 1989, Kōno's name came up in the LDP's search for a "clean" successor to Prime Minister Uno, but he was passed over for Kaifu Toshiki.

31. The two-term limit on the party presidency set in 1977 has remained in place, though an exception to it was made for Nakasone, who was granted a one-year extension in 1985, after serving two terms.

stance (which was, it will be recalled, a central policy issue in their protest) made headway despite the opposition of key LDP leaders and their followers: Liberal Democratic strongman and former prime minister Tanaka Kakuei was arrested in 1976, only half a year after the Kōno group's defection, on charges deriving from the Lockheed scandal. Although the indictment caused Miki Takeo, prime minister at the time, to be forced out of office by his opponents within the party, nevertheless some of the housecleaning changes proposed by the Kōno group did occur.[32] The party also addressed the charges of "money politics" with the 1976 revision of the Public Offices Election Law, which among other things regulated political contributions.

Steps toward reform on the issue of the party president selection process were taken after the Kōno group left the party as well. In 1977 under Fukuda, the LDP officially adopted a party primary system:[33] in elections in which there were more than two candidates, an electorate made up of dues-paying LDP members (1.5 million in 1978) could choose the two top candidates; from these two contenders, then, the party convention (made up of LDP Diet members) selects one as party president. Subsequent changes in party primary rules have led to its more restricted use; since 1981, for example, four candidates have been required for a primary to be held. In any case, the party primary system today remains as an alternative to backroom politics for choosing the party president.

It would be absurd to hold that pressure from the Kōno group alone was enough to bring about any of these changes. Recognition of the PRC, for example, resulted largely because a strong proponent of this policy, Tanaka, was selected as prime minister in 1972, thus ending many years of party dominance by Satō Eisaku, who had been close to the Taiwan lobby. Both the Public Offices Election Law revision in 1976 and the introduction of the party primary system the following year were the product of many forces, including the need for a "cleaner" image, as well as for greater openness in the party (hence the primary), following the LDP's poor showing in the January 1976 election and, in the case of the primary system, the desire of Fukuda to break Tanaka's power by reducing the role of

32. Only four months after Tanaka's indictment, Miki was pushed from office in what was known as the "down with Miki" (*Miki oroshi*) campaign. His critics within the LDP held that he should have utilized special powers available to him to prevent Tanaka's arrest—powers that had been used successfully to protect Satō in the shipbuilding scandal during his administration. See Curtis, *Japanese Way of Politics*, 163.

33. The idea was originally Miki's, but he lacked the political clout to see it implemented during his term (1974–1976). His successor, Fukuda Takeo (1976–

"money politics" in deciding the party presidency. In the 1970s many forces other than Kōno's group were propelling the LDP toward internal reforms, from citizens' movements protesting the LDP's hand-in-glove relationship with big business to demographic changes that forced the party to reach out to reform-minded urban middle-class voters, not to mention many voices within the party itself.[34] It remains significant, however, that virtually every major criticism relating to party policy and decision-making practices that Kōno's group of dissidents had raised prior to 1976 was addressed in some way between 1976 and 1978.

With this said, we might also ask whether any of these party reforms has permanently altered the way the LDP conducts its business. The argument that the reforms were mainly cosmetic is quite persuasive. Despite the party's steps against corruption in 1976 through the campaign financing law and the decision not to contest Tanaka's indictment, money politics has continued to be a reality of Japanese political life. LDP Diet members still rely overwhelmingly on corporate funding sources, and scandals over money politics surface even today. Indeed, the Recruit Cosmos scandal that broke in 1988, involving questionable stock purchases by a host of LDP seniors (and others), was in many ways the worst case to date of "dirty money" politics.[35] The party primary system, despite its existence on the books, has not been used since 1982, and behind-the-scenes maneuvering by a small circle of seniors still decides the party president.

In the end, then, the reforms instituted by the party in the late 1970s represent an impressive example of preemptive concession-making. Faced by rising criticism from the media, middle-class and urban voters, and citizens' movements, as well as from internal critics such as Kōno, the party through these reforms laid the groundwork for a resurgence in the 1980s. In that sense, it was indeed responsive to a rising level of social discontent in the early to mid 1970s as, fearing an electoral backlash, it opted for image-enhancing reforms that bespoke a certain "creative conservatism."[36] But in so doing it made few lasting changes in party decision-making

---

1978), adopted the reforms, ostensibly as a way to lessen the role of backroom "money politics" in deciding the party presidency. See ibid., 101–104.

34. On the forces at play in this turbulent era of LDP history, see ibid.; Satō and Matsuzaki, *Jimintō seiken*; Baerwald, *Party Politics in Japan*; Tagawa, *Dokyumento Jimin dattō*; and Itō Masaya, *Jimintō sengokushi*, vol. 1 (Tokyo: Asahi Sonorama, 1982).

35. For an early account of the scandal, see the *New York Times*, 7 July 1988.

36. The phrase is used by T. J. Pempel, *Policy and Politics in Japan: Creative Conservatism* (Philadelphia: Temple University Press, 1982).

on internal matters or in relations with business interests, the latter issue having been a point of particular public criticism in the first half of the 1970s.

As many writers note, various factors—such as increased internationalization with regard to policy matters and the rise within the party of so-called *zoku* (tribes), or groups of members with specific policy interests—have reduced the factions' hold over their members and increased party pluralism.[37] Yet the reward system has not fundamentally changed; indeed, the principle of seniority is now more institutionalized than in the past, with its minimum guarantees to all regardless of ability.[38] Nor has the route to top positions of political power altered; loyalty to mentors and a cooperative spirit are still more effective in gaining advancement than bold or critical policy stances or independent power jockeying. Conspicuously absent from the LDP's reforms, in fact, are new channels for broadening party participation in the distribution of posts. The introduction of a party primary system opening up the contest for party president represented a step in that direction, but subsequent restrictions, not to mention the fact that the system has been ignored in recent elections, raise doubts about the meaningfulness of this reform. In the final analysis, then, preemptive concessions functioned extremely effectively to allow the party's resurgence without fundamentally altering the hierarchical basis of power allocations.

In the case of the tea pourers' rebellion, too, the gains present a mixed picture. The key participants claimed a signal victory because, for four or so years following the struggle, until the leaders either married and left the city office or were transferred to other divisions, the tea-serving rituals *did* change. Further evidence of significant gain was found in the recognition accorded the protesters by numerous women's groups at a Kyoto meeting held some eight months after the rebellion. By most other measures of success, however, the outcome hardly constitutes a victory.

Any prospect for fundamental change died when the rebellion failed to spread to other divisions. In the summer of 1964, just when the participants were feeling the full flush of victory, union members representing various youth and women's bureaus in the city office went on a retreat. At the meeting, Kawata, the retreat organizer, held up the Housing Division as a model, urging the (mainly male) bureau representatives to go back to

37. See Satō and Matsuzaki, *Jimintō seiken*, 92–94.
38. Curtis, *Japanese Way of Politics*, 88–90.

their divisions and convince the young men to pour their own tea. By his own report, Kawata's suggestion was met with a mixed response; at any rate, it was not implemented.

Why did the union's central office not endorse the women's efforts and urge all divisions to follow suit? The Kyoto City Employees' Union, after all, was the formal "parent" of the women's section, and its support might have made all the difference in validating the cause. Yet union officials deliberately avoided getting involved, treating the rebellion simply as a division-specific, shop-level struggle without broader implications. They gave three reasons for this stance: first, because only four sections were involved, the dispute was considered too localized to merit union involvement; second, the women's grievance, unlike such issues as equal pay for equal work or maternity benefits, was deemed to be outside the proper concerns of the union; and third, the issues were just "not serious enough" to receive union attention. Although officials acknowledged that most of the two thousand women in the eight-thousand-member union have various tea-related duties and that numerous other complaints at the section level had surfaced, the union's position on this point has been unyielding.[39]

In this struggle, then, no channels for the resolution of future similar conflicts were opened, nor did a dialogue develop between women office workers and their male superiors. Indeed, in the entire course of the rebellion, from its inception to its final hours over four years later, when the last of the original protesters left the Housing Division, there is no evidence that any direct communication, much less formal dialogue, ever occurred between the rebels and their seniors. Nor was the long-term yield on the tea-serving issue significant. In certain large Japanese offices beverage machines have been installed, freeing women from their former duties entirely, or else the number of daily tea servings has been reduced or (as in the city office after the struggle) new equipment has been purchased to make tea preparation quicker, thus at least easing the women's chore. But among male bureaucrats and, of course, many women workers, especially of older generations, the view persists that "it is women's duty to pour tea."[40]

In postwar Japan several channels of conflict resolution have taken up issues relating to women's status in the workplace. Using constitutional

39. Interviews with officials of the Kyoto City Employees' Union (Kyōto-shi Shokuin Rōdōkumiai), Kyoto, 4 July 1978.

40. In a survey reported in 1978, over 50 percent of the Japanese men questioned indicated that they saw tea making as an integral part of women's work in the office; *Asahi Evening News*, 7 July 1978, 5.

provisions and the Labor Standards Act as resources, women plaintiffs backed by feminist lawyers in the mid 1960s embarked on a litigation campaign against discriminatory practices in economic life, with numerous successes, particularly in the domains of forced early retirement and "equal pay for equal work" violations (see chapter 4). The Labor Standards Bureau of the Ministry of Labor, too, by means of "administrative guidance"—a combination of exhortation and prodding within the close consultative context of bureaucratic-business relations—has succeeded in gaining active compliance with court decisions in suits brought by women workers.

The Women's and Young Workers' Bureau in the Ministry of Labor, which dates from the Occupation, has played a key role in monitoring the situation of women in the workplace as well, both through its surveys and publications and by linking Japan to international efforts to raise working women's status.[41] This bureau, for example, took the lead in hammering out an antidiscrimination statute, which, as part of observances for the United Nations Decade of Women (1975–1985), Japan had pledged it would ratify by the time the 1985 Convention on the Elimination of All Forms of Discrimination Against Women met. To the bureau fell the task of drafting the statute and of presiding over the stormy consultations among bureaucrats, business groups, unions, and feminist groups that preceded the final emergence of the Equal Employment Opportunity Law (EEOL). Although the EEOL carries no sanctions for violations, it opens the way for a key mediating role to be played by the Ministry of Labor in pressing employers toward compliance.[42]

When viewed in the context of the worldwide struggle for equality since World War II, the gains in Japan seem modest indeed. The women's movement there has not been broad and sustained, but dozens of women's organizations and feminist groups have pressed for various measures that would improve women's status in the workplace. Women plaintiffs have likewise been coming forward since the 1960s, despite many disincentives, including long court delays and exceedingly small monetary rewards even in the event of favorable decisions. Meanwhile, Japan's rising importance in the world and its participation in such forums as the United Nations and the International Labor Organization have given increased visibility

41. This latter role is quite significant, given Japanese responsiveness to pressures from abroad (*gaiatsu*) and sensitivity to foreign criticism. See chapter 10.

42. The developments leading to the EEOL are well summarized in *Problems of Working Women* (Tokyo: Japan Institute of Labor, 1986). See also Upham, *Law and Social Change*, 148–156, for an account of the debates leading up to the law.

to the problems of Japanese working women and to the underrepresentation of women in managerial and other leadership positions in business, bureaucracy, and political life.

Despite these pressures, the degree of official accommodation has been relatively minimal. The most impressive successes have come as a result of the litigation campaign, but even there only a few issues have been addressed. Indeed, the courts have been highly reluctant to develop new doctrines that would open the way for deliberation of major problems, such as discriminatory hiring practices, that have been at the center of working women's struggles elsewhere.[43] The range of practices not yet addressed definitively by the courts includes virtually all the issues dealt with in our case study, most notably job content, including the assignment of tea-serving and custodial duties to women, and work environment as it affects women workers' psychological well-being.

The problem that women encounter when they turn to the courts for conflict resolution is well illustrated by one of the few cases concerned specifically with women's work issues. In *Yamamoto vs. Suzuka City*, a female city office employee sued over discrimination in promotion and in the granting of family allowances, as well as in the city office practice of assigning tea-serving and custodial duties to women workers. The Tsu District Court in 1980 found for the plaintiff, agreeing on the basis of her statistical evidence that she had indeed been systematically discriminated against. On appeal, however, the Nagoya High Court in 1983 reversed the decision, accepting the defendant's argument that promotions were discretionary and that the plaintiff, despite her excellent work record over twenty years of employment, "lacked a cooperative and enthusiastic personality and had difficulty with interpersonal relations."[44] The case is currently being appealed to the Supreme Court.

One problem with legal conflict resolution is the limited sphere in which the courts have been prepared to act. Another even more serious problem is the adverse consequences suffered by working women as employers have sought to head off litigation or avoid the impact of legal judgments. In the 1970s, for example, many employers responded to the courts' assault on forced early retirement practices by ceasing to hire women at all as permanent employees, hiring them instead only on a part-

43. The only areas well covered so far by court-developed doctrines are wage and retirement discrimination; a major problem for plaintiffs is how to fit a great many issues such as promotion and hiring discrimination within the framework of established doctrine, since the courts are so reluctant to expand their mandate through doctrinal innovation. See Upham, *Law and Social Change*, 134–143.

44. Ibid., 142.

time or temporary basis. To avoid charges of unfair compensation, moreover, some employers shifted from compensation systems based on seniority (which gave women grounds for claiming equal treatment) to ones based on function; they then assigned all women to low-paying jobs. Companies also retaliated against lawsuits brought by college-educated, career-minded women by simply ceasing to hire female university graduates. A new round of litigation since 1975 has sought to attack some of these new policies, but so far with only limited success.[45]

At the same time, bureaucracy too has been a weak ally for working women who pursue social change, having lacked the clout to pressure employers to end discrimination. Administrative guidance, although applied aggressively and effectively in many other domains of policy, has been used only sparingly on behalf of working women. Even the one major Ministry of Labor success—that of inducing employers to drop early retirement policies—came only after a contentious ministry-level struggle between officials of the Women's and Young Workers' Bureau, who sought a more active role for the ministry, and other bureaucrats who resisted assuming that responsibility. Internal opposition was so great that the finally victorious Women's and Young Workers' Bureau took on the task itself rather than going through the Labor Standards Bureau—whose cooperation would have given the initiative more clout.[46]

The ministry still maintains a low posture on the problems of working women today, as its lack of response to the new round of discriminatory policies adopted in the 1970s demonstrates. It remains to be seen how active the ministry's role will be in the wake of the EEOL. The very existence of the law, coupled with Women's and Young Workers' Bureau efforts to push and persuade employers into compliance, may well be leading to some changes, however. For example, a Ministry of Labor survey reported that between fiscal 1986 and fiscal 1987 the percentage of companies prepared to hire female college graduates increased from 32.4 percent to 72 percent, a dramatic jump.[47] Changes have occurred in job advertising as well: in 1986, for instance, the ministry, using administrative guidance, mounted a strikingly successful effort to end sex-based job listings.[48] But new forms of employer evasion have also appeared, in the form of "multi-track employment systems" that classify regular employees into two categories: the managerial (sōgōshoku) track and the "general em-

45. See ibid., 138–142, for a discussion of employer policy changes in the 1970s as a response to women's court successes.
46. Ibid., 147.
47. *Daily Yomiuri*, 28 December 1986, 2.
48. Japan Institute of Labor, *Japan Labor Bulletin* 3 (1 October 1987): 5.

ployee" (*ippanshoku*) track for clerical workers. In some firms there is also a third track for "specialized employees" (*senmonshoku*). A recent survey indicated that 21 percent of firms that had no such classification system before the EEOL have since instituted one, thus raising doubts about the positive gains forthcoming from the EEOL for working women.[49]

The general pattern of response by the courts and the bureaucracy—and indeed by management as well—to women's pressures for greater equality in the workplace suggests the difficulty of achieving gains through overt actions. The number of legitimate avenues available to women who seek redress for grievances has increased very little; moreover, the EEOL lacks provisions for enforcement and, more significantly, offers few channels for the pursuit of remedies. There is no real equivalent to the Equal Employment Opportunity Commission, provided for in Title VII of the U.S. Civil Rights Act of 1964, which provided a new resource to women and minorities in affirmative action cases. Article 13 of the EEOL, in contrast, simply urges employers charged with discrimination to "strive" (*tsutomenakereba naranai*) to deal with the complaint within the company through a specially constituted labor management body. Additionally, if either the employer or woman employee so requests, the director of prefectural branches of the Women's and Young Workers' Bureau can offer advice and recommendations, but both sides must agree if actual mediation (*chōtei*) is to be conducted; this would be done through an Equal Opportunity Mediation Commission set up on a case-by-case basis.[50] Inherent in this approach to conflict resolution is a preference for dealing with disputes individually and avoiding methods that would generate broadly applicable principles. Even the courts, despite the important role they have played as a forum for women's grievances, have limited their accessibility and effectiveness through narrow definitions of what they will hear, through minuscule settlements for successful plaintiffs, and through judicial procedures that keep cases in the courts for years.[51] From the protester's standpoint, then, significant gains are unpromising if pursued through conventional channels of Japanese society.

49. Ibid., 5–6.

50. Such a commission would consist of three persons appointed by the Ministry of Labor from among "persons of learning and experience," who would hear out the case and could propose settlements; see Upham, *Law and Social Change*, 153.

51. Typically the settlements are limited to back pay, damages, and legal fees. The award of the Tsu District Court in *Yamamoto vs. Suzuka City* in 1980 was a total of ¥1,426,150, or $7,100; when the higher court reversed the decision, the plaintiff's side, of course, had to cover the legal fees. In particular, the awards of damages for mental suffering are exceedingly small by U.S. standards. See ibid., 140–141.

The outcome of the Yōka High School conflict, finally, likewise yielded little in the way of benefits for the burakumin activists. Indeed, most observers agree that the league's efforts in the entire region suffered a setback as a result of the struggle and the violence that marked the final clash. Those protesters at the front line of the struggle—league-affiliated burakumin students who stayed on at the school—undoubtedly suffered the most. Several commented on an atmosphere of tension that persisted until they graduated. Said one: "The teachers didn't express their hatred or retaliate directly in front of us students. But when we ran into them unexpectedly in the hall or someplace, their faces froze and they glared." Said another: "The atmosphere wasn't exactly tense, but [if you were a burakumin] you could only talk with people superficially. There was a wall and you couldn't get beyond it."[52] After the conflict, moreover, burakumin students were dispersed throughout the school so that no more than one or two were ever in a given classroom. Meanwhile, the thirteen league activists who were arrested following the 1974 confrontation went on trial and, in 1988, were found guilty of many of the charges against them. The case is now being appealed to the Supreme Court.[53]

The conflict had several immediate political outcomes, none positive. One was the breakdown of the league's alliance with the local administration of Yōka Town as, in the election of 15 February 1975 held less than three months after the confrontation, power was transferred from the Socialists to the league's archenemies, the Communists (with the Communist candidate receiving a full 92.3 percent of the vote). Another related outcome was the dissolution of the entire network of affiliation between the league and other regional organizations. Not only did the new Communist mayor immediately accept the resignation of the five-member school board that had backed the league in the struggle, but within the town office a major reshuffling occurred as well in which 80 out of 130 employees were assigned new positions.[54] With the power of the Japan Socialist party thus effectively broken within the town office, the league lost its crucial external base of support for educational initiatives in the region.

At the same time, more extensive JSP-linked organizational support fell sharply away, with only Sōhyō, the Union of Trade Organizations, still cooperating with the league's *kyūdan* sessions. Nor were the repercussions limited to the town. Local league activists noted, for example, that

52. Interview with former hunger strikers, Tajima regional headquarters, Buraku Liberation League, August 1978.
53. *Buraku Kaihō Newsletter*, 1984; *Asahi Shinbun*, 30 March 1988, 22; and *Mainichi Daily News*, 1 April 1988, 1.
54. Interview with JCP-affiliated Mayor Hosokawa, Yōka Town, August 1978.

Communist mayors had been voted into power throughout the wider region following and as a direct result of the conflict: "They got there by attacking the league. People feel that burakumin activities should be controlled."[55] Maruo Yoshiaki, the leader of the struggle, summed up its tragic results from the protesters' perspective: "We have returned to the buraku. Because of oppression from authorities, we have fewer persuasive powers. So we're back among ourselves. We're trying to form a strong group among burakumin themselves."[56]

The single gain for the activists (to the extent that it was one) was the trial itself, in which the league succeeded in laying out evidence of discrimination in Japanese society. Indeed, in the first hearings on the case in May 1985 in Kobe District Court, the accused all refused to take off the *hachimaki* (headbands) symbolizing their protest until the chief justice made a statement acknowledging that, despite the Constitution of 1947, discrimination against burakumin persists in Japan.[57] Over the postwar years, the league—although it has not seen litigation as a major route to social change—has used the various cases brought by burakumin to trace and document the history of discrimination in Japanese society. In a country where a great many people continue to deny that prejudice against burakumin exists, such legal proceedings, independent of their actual outcome, represent important forums for the league as it makes its case publicly.[58]

The Yōka struggle brought no additional gains for the league. Instead, the league's efforts to gain recognition as the single legitimate spokesman on discrimination in education and to demolish the claims of Japan Communist party–allied groups and organizations lost ground in the Tajima region. In Yōka High School, the league-organized study group (never officially approved) continued to meet only until the last of the student participants in the struggle graduated in 1977. The most serious setback to the league's fight to have a voice in educational matters in Tajima was perhaps the Hyōgo Board of Education's January 1976 decision to separate the general courses from the vocational courses (stockbreeding, agriculture, home economics, and so on) at Yōka High School. By April, the new Tajima Agricultural High School was holding classes in a temporary building two kilometers from the senior high school proper.[59] Since burakumin

55. Interviews with Buraku Kaihō Dōmei officials, Wadayama, 17 August 1978.
56. Maruo Yoshiaki, interview with author, Wadayama, August 1978.
57. *Mainichi Shinbun*, 31 May 1975.
58. Maruo Yoshiaki resolutely defended the utility of the trial from that standpoint.
59. Interviews with Yōka High School teachers, Yōka Town, August 1978.

students, especially males, were heavily concentrated in the vocational track, this action effectively removed a great many past and future league activists from one of the prefecture's most prestigious high schools. By 1977, when the last of the original student protesters graduated, only a handful of burakumin students, mostly female, remained in the school. Although girls had predominated among the original activists, the small core group remaining was hard pressed to continue the study group with the overall number of burakumin students at the school so diminished. According to Maruo, these students took a public stand in favor of keeping the group alive, but it nonetheless soon ceased to be active.[60]

In the final analysis, it seems reasonable to say that the Yōka protest effectively backfired. With the burakumin student population divided in the region's major senior high school, with the support of the local administration and of the school board gone, with its once-large network of supporting organizations no longer in place, the league lost its access to educational policymaking. Yet interestingly, this loss of power applied not only to the league, but to the JCP as well. According to several PTA members, burakumin education became a taboo subject in the community following the struggle; the debate that had gone on prior to 1974 over which approach to burakumin education, the league's or the JCP's, was more suitable had effectively ceased. According to one parent, the situation regarding burakumin discrimination was virtually set back fifty years in the region.[61]

In considering the issue of success in relation to the outcome of a particular episode, however, a distinction must be made. Whereas the Yōka struggle represented a worse immediate outcome for the protesters as compared with the other two episodes we have studied, burakumin and the league itself have undoubtedly gained far more overall from organized protest efforts in postwar Japan than have either women or age inferiors. By organizing, mobilizing, and forging alliances with other national organizations and opposition political parties, burakumin movements, both Socialist- and Communist-party allied, have achieved widespread recognition as representatives of burakumin interests. Even if many specific protest tactics (such as *kyūdan*) do not enjoy full legitimacy, the yield to burakumin from the movements' activities is impressive.

60. Interview with Maruo Yoshiaki and Yōka High School teachers. Maruo's account is supported by an article in the league's primary publication: "Jikengo sannenkan no tatakai," *Buraku Kaihō*, June 1978, 129–134.

61. Interview with two PTA members, Tajima, August 1978. The JCP-affiliated mayor, league officials, and parents generally agreed that discrimination against burakumin had increased as a result of the incident.

The most important gain has been the Law on Special Measures for Dōwa Projects (Dōwa Taisaku Jigyō Tokubetsu Sochihō), passed by the Diet in 1968 and extended by two subsequent special measures laws through 31 March 1992.[62] As of 1988 under this series of laws, the government had allocated 3 trillion yen (approximately 13.9 billion dollars) on physical improvements to roads, schools, housing, and recreation centers, and on the promotion of education and so on in designated buraku. The Buraku Liberation League has hailed the special measures laws as one of its great achievements; indeed, it is now beginning to push for a Fundamental Law for Buraku Liberation (Buraku Kaihō Kihonhō) that, if adopted, would go into effect when the current and final special measures law expires in 1992. The new law, unlike its predecessors, would have no time limit and, in addition to providing funds for buraku projects, would provide for criminal prosecution of discriminatory acts.[63]

Nevertheless, a key question remains: has discrimination against burakumin in fact diminished or the remedial channels available to burakumin improved as a result of the government's response to date? In many ways, the special measures laws bear all the marks of preemptive concessions granted in the turbulent late 1960s to head off future protests. Despite real improvements in living conditions, it is difficult to see how these measures, targeted as they are at closed buraku worlds, have addressed the concrete problems of discrimination in employment and marriage encountered by burakumin who leave the ghetto. Indeed, a cynical view would hold that the special measures laws have actually increased the incentives to stay in the buraku, thus calling into question the laws' presumed intent: the promotion of *dōwa* (merger with society) of burakumin.

Nor can it be said that this legislation has transformed the role of burakumin in social bargaining, a role that today is not unlike that played by the burakumin leadership in the Tokugawa period. Buraku leaders presently enjoy rather complete autonomy with regard to how allotted funds are actually to be used—much as in the past they exercised the power of taxation over their areas. At the national level, the funds flow down to the recipients through a bureaucratic system controlled by majority Japanese. Thus, fundamental power relationships are unchanged.

The major channel for articulating grievances in instances of discrimi-

62. Tagami Kazuyoshi, "1989–nendo chiiki kaizen taisaku yosan omiru," *Buraku* 41 (March 1989): 46; and Sōmuchō Chōkan Kanbō Chiiki Kaizen Taisakushitsu, *Dōwa mondai no genkyō*, 1987 (Tokyo: Sōmuchō, 1987), 46. Dollar figure is based on the yearly average yen-dollar rate from 1969 to 1988.
63. *Daily Yomiuri*, 6 December 1987, 6.

nation continues to be the denunciation session, in which burakumin in effect "take the law into their own hands" to try to bring about social change. The courts' support for "the right of denunciation" (*kyūdanken*) indicates the willingness of government authorities simply to delegate their responsibilities and let burakumin defend themselves from oppression. In upholding *kyūdanken* in a key case of 1975, the court stated its position in almost precisely those terms: "Legal remedies against discrimination are definitely limited. Their scope is narrow and frequently there is nothing that can be done. In light of these circumstances, it's justifiable for society to accept the process called denunciation as long as the methods and tactics don't exceed reasonable limits."[64] The special measures laws and the courts' response to *kyūdan* thus reveal a preference for keeping discrimination cases, wherever possible, outside the established channels of conflict resolution and for seeing them dealt with on a strictly case-by-case basis.

Prospects for Equality: Obstacles to Victory in Status-based Protests

"It should not be taken for granted . . . that individuals will . . . organize to pursue their interests. On the contrary, they will not, except under special conditions."[65] With these words William Gamson sums up the cumulative wisdom of students of social and political protest, whatever the setting. In ordinary life outside a revolutionary context relatively few people become involved in organized protests, however much they may espouse a cause or however acceptable protest itself may be in that society. Indeed, writers such as Mancur Olson suggest that under certain conditions participating in a protest is actually irrational, since people can gain just as much from not participating.[66] The disincentives that keep most people from being drawn into protest movements, then, are far-ranging.

If the disincentives for engaging in protest are numerous in most settings, moreover, they are even more numerous in Japan, for reasons discussed earlier: the cultural emphasis on social harmony; the relatively short period of time in which basic freedoms, including the right to or-

64. From the lower court's opinion in the Yata case, 3 June 1975; cited in Upham, *Law and Social Change*, 98. The high court reversed the decision but upheld the right of *kyūdan*, holding merely that it had exceeded reasonable limits. (See chapters 5 and 7 for additional discussion of *kyūdan* and the Yata case.)

65. Gamson, *Strategy of Social Protest*, 57.

66. Mancur Olson, *The Logic of Collective Action* (Cambridge, Mass.: Harvard University Press, 1975).

ganize and protest, have been guaranteed; and the consequent lack of full legitimation for protest even today, as compared to other industrial democracies with stronger traditions of grass-roots protest and longer democratic backgrounds. Indeed, the negative view of conflict in Japan gives rise to what might be called a "negative free rider" problem: not only do many individuals have little to gain from actively engaging in protest, but they have everything to lose, since everyone even remotely connected with a conflict—independent of whether they are "right" or "wrong"—will be "contaminated" by association. Of the various types of protest that surface in Japan, clearly status-based protests confront the most serious obstacles of all.

The first set of obstacles to favorable protest outcomes arises from the very multidimensionality of goals in status-based conflicts—symbolic, affective, and concrete. Such protests, however modest the specific concrete goals, challenge the very basis of hierarchically ordered social arrangements in Japan; that the authorities recognize this fact, moreover, is suggested by their greater willingness to yield on concrete concessions than on symbolic ones. To use the categories established by John Wilson, who distinguishes among various types of social movements according to the locus of change sought (in the individual or in the social structure) and the amount sought (partial versus total), even those more limited status-based protests in Japan—that argue not for "equality" along Western lines but for more subtle renegotiation of the terms of social relations—are more structurally targeted and "totalist" in their implications, since they challenge the most fundamental terms of Japanese status relationships.[67] Similarly, they are "radical" in Roberta Ash's sense in that they attack the present distribution of power in Japanese society.[68]

At the same time, these multifaceted goals constitute a major impediment to the mobilization of support in Japan, given cultural traditions and the ideal model of protest that has developed in Japanese political culture. Almost by definition, status politics represents an assertion that the would-be beneficiaries of the protest movement are entitled to more than they are currently getting. Implicit or explicit as well is an assertion of self and self-interest that challenges the cultural ideal of protest as involving sacrifice, preferably in the name of higher aspirations. Charges

67. John Wilson, *Introduction to Social Movements* (New York: Basic Books, 1973), 23–27.
68. See Roberta Ash, *Social Movements in America* (Chicago: Markham, 1972), 12.

that women who refuse to pour tea are selfish or lazy, or that younger politicians are spoiled and greedy for desiring political rewards sooner rather than later, reflect these cultural attitudes and suggest the powerful obstacles that protesters in status politics issues meet when seeking support for their cause. Few activists for equality, regardless of the particular society, are strangers to the charge of "uppityness" or of not "knowing their place." Japan's long tradition emphasizing the group over the individual and encouraging cooperation over self-assertiveness leaves protesters only limited cultural ammunition with which to counter such charges and win support for their "selfish" goals.

A second set of obstacles in status-based protests arises from the locus of the problem, which typically centers at least in part on problems lying not in the law or in articulated rules and policies but in everyday life. The dilemma the tea pourers met with in identifying targets for their struggle illustrates this point especially well, for no particular official supervised the performance of tea-serving duties, no formal statement in the women's job descriptions required them to pour tea, and no official could even be singled out as ever having ordered the women to perform this task for their fellow workers. Similarly, when Kōno's group challenged the LDP decision-making process, they were not challenging formal rules; even the factions, which form the basis of party decision-making and power arrangements, have no formal, legal existence. And burakumin, for their part, face virtually no legal barriers of any kind. The most serious problem for burakumin, as league leaders say freely, is a subtle form of discrimination; the problem, they say, lies "in the hearts and minds of the people."[69]

The absence of obvious, identifiable legal foundations for behavior or practices to which the status-deprived object poses numerous obstacles to protesters: not only may there be no rule to overturn, but there may be no clear enemy either. Moreover, since the practices being questioned may be a routine part of daily life, the status-deprived often cannot get a serious hearing for their grievances. As in the case of the union position on the tea-pouring issue, potential allies may see the protesters' goals as "not serious," and protesters may themselves come to doubt the appropriateness of their actions. At the same time, without clearly stated rules and policies, status inferiors have difficulty proving their case—that, for instance, even though pouring tea is not an "official" responsibility of women office

69. Interviews with officials of the Buraku Liberation League, Kyoto and Osaka branch offices, 1978.

workers, it is nevertheless a de facto job requirement. As civil rights litigation in the United States has shown, it is far more difficult to press a case
when there is no clear evidence of intent to discriminate.[70]

A similar problem is that status-based conflicts most often arise in the
context of close interpersonal relations, in a society where the maintenance of good relations receives extraordinarily strong emphasis. Takie
Lebra has held that Japan is the ultimate "relational" society—that is,
there, social relations are the main reality.[71] Thus, it may be far easier to
release anger on a distant enemy—such as the state in the case of the
Narita Airport struggle, or an anonymous company president in a pollution case—than on an immediate superior, one's teachers, or one's own
faction head. As Coser suggests, the existence of intimate relations between parties to a potential conflict necessarily constrains behavior,[72] a
factor that has long been used to explain the moderate nature of labor demands in enterprise unionism in Japan.[73] Status-based struggles face the
same obstacles but even more so, given the lesser legitimacy that status
issues have as compared with material issues.

Specific features of Japanese social relations may pose their own obstacles to protesters in status-based conflicts. For example, because the nature and dynamics of group behavior in Japan assume that group attachments are to be long term, there is a corresponding notion that the time
horizon for resolving conflicts is equally long.[74] Status inferiors prepared
to press their case immediately may therefore be enjoined by others to
wait, as the experience of junior LDP members in the distribution of posts
reflects. Similarly, the vertical nature of social relations within the ranks of
protesters themselves poses its own constraints, ultimately having a mod-
erating effect on activism[75] or obstructing the protesters' efforts to forge
organizational alliances (as seen also, within the "official sphere," in the
difficulty with which political coalitions are formed in Japan).[76]

The difficulty of engaging in conflict behavior within an organizational

70. See Juanita M. Kreps, ed., *Women and the American Economy* (Englewood
Cliffs, N.J.: Prentice-Hall, 1976).

71. T. Lebra, *Japanese Patterns of Behavior*.

72. Coser, *Functions of Social Conflict*.

73. See, for example, Ronald P. Dore, *British Factory—Japanese Factory* (Berkeley and Los Angeles: University of California Press, 1973).

74. I am grateful to David Plath for this point; see David W. Plath, *Long Engagements: Maturity in Modern Japan* (Stanford: Stanford University Press, 1980).

75. Coleman, *Community Conflict*.

76. See Nakane, *Japanese Society;* also Michael Leiserson, "Factions and Coalitions in One-Party Japan: An Interpretation Based on the Theory of Games,"
American Political Science Review 62 (September 1968): 770–787.

context may, moreover, be matched by the high costs of waging such a protest. Apart from the potential threat to livelihood that a workplace protest presents, any protesters who know the enemy personally run the risk of social isolation—a high cost in any society, but particularly so in a group-oriented one like Japan's. Witness only the sad accounts by league-affiliated Yōka High School graduates of their years of loneliness and ostracism following the struggle there.

Finally a formidable obstacle to victory consists in the response of authorities to status-based protests. Indeed, all but the most committed activists are apt to have difficulty withstanding the authorities' conflict tactics. The quick resumption of tea-pouring duties among some women in the Kyoto city office and the decision by numerous longtime Kōno associates to stay in the party rather than follow him out are reminders of the powerful counterpressures that authorities can wield, even against those sympathetic to a cause. The reluctance of authorities to yield on symbolic goals, their efforts to contain conflict and keep it outside the established channels for resolution, and their tendency to grant concessions preemptively rather than in ways that directly acknowledge the protesters' concerns and widen the decision-making circle, have particular bearing on status inferiors contemplating protest activity for the first time.

When we look at protest outcomes in the postwar era, it is hard to find examples in which Japanese status-deprived have emerged clearly victorious. There are no guarantees: when moving forward into combat, as Kōno Yōhei put it, the path ahead is indeed treacherous. Only a leap of faith can provide the courage needed to press ahead into the unknown in the face of so many obstacles.

10

Social Conflict, Authority, and the State

From Marx and Weber to social psychologists today, a long tradition in the social sciences has heralded the positive functions of social conflict, both for political systems and for the individuals within them. Indeed, many writers argue that the principal role of the state is to mediate clashes of interest: the state is the "arena of routinized political competition in which class, status, and political conflicts representing both elite and popular interests are played out."[1] In this view of the world, conflict is both natural and legitimate, and the resolution of conflict becomes the force behind statemaking itself.

The advantages to the political system and to society more broadly from the clash of interests and its subsequent resolution are thought to be multifarious. When conflicts emerge and conflicting parties (unlike those described in this volume) cooperate to reach a mutually satisfactory outcome, "open and honest communication" is aided, which in turn heads off "the development of misunderstandings that can lead to confusion and mistrust" in the future. Such cooperation encourages the various parties to recognize the legitimacy of one another's interests, and "stimulates a convergence of beliefs and values." Moreover, from the standpoint of those in authority, supposed long-term benefits ensue, for in the process of conflict resolution elites who might have been satisfied with the status quo "may be aroused to recognize problems and be motivated to work on them as opposition from the dissatisfied makes the customary relations and ar-

---

1. Charles Bright and Susan Harding, eds., *Statemaking and Social Movements: Essays in History and Theory* (Ann Arbor: University of Michigan Press, 1984), 3–4.

rangements unworkable and unrewarding."[2] When conflicts, however rancorous, are ultimately terminated, a "shared universe of discourse" is established that presumably can serve as a bridge in the resolution of future conflicts.[3]

Political scientists have joined with sociologists and social psychologists in noting the numerous positive consequences of conflict. Government, E. E. Schattschneider observes, "is a great engine for expanding the scale of conflict"; free societies maximize "the contagion of conflict" and give "a high priority to the participation of the public in conflict."[4] It is a major theme in much political inquiry that conflict is the indispensable basis for change within a political system; without it, by implication, a tenacious clinging to the status quo, lack of innovation, and, ultimately, stagnation result.[5] This positive view of conflict was taken to its logical extreme in the work of, among others, Franz Fanon on creative uses of violence.[6] The social science view is also mirrored in the everyday language of Western societies, where, for example, the salutary effects of "clearing the air" and getting something "off one's chest" are noted.

If everyday language and much Western social science analysis point to positive, even creative, functions for protest, conflict, and dissent, practically speaking there is a powerful ambivalence toward conflict in the West, even in societies such as the United States that are most apt to be seen as litigious and conflictual. Nixon's public labeling of antiwar protesters as "bums" is a reminder of the deep repugnance many people feel toward social activism when the opinions expressed are not their own.[7] Protracted struggles by labor and other groups to gain legitimacy for their demands in the United States, Britain, and Germany likewise signal a deep antagonism toward protest, whatever the rhetoric about dissent more gen-

2. Deutsch, *Resolution of Conflict*, 363, 361.

3. Coser, *Continuities*.

4. E. E. Schattschneider, *The Semi-sovereign People: A Realist's View of Democracy in America* (New York: Holt, Reinhart and Winston, 1967), 13, 5. For a useful discussion contrasting Schattschneider's views of conflict with those evident in prewar Japanese decision-making, see David A. Titus, *Palace and Politics in Prewar Japan* (New York: Columbia University Press, 1974), 311–313.

5. DiPalma states this view in *The Study of Conflict in Western Society*. Another typical statement is found in Evelyn P. Stevens, who sees an "interest in the question of protest and response" as "an inquiry into the arrangements for institutionalizing change" (*Protest and Response in Mexico* [Cambridge, Mass.: MIT Press, 1974], 6–7).

6. Franz Fanon, *The Wretched of the Earth*, (New York: Grove Press, 1968).

7. Marx, "External Efforts to Damage or Facilitate Social Movements."

erally.[8] Western political elites typically draw a sharp distinction between routine politics on the one hand and protest and opposition on the other, generally treating activists as if they were somehow "outside" the state rather than part of a basic participatory political system.[9] Even in societies with a relatively recent revolutionary tradition such as Mexico, decision makers are often quick to charge that a given attempt at change has "gone too far." Indeed, the revolutionary tradition may itself be recycled; thus reformers in Mexico are "branded as counterrevolutionaries, protesters are convicted as subversives, and supporters of established policies call themselves true revolutionaries."[10] If, to writers such as Schattschneider, the ideal response of political elites and authority figures more generally to social conflict is one of openness and willingness to negotiate, Anselm Strauss reminds us that in reality all societies present mixes of responses to clashes of interests. Negotiation, for example, is only one of a mix of strategies that includes "persuading, educating, manipulating, appealing to the rules or to authority, and coercion," all of which are likely to be in use in any one political system, even if particular situations may favor some modes over others.[11]

The Japanese Solution: Privatizing Social Conflict

The notion that conflict is desirable—that, like bitter medicine, it is ultimately good for body and soul, and for the state itself—is profoundly alien to Japanese, be they social theorists, politicians, or ordinary citizens. Rather than seeing conflict as creating bridges among disparate social interests or between society and the state, or as providing a crucial mechanism for change, the Japanese today still appear to adhere to the words of the seventh-century Prince Shōtoku: "Above all else esteem concord; make it your first duty to avoid discord."[12] Even protesters voicing social concerns are apt to see conflict as negative, disruptive, and regrettable. Perhaps no major nation in the world places a greater cultural emphasis on conflict avoidance.

8. Herbert W. Simons and Elizabeth W. Mechling, "The Rhetoric of Political Movements," in *Handbook of Political Communication*, ed. Dan D. Nimmo and Keith R. Sanders (Beverly Hills, Calif.: Sage, 1981), 419. See also Schelling, *Strategy of Conflict*; and Rimlinger, "Legitimation of Protest."

9. Bright and Harding, *Statemaking*, 5.

10. Stevens, *Protest and Response in Mexico*, 285, 284.

11. Anselm Strauss, *Negotiations: Varieties, Contexts, Processes, and Social Order* (San Francisco: Jossey-Bass, 1978), x.

12. Cited in Blaker, *Japanese International Negotiating Style*, 5.

The preferred method of decision making in Japan, involving the consensus of a rather small number of participants, operates most effectively when it includes parties with long-term, face-to-face relationships of the kind fostered in the lifetime employment pattern typical of large companies, the bureaucracy, and Japan's ruling party. As John Creighton Campbell has observed, it seems that authority figures "carry around a distinctively Japanese 'implicit theory' of decision-making and conflict resolution," which sees the consensus model as producing the most satisfactory solution to a problem.[13] When conflicts occur within such a circle, a search is launched for a consensus that accommodates the various competing needs and viewpoints represented in the group, with participation in the process based on status. In that a strenuous effort is made to consider all points of view, the Japanese search for consensus is egalitarian and democratic by many standards. Yet even within such an in-group of persons with similar backgrounds and long-term, direct relations, overt forms of conflict are assiduously avoided; the real goal, then, is not so much conflict resolution as it is conflict accommodation.[14] As Campbell notes, when officials, politicians, or other in-group circles fail to reach a consensus, they are likely to abandon the hope of resolving the conflict and engage instead in conflict avoidance.[15]

If finding accord through consensus within a small circle of insiders is sometimes fraught with difficulties and may lead to conflict-avoidance behavior, and if the natural reflex of authorities is to restrict rather than open up conflict, then the problem of expanding the decision-making circle from *uchi*, or insiders—those included in the "we-ness" of a particular group—to *soto*, outsiders, emerges clearly. In short, the consensus method is inherently exclusionary: opening up the circle to bring in outsiders who may mount a challenge to the status quo runs counter to the basic approach to dealing with conflict in Japan and to the values surrounding it. To attempt to create a permanent "universe of discourse" between insiders and outsiders—the route that Western conflict theorists point to as leading to conflict termination and resolution—would stretch the consensus approach beyond its capacity and in a direction it is not intended to go.

The Japanese approach thus is aimed fundamentally at privatizing social conflict.[16] When faced with a social protest, authorities tend to re-

13. John Creighton Campbell, "Policy Conflict and Its Resolution Within the Governmental System," in *Conflict in Japan*, ed. Ellis S. Krauss, Thomas P. Rohlen, and Patricia G. Steinhoff (Honolulu: University of Hawaii Press, 1984), 311.

14. Ishida, "Conflict and Its Accommodation."

15. Campbell, "Policy Conflict," 311.

16. See Titus, *Palace and Politics*, 311–333, for his development of this term.

spond by ignoring it; if avoidance fails, they work to contain the conflict, to keep it outside existing channels of resolution, and to discourage others from joining in. They strongly prefer to deal with conflicts case by case, and their favored methods are informal rather than formal. Whenever possible, they skirt solutions that might extend legitimacy to the protesters, which would have repercussions in the future on how problems of a similar nature should be resolved. Avoided also are solutions that generate principles having broad applicability across cases. As a result, outsiders remain outsiders and any gains achieved by protesters in a specific conflict episode have only a limited chance of becoming general. Despite all the rhetoric on the positive virtues of conflict, one could argue that authorities, whatever the national setting, would prefer to privatize social conflict in precisely this way. If so, the distinctiveness of the Japanese case is not in what the authorities try to do, but in how often they actually succeed.

More broadly, the dominance of a strategy aimed at privatizing social conflict reflects a particular type of relation between state and society in Japan, one that evolved over centuries of feudalism and has been adapted (in many ways, with remarkable success) to the needs of a modern industrial democracy. In this respect the Japanese state presents an extraordinary anomaly. On the one hand, Japan's history of centralized feudalism puts it squarely in the "strong state" tradition. Given the scope of authority exercised by the Tokugawa government and its penetration into everyday life, with regulations set on matters ranging from local travel to women's hairstyles, late Japanese feudalism is in some ways better compared to twentieth-century totalitarianism than to the much earlier, more decentralized feudal systems of Europe. This strong-state tradition was carried into the modern era by a powerful bureaucracy and by one hundred years of virtually unbroken conservative rule. On the other hand, Japan in the 1980s was winning accolades for its seeming ability to maintain "small government" at a time when many of its fellow industrial states were struggling with the purported excesses of "big government." Certainly, in economic terms alone, there is no question that the Japanese state is small, comparatively speaking. Less of Japan's gross domestic product (GDP) went for governmental outlays than in any other of the twenty-three OECD nations, and it ranked twenty-first (above only Turkey and Spain) in tax revenues as a percentage of GDP.[17]

It is in the seeming incongruity of Japan as a country that manages to combine big government—in terms of the sheer authority and scope of state power—with small government—in terms of its actual size, budget,

17. *Wall Street Journal*, 13 September 1984.

and tax bite—that the key to how and why Japan privatizes conflict lies. In Western countries, big government developed in part when the state, responding to the welfare consensus that arose, especially in Europe, at the end of World War II, expanded first the public domain and then the reach of state power into the civic domain in the course of formulating new social policies and monitoring their implementation.[18] Big government also grew, especially in the United States, with the taking on of major defense commitments in the postwar era, in recent years at 5–6 percent of the gross national product. With the growth of the defense establishment, increasing numbers of civilians have entered the public domain and more lives have been affected—for example, through industrial dependence on defense contracts—thus spurring the state's reach into society. The whole notion of "big government" in Western countries, in short, has rested on the idea of a boundary between the public and private domains: when government, through regulatory activity or expansion of the public sector, extends its reach at the expense of the private domain, then is the charge of big government raised.

In Japan, in contrast, the boundary between the public and private domains has never existed quite as in Europe and the United States. Under Confucianism, which provided the philosophical basis of Tokugawa rule, no clear distinction was made between state and society, public and private; rather, the state was seen as encompassing the whole of society in its familistic embrace.[19] Given this tradition, the Japanese state has functioned essentially through a type of enlightened conservatism, in which a relatively small number of political and administrative elites have left the actual maintenance of society—including the handling of conflict—to the workings of traditional social relations. Responsibility for carrying out the goals of the state—including that of maintaining social harmony—was passed down to lower-level authority figures, whether factory managers, school officials, or village heads. Through the workings of social control based on norms and values shared by political elites, authority figures more generally, and the populace at large, those goals could be met without "big government" in the Western sense, while the "strong state" tradition was still maintained. In Japan one finds this principle of delegation in other domains as well. For example, despite the common view abroad of a strong Japanese state "directing" the private sector, the reality, as

18. Offe, "New Social Movements."
19. Peter Duus, "Liberal Intellectuals and Social Conflict in Taishō Japan," in *Conflict in Modern Japanese History: The Neglected Tradition*, ed. Tetsuo Najita and J. Victor Koschmann (Princeton: Princeton University Press, 1982), 419.

Richard Samuels has shown, is much more along the lines described here: the state shares authority with the private sector in a pattern of "reciprocal consent."[20]

The principle of delegating responsibility for conflict management thus provides the basis for the privatization of social conflict. Just as public officials and bureaucrats at the national level make decisions and work to resolve conflicts in the context of small, closed circles, authority figures at lower levels are expected to do the same. At any given level of society, whether in a school, a section of city bureaucracy, or a political party, the aim of authorities is to maintain harmony within their own bailiwick, and to restore it in the event of discord. Although institutionalized channels for handling social conflict exist, or can be established to meet new situations, authorities at all levels prefer to avoid going this route whenever possible. Ideally, any conflict episode should be isolated and dealt with individually, by the authorities most directly concerned. With protesters, even those who "win" their case, kept outside the conflict-resolution process and decision-making circles remaining closed to "outsiders," elites at the national level successfully control the pace of social change.

Managing Social Conflict in Hierarchical Societies: Comparative Perspectives on Britain and Germany

Privatization as an approach to social conflict would appear to be well suited to a political system and social order characterized by an emphasis on hierarchy and a tradition of benevolent paternalism. In contrast, an approach that rests on opening up conflict, with negotiation and discourse among the various segments of society encouraged, would seem more appropriate to political systems and social arrangements characterized by an emphasis on individual rights and a tradition of grass-roots participation. In that light, it makes sense to explore the experiences of other countries with strongly hierarchical social relations and to compare those experiences with that of Japan.

Both Britain and Germany qualify in this regard, being countries in which the exercise of authority by elites on behalf of society was, at least historically, thought to be natural and legitimate. Robert Scalapino notes that in Western Europe more generally, the medieval feudal ideal included a notion of organic unity similar to that underlying the ideal of social har-

20. See Richard J. Samuels, *The Business of the Japanese State: Energy Markets in Comparative and Historical Perspective* (Ithaca, N.Y.: Cornell University Press, 1987), 8–19.

mony in Japan today. As he points out, there was no place in such systems for "nonconformity or individualism—no place for theories of accepted differences of competitive ideas."[21] It therefore seemed natural that superiors should exercise authority on behalf of those below. In that sense, both East and West had a common heritage of ideas about social relationships, authority, and the goals of a political system, arising out of similar political and economic institutions developed in the feudal era. Joseph Strayer, too, is struck by the similarities of feudalism in Japan as compared to Europe, the major difference being, in his estimation, the persistence of the principle of benevolent paternalism in Japan long after its European counterpart had undergone profound change. As Strayer notes, by the twelfth century a European vassal would have considered it an insult to be "called the 'child' of his lord," whereas in Japan "the filial relationship was the most highly honored of all" well into the nineteenth century.[22]

In Britain, even as social hierarchy and the notion that elites held natural and legitimate authority persisted, a parallel tradition of individual rights developed by elites themselves from the Renaissance through Hobbes and Locke increasingly came to challenge these principles. Added to this pressure was a legacy of humanism, Roman law, and Judeo-Christian philosophy that cumulatively shaped a set of values deeply espoused by elites.[23] With the new forces of capitalism in the Tudor period and of industrialization, a process of social differentiation was set in motion that Japan would experience only much later.

By the nineteenth century, patterns of social hierarchy coexisted in England with a highly developed moral code based not on rule by status, as in contemporaneous Japan, but on individualism and rule by law. Thus, as groups on the lower rungs of society began to seek redress from the dislocations and inequities of industrialization, both features of the system were before them: on the one hand, they faced authorities who harbored a strong belief, which society widely shared, in their own natural superiority; on the other, they had at their disposal a well-entrenched value system, one fully accepted by those same elites, based on individualism, the rule of law, and the rights of man. The task of social inferiors in Britain,

21. Scalapino, *Democracy and the Party Movement*, 395.
22. Joseph R. Strayer, "The Tokugawa Period and Japanese Feudalism," in *Studies in the Institutional History of Early Modern Japan*, ed. John Whitney Hall and Marius B. Jansen (Princeton: Princeton University Press, 1968), 8.
23. Scalapino, *Democracy and the Party Movement*, 396. See Quentin Skinner, *The Foundations of Modern Political Thought* (Cambridge: Cambridge University Press, 1978).

then, was to see that value system applied to their own situation. Indeed, the very availability of such a tradition that new groups could commandeer is often cited as the reason for the success of British workers, and of other socially inferior groups since then, in gaining rights and entering into a bargaining relation with authorities. As E. P. Thompson succinctly puts it, English culture offered workers the legacy of the "rights of a freeborn Englishman."[24] While British miners, for example, continued to rely "on their opponents' ideological arsenal," employers, the state, and public opinion soon became accustomed to the workers' role as a force in industrial society.[25] Andrew Gordon shows that whereas Japanese workers, too, drew on older values—those of Tokugawa feudalism and Confucianism—to attempt to construct their own ideological basis for challenging authority, the weapons available to them and to subsequent generations of protesters were far weaker.[26]

Perhaps no major European country was as successful as England in integrating the lower classes into the existing political order while still retaining their allegiance, and it was in that sense that the basis for preserving hierarchy in society was laid.[27] At the same time, though, the extension of new rights to social inferiors meant that new types of bargaining relations became necessary. Any approach to social conflict based primarily on privatization and on restricting access to available channels for resolution was foreclosed by virtue of all Englishmen having been made privy to the full rights tradition. In addition, because pressures to accommodate new groups came early in England, protest there has had a longer time to gain legitimacy than in late-developing countries such as Germany and Japan.

Developments in Germany more closely parallel those in Japan than in any other major European country. Aspects of feudalism were still in place in Germany long after the system had ended in Britain and France. At the close of the eighteenth century, for example, serfdom had not been fully abolished anywhere in Germany, and peasants were still bound to the land as they had been in the Middle Ages. As late as 1788, Tocqueville notes,

24. E. P. Thompson, *The Making of the English Working Class* (New York: Vintage Books, 1963), 11.

25. Rimlinger, "Legitimization of Protest," 375. See also Reinhard Bendix, "The Lower Classes and the 'Democratic Revolution,'" in *Protest, Reform, and Revolt*, ed. Joseph R. Gusfield (New York: John Wiley, 1970), 210–211.

26. Gordon, *Evolution of Labor Relations in Japan*, 6, 431–432.

27. Guenther Roth makes this argument in *Social Democrats in Imperial Germany: A Study in Working-Class Isolation and National Integration* (Totowa, N.J.: Bedminster Press, 1963), 7.

"the peasant was not allowed to quit his lord's estate" and "could neither better his social position, change his occupation, nor even marry without his master's consent."[28]

Paternalistic authority was likewise fully in force in Germany through the mid nineteenth century. Laborers in state-run mines, Gaston Rimlinger shows, were urged by civil servants to show "esteem, obedience, and respect for their superiors, and to greet them properly at all times."[29] These miners, moreover, whose work conditions were severe, embarked on relatively few protests in Germany before 1850; in fact, many workers were at that date pleading not for autonomy and bargaining power but for greater paternalism—again paralleling the situation and pace of development in Japan.[30] In both countries, the human rights tradition that was by then fully accepted by British authorities was missing.

Even the pattern by which early social welfare gains were achieved in Germany closely resembles that of Japan, for Bismarck granted such reforms unilaterally and magnanimously in a manner reminiscent of pre-emptive concession-making.[31] As noted earlier, the German approach to accommodating the lower classes and protest is one that Roth has characterized as "negative integration": as in Japan, the institutionalization of conflict was avoided; although interest groups and protest groups were allowed to exist, and in that sense were integrated into the system, they lacked real legitimacy.[32]

On closer examination, however, many aspects of the German view of and response to social conflict differed sharply from the Japanese experience. Most notable, perhaps, was the lack of a parallel in Germany to the Confucian-based familism and state-society overlap that underlay the Japanese political universe—features that enabled elites in the capital to leave conflict resolution to the workings of social relations at lower levels of the national pyramid. The boundaries between *der Staat*, with its powerful authority claims, and society were in contrast very clear in Germany, in part because of the influence of thinkers such as Hegel, who gave the notion of the state a quasi-religious meaning, but also because of the cen-

28. Alexis de Tocqueville, "The Old Regime and the French Revolution," in *Protest, Reform, and Revolt,* ed. Joseph R. Gusfield (New York: John Wiley, 1970), 70.

29. Rimlinger, "Legitimation of Protest," 371.

30. Ibid., 372, 373. See also Gordon, *Evolution of Labor Relations in Japan.* Note too the early appeals of the prewar burakumin liberation movement for greater paternalism and protection, as discussed in DeVos and Wagatsuma, *Japan's Invisible Race,* 33–67.

31. See Peter Flora and Arnold J. Heidenheimer, eds., *The Development of Welfare States in Europe and America* (New Brunswick, N.J.: Transaction Books, 1981).

32. Roth, *Social Democrats in Imperial Germany,* 7–8.

tralizing role the German state had played in creating one society out of a conglomeration of diverse principalities.[33] The great heterogeneity of Germany, with its major religious, ethnic, and regional cleavages, foreclosed the possibility that any such delegation of authority could have occurred there, even if such a pattern had been more consistent with German traditions. Thus, authority figures at the national level had to evolve methods for mediating among the competing interests of society.

In addition, lower-class insistence that their needs be accommodated was apparently far greater in nineteenth- and early-twentieth-century Germany than in Japan. After 1850, in the absence of a fully accepted rights tradition such as that found in Britain, German protesters pressing for greater civil liberties found support in several ways. One major route was through commitment to the totalist ideologies of the Social Democratic party and the Christian Social Movement.[34] Although many Japanese protesters, including several wings of the labor and burakumin movements of the 1920s, adopted the same approach, leftist activity was far more advanced in Germany than in Japan, for socialist movements and Marxism itself had an immediate contagion effect in Europe that gave social reform efforts a great momentum. In contrast to the proletarian parties of prewar Japan, which cumulatively never managed to capture more than 8 percent of the vote in any given election, the German Social Democrats, for example, quickly achieved and maintained a large and loyal following during both the Hohenzollern and Weimar periods.[35]

Even if Roth is correct in arguing that the integration of diverse interests into pre-Nazi German society was essentially "negative," the legitimacy achieved by protesters there, including the parties of the left, appears well advanced relative to the situation in prewar Japan. It was only because a multiparty system was well enough established prior to the Nazi takeover, for example, that a turnover system, with parties alternating in power, could be quickly established after the war. In Japan, by contrast, the prewar legacy of weak opposition has made it difficult for opposition parties to have a real turn in power. Furthermore, despite the curtailment of dissent and the forced unity of the Nazi era, the basis for a participatory system in which protest is accorded full legitimacy was apparently firmly

33. The Meiji state, too, played a centralizing role, but a far less demanding one than in Germany; I am grateful to David Titus for pointing out these key differences in state-society relations in Germany as compared to Japan. See also Leonard Krieger, *The German Idea of Freedom* (Boston: Beacon Press, 1957).

34. Rimlinger, "Legitimation of Protest," 373.

35. Lewis J. Edinger, *Politics in Germany*, (Boston: Little, Brown, 1968), 256–257.

in place again at the very outset of the postwar era.[36] Indeed, Dorothy Nelkin and Michael Pollak, in their study of German and French anti-nuclear protest, describe far more accommodation to protesters in Germany than in France; and in both countries, "reforms of decision-making procedures" were a common response to protest.[37] Despite its traditions of hierarchy and paternalism, and despite a pattern (compared to that of Britain) of negative rather than positive integration of new social forces into the political order, Germany appears to have made more resources, ideological and otherwise, available to protesters in the postwar era—and thus given protest far greater legitimacy—than has Japan. At the same time, because of the particular "strong state" tradition that operates in Germany, in which government has sought to extend rather than share its authority, the state has come to seek an active role in resolving conflicts in society. In short, then, Germany—like Britain—does not possess the conditions that permit the privatization of social conflict and in this sense differs markedly from postwar Japan.

Advantages of the Japanese Approach

The benefits of opening up conflict—the Western approach—have been much studied by political scientists. Yet the privatization of conflict—the Japanese approach—despite certain costs, has numerous advantages as well and deserves closer consideration. As we saw in chapter 8, by handling status-based conflicts in ways that result in containment and that deny the legitimacy of the protest itself, authorities themselves benefit, for by doing so they maintain their own prerogatives. More significantly, however, privatization has certain distinct advantages for state and society collectively, which cannot be ignored.

First, there is no question that the Japanese approach to conflict is extraordinarily successful at providing stability without reliance on coercion. Through privatization and limits on the spread of conflict, traditional patterns of authority relations are maintained. The creation of institutionalized channels for conflict resolution, in contrast, for all its benefits, almost inevitably generates principles that can be applied broadly, thereby inviting application to new groups and opening the way to new demands from old groups.[38] This process undoubtedly contributes to what many

36. Nelkin and Pollak, *The Atom Besieged*, 168.
37. Ibid., 178.
38. On this process, see Jo Freeman, *The Politics of Women's Liberation* (New York: David McKay, 1975), 230–244.

writers see as a major problem in numerous industrial nations, including the United States—namely, the overload of social demands on formal institutions.[39] Indeed, a fundamental question that has been raised to challenge liberal democratic theory in the climate of fiscal austerity and conservatism of the late 1980s is whether the state any longer has the resources or the mandate to appease all groups.[40] Thus far, the traditional Japanese formula for conflict management has been extremely effective in that country for containing social demands. Without necessitating coercion as a major instrument of control, the formula keeps overall levels of conflict in society manageable, thereby contributing to the overall stability of the social and political order.

A second advantage of the Japanese approach is one on which Chalmers Johnson has focused—that is, its effect of freeing public officials for the pursuit of other state goals. By privatizing social conflict and leaving its resolution to lower levels of society, national elites—operating within their own relatively closed decision-making circles—are buffered from the constant dialogue and negotiation which the more open Western approach demands. Johnson argues persuasively, for example, that Japan's economic success has rested in part on the freedom bureaucratic elites have had to devote their full energies to spurring economic performance:

> the effective operation of the developmental state requires that bureaucracy be protected from all but the most powerful interest groups. . . . A system in which the full range of pressure and interest groups exist in a modern, open society [and have] access to government . . . will surely not achieve economic development, at least under official auspices, whatever other values it may fulfill.[41]

Opening up conflict, in other words, requires the creation of precisely those channels of access and patterns of accommodation to social demands that Johnson sees as impeding the pursuit of economic growth as an overriding national goal.

A third advantage of the privatizing approach to conflict consists in its preemptive-concessions mechanism, which allows Japanese authorities to manage social problems without incurring the cost of major social disruption. As suggested earlier, many Western social scientists see the open-

39. See Crozier, Huntington, and Watanuki, *The Crisis of Democracy;* and Huntington, *American Politics.*

40. See Verba et al., *Elites and the Idea of Equality,* 145–156 and 271–276, for a discussion of the 1980s attacks on equality struggles on just such grounds, in Sweden, the United States, and elsewhere.

41. Johnson, *MITI and the Japanese Miracle,* 44.

ing up of conflict, together with the creation of bridges and patterns of accommodation among parties to a conflict, as crucial to bringing about innovation and change in a political system. By implication, then, the privatization of conflict would seem to involve a high risk—namely, that authority figures would be cut off from new ideas and new forces in society, thus inviting political stagnation.

In the Japanese formula, however, a number of built-in correctives diminish such risks and provide for change and innovation on a different basis. The first check arises out of the particular set of prerogatives and responsibilities attached to authority figures' roles. For even if authority figures make only limited direct concessions in a conflict and avoid bringing protesters into permanent dialogue, they are nevertheless under considerable pressure to respond in *some* way because of their own traditional responsibility to preserve social harmony. Peter Duus notes, "The lack of a clear distinction between state and society in Confucianism might encourage the idea that society should be subordinated to the needs of the state, but it could also imply that those in authority had a responsibility not to rend the social fabric by despotic action." One factor that stands out in Japan's case is that conflicts seldom divide the parties involved into clear winners and losers because everyone, including those in authority, are negatively implicated for the simple reason that a dispute has occurred at all. Authority figures are therefore under enormous pressure to end any conflict that surfaces and to head off future outbreaks of protest. Indeed, the traditional ideology of superior-inferior relations puts the responsibility for maintaining harmony squarely on the superiors' shoulders. As Duus observes, the cultural emphasis on maintaining social order is not inherently a conservative idea, "especially if the burden of blame for disharmony was shifted from the ruled to the ruler."[42] Even if this weighty responsibility sometimes leads to conflict avoidance behavior or strategies of protest containment, it also spurs those in charge to seek solutions to the problems that protesters raise.

As we have seen, preemptive concession-making is a common approach used by Japanese authorities faced with potential conflict. From the standpoint of protesters, such a response—to the extent that preemptive concessions deny the legitimacy of the protest itself, discredit the protesters' efforts to achieve reform, and deny them access to future decision making—is obviously less than satisfactory. From the broader perspective of society and the political system as a whole, however, this approach does have certain advantages that "open society" advocates overlook. By engaging in a

42. Duus, "Liberal Intellectuals and Social Conflict," 419.

dialogue with dissenters and granting their protest legitimacy, authorities are put in the position of having to respond to, and give credence to the views of, those individuals in society who are most committed to effecting a change in the status quo and who indeed may have the least to lose in actively protesting. In a country like Japan, the cultural disincentives to overt protest are great, the obstacles to forming a broad-based social movement high; thus, those who come forward to wage a protest and who stay committed even in the face of such deterrents may have extreme views (relative to those of ordinary people) on the issues at stake. Public debate and litigation in more open, conflict-oriented societies offer much evidence of the consequences of this dilemma. In the United States, for example, much time, tax dollars, and energy are expended in public hearings to hear out activists who would halt all medical experimentation in the name of animal rights, end all human uses of public lands to restore ecological balance, or reclaim entire states on the basis of early treaties between native Americans and European settlers. Social legislation and court rulings have likewise often been far to the left or right of the popular consensus, pulled there in part because of the view that the state should be responsive to all interests.[43]

The preemptive-concessions strategy allows authorities to sidestep the potential problem of having to go to extremes in responding to social problems, providing them with a way to introduce social change on their own terms. In fact, the very notion that innovation and change result from the open clash of interests in society is belied in the Japanese case. Japan's astonishing 70-fold increase in social welfare spending over the period 1955–1978, for example, owes far more to bureaucratic initiative than to protest efforts. Likewise, the 121-fold increase in aid to the elderly and 335-fold increase in governmental support for social insurance, including medical insurance contributions, over the same period are better understood as preemptive concessions granted by a bureaucracy with its eye on trends in other countries and on the possibility of future social disaffection in Japan than as a response to organized pressure from within society.[44]

43. Prohibition is an example of the pull to the right, whereas affirmative-action legislation, with its checkered history of attempts to gain public acceptance and compliance, exemplifies the pull to the left. In the United States, the struggle of a conservative Republican administration to accommodate the religious views of its well-organized, far-right supporters likewise demonstrates the difficulties that authorities encounter in political systems which place a high value on "responsiveness."

44. Bradley M. Richardson and Scott C. Flanagan, *Politics in Japan* (Boston: Little, Brown, 1984), 412–413.

Finally, several political scientists have noted that in complex societies where effective protest requires an enormous expenditure of time and money and a mastery of technical detail, the ideal of participatory democracy places an onerous burden on the public.[45] The inherent danger here is that authorities will regard themselves as free to pursue any course they choose so long as the public raises no hue and cry—a danger that becomes even greater as the sheer volume of public policy grows and as the technical sophistication required to understand it increases exponentially. The Japanese approach, in contrast, relies on the high ideals of public service held by an elite and efficient bureaucracy; the burden for good policy therefore resides firmly with the authorities, not with society. Ultimately this approach to social problem-solving may in fact be the more realistic and responsible, given these concerns.

Is Japan a model for other countries in its formula for handling social conflict? In general, the answer appears to be no. There is no reason to believe that an approach that works in one cultural setting can be readily adapted to another. Denying the legitimacy of social protest wherever possible; waiting out protests until all but the most stalwart drop away while avoiding coercive measures that might stir public support for the causes raised; engaging in strategies that prevent protesters from forging a broader base of support; and keeping social protest out of institutionalized channels for resolution, thereby limiting the social impact and contagion effect of any given protest action—collectively these measures constitute a workable formula, so long as they are accompanied by efforts to head off future protests through preemptive concessions. The same formula, however, would work less well, or not at all, in other countries where the cultural and historical forces that define society differ markedly from those at work in Japan.

The tactic of "undercutting" by using language and behavior that puts protesters "back in their place," for example, works best in a setting where both protesters and the public at large are vulnerable to traditional values that see social inequality as natural and legitimate. In societies such as the United States, Britain, France, or Sweden, where over several centuries egalitarianism has had the force of a dominant ideology, such a technique

45. For statements of this view, see Samuel H. Beer, "Federalism, Nationalism, and Democracy in America," *American Political Science Review* 72 (March 1978): 9–21, and "The Modernization of American Federalism," *Publius* (Fall 1973): 48–95. Also see Vincent Ostrom, "Nonhierarchical Approaches to the Organization of Public Activity," *Annals of the American Academy of Political and Social Science*, no. 466 (March 1983): 135–148.

would simply not work or—worse, from the elites' standpoint—would backfire to spur public support for a beleaguered minority. Similarly, containing a conflict by restricting access to established dispute-resolution channels is far more effective in a country like Japan where informal methods are generally preferred in any case over more formal, legalistic channels such as the courts. Even preemptive concessions—which ultimately are what make the "Japanese formula" so effective in status politics disputes—offer no particular advantage in countries where the right of status inferiors to protest the terms of status relations and to make demands on superiors has been established over centuries of struggle, whether revolutionary as in France or evolutionary as in Britain, over the issues of human equality and political participation. Since status-based protest is already fully legitimized in most industrial nations and authorities there feel great pressure to be responsive to disadvantaged groups demanding civil rights, there is little to be gained from the granting of concessions independent of the protest itself; indeed, such an effort actually might create a window of opportunity for protesters to press for even more concessions. In a society with a strong grass-roots tradition, moreover, authorities who grant settlements preemptively run the risk of being perceived as weak, and the concessions as suspect—why, after all, wasn't the public consulted?

Of those strategies favored by Japanese elites, the one perhaps most worthy of study outside Japan is the creative use of delay in the final stages of a social conflict. From the use of police dogs against black protesters in Birmingham, Alabama, and of mace and fire hoses against antiwar activists at the 1968 Democratic convention, to the actual bombing of a radical group's hideaway in a crowded Philadelphia neighborhood in 1985, authorities in the United States have a long record of resorting to coercion when social conflict arises—a strategy that has often backfired and contributed to the protesters' ultimate success in mobilizing support for their cause. A close study of postwar Japanese history, in contrast, brings to light few comparable examples. The predisposition of Japanese authorities to tolerate ambiguity and to wait out protests—whether it is a rebellion by women office workers, a paralyzing national railway strike as in 1975, the twenty-year struggle at Narita Airport, or the lengthy sit-ins by students at university campuses in the 1960s—has clearly worked to their advantage, keeping the overall level of conflict manageable.

Conditions Supporting the Japanese Approach

It is important to make explicit the broad conditions on which Japan's preferred approach to social conflict management rests. First and perhaps foremost is the condition set by political culture, which itself operates to limit the number of conflicts that arise, discourages dissidents from drawing out a protest activity, and deters the public from joining the cause. Even many activists who have opposed the status quo and advocated broad social reform in Japan have adopted positions consistent with the pervasive cultural preference for harmony and unity. Peter Duus found liberal intellectuals in prewar Japan discussing political life "in the language of togetherness, unity, solidarity, commonality and the like" in a way that revealed "an implicit assumption that the normal impulses of mankind were toward social harmony and that the proper mission of political theory was to analyze how such harmony might be achieved."[46] To them, democracy and constitutionalism were far more a means to collective harmony than a way of securing protections for diverse views. Even today, participants in status-based protests, right down to the most militant among them, are far more likely to play down the disruption they have caused than to justify it in the name of a right to state their case or to fight injustice.[47]

Other features of the political culture support the Japanese approach as well. The cultural expectations that drive authorities at all levels of society to behave paternalistically and work to preserve harmony, for example, serve as an important corrective on elites who might otherwise ignore protest altogether, meet it with coercion, or otherwise fail to address the issues raised. It is extraordinary that in Japan, where a one-party dominant system actively affirms and supports prevailing patterns of authority relations, authority figures display such sensitivity to the public mood. Indeed, in few countries are leaders as attentive to public opinion surveys as in Japan, where it is considered quite reasonable for a high-ranking bureaucrat or politician to state that no action will be taken on a given measure until the public's views are known.[48]

Similarly, the cultural homogeneity of Japan is an important asset to authorities in carrying out their mandate. In a society where elites are not expected to be directly responsive to the public and where the direct articulation of grievances by social subordinates is discouraged, this homogeneity enables elites to understand and anticipate the needs of those subject to their authority. In exploring the introduction of quality control into

---

46. Duus, "Liberal Intellectuals and Social Conflict," 418.

47. Buraku Liberation League activists who were involved in the Yōka High School struggle are a case in point. League publications tried hard to discredit the teachers' reports concerning their injuries, in an effort aimed more at minimizing the level of the conflict than at justifying their right to protest discrimination.

48. Shigeki Nishihira, "Political Opinion Polling," 165–166.

Japan, Robert E. Cole notes how important the ties that bind managers and workers—ties based on cultural unity—were in assuring that managers would devise a management technique that workers would accept. Because the notion of quality control fit the values and common background that both workers and managers shared, it was considered a workable innovation.[49] These factors, then—the pressure for the "good" authority to be alert to (if not always directly responsive to) the needs and wishes, both stated and unstated, of those below, along with the cultural homogeneity that allows authorities to comprehend those needs—would seem to be crucial to the workability of Japanese social conflict management.

In any national setting, Anselm Strauss shows, a key question is whether negotiation will be elected or—as in Japan—avoided as a strategy for resolving differences. The choice depends primarily on what alternative modes of action are perceived to be available. If, as he notes, "the potential or actual parties to negotiation perceive that they can attempt persuasion, make an appeal to authority, manipulate political or social events, and so forth, then their choices of these alternative modes will either prevent them from entering negotiation" or "affect what transpires during the course of negotiation."[50] It is in precisely that way that political culture structures the options open to authorities in Japan and makes possible the choices they elect.

A second condition underlying Japanese conflict management is the particular history of repression in Japan, together with its legacy. One overarching characteristic of the Japanese political system today is the weakness of the political opposition. In contrast to virtually every other major democracy, up until 1945 Japan had no experience with a legitimate and organized opposition that competed successfully for power. The two conservative political parties that arose after the promulgation of the 1889 constitution were more like competing factions of the same party than distinct parties representing real alternatives. Indeed, in 1955 their successors merged to form the ruling LDP, thus carrying the same legacy into the postwar period.

Meanwhile, for long periods over the prewar era both labor unions and the proletarian parties—the real analogs to European opposition parties—faced repressive measures that marginalized them and kept their full legitimacy in question. After the war, the suppression of Japan's first gen-

49. Robert E. Cole, "Diffusion of Participatory Work Structure," in *Change in Organizations*, ed. Paul S. Goodman and Associates (San Francisco: Jossey-Bass, 1982), 208.

50. Strauss, *Negotiations*, 100.

eral strike in 1947 by Occupation authorities once again undercut labor unions' efforts to launch a renewed struggle. The pattern of Japanese accommodation to proletarian parties and the labor movement in prewar Japan closely conforms to what for Germany Guenther Roth called "negative integration," in which a political system "permits . . . hostile mass movement[s] to exist legally, but prevents [them] from gaining access to the centers of power." As Roth notes, negative integration may be contrasted "with the institutionalization of conflict among genuinely legitimized interest groups" in such nations as England and the United States.[51]

As a result of this particular pattern of conflict containment, various forms of protest—ones relatively well established and accepted by the end of World War II in most major countries—have been slow to gain legitimacy in Japan. Many interests, of course, such as big business and rural landowners, who were already insiders as of the Meiji period, are fully sanctioned and play a large role in the decision-making process. Even labor has gone much further than most social groups in gaining policy access. But corporatist arrangements of the type found in many European countries, in which full legitimacy is granted to both economic and noneconomic interests, which then become a permanent part of institutionalized decision-making arrangements, contrast sharply with arrangements in Japan, in part because of the historical legacy of repression.

A third and related condition supporting the Japanese approach concerns the timing of developments in Japan's emergence as a welfare state. As noted earlier, the growth of "big government" (in the Western sense) started quite early in Europe, and to a lesser extent in the United States, as most liberal democracies adopted the provision of social welfare as a major goal. Claus Offe has argued that the postwar policy agenda in Western Europe was shaped by three major concerns: economic growth, the distribution of benefits and social welfare protections, and security. Ultimately, the shape taken by the social, economic, and political orders in Western European countries rested on a "highly encompassing liberal-democratic welfare state consensus" that went unchallenged by either the right or the left.[52] On the strength of this consensus, then, it made sense for a conservative nationalist like DeGaulle to expand the reach of the welfare state at the same time that he turned his attention to both national defense and the revitalization and modernization of the postwar French economy. No-

---

51. Roth, *Social Democrats in Imperial Germany*.
52. Offe, "Challenging the Boundaries," 66.

where among the major countries of Europe was it possible for the state to sidestep or table a response to public pressure for more social welfare provisions.[53] And inevitably, the public domain expanded in response to these new tasks—a fact that is reflected, for example, in the percentage of GDP that the government absorbs through taxation (around 40 percent for most of Europe and as high as 50 percent for northern European countries such as Sweden) or that it actually spends (45 percent for Britain in recent OECD figures, and 60 percent for Sweden).[54]

The popular consensus that in Europe forced security and social policy onto the public agenda alongside economic growth following World War II was, however, lacking in Japan. There, responsibility for providing social welfare—like that for maintaining social harmony or managing social conflict—was privatized, that is, it was left to civil society, notably to the company and the family. Japan's "small government" then centered its energies on attaining the one goal fully backed by a popular consensus: economic recovery and growth.[55] Only here did the domain of public action expand, in the form of an intense working relationship among bureaucracy, the ruling party, and the private sector in pursuit of that goal. In this one domain the state's presence has been "pervasive," in a relationship with the private sector characterized by "reciprocal consent."[56]

The choices made by Japan's government in electing to fill the "space of political concern" with issues of economic performance and to delegate or defer many issues of social policy help to explain why the Japanese approach to social conflict is so different from that in many other industrial democracies. For better or worse, one of the most profound consequences of big government in the West has been state penetration and a regulatory presence in many domains of daily life. The state takes over welfare tasks that formerly were left to the family or factory management to perform or not perform. Social programs extend new benefits to the disadvantaged, the unemployed, or the handicapped or ill, which means establishing criteria for identifying who is disadvantaged or discriminated against and who is not. Such governmental penetration of society, whatever else it may entail, carries with it extensive new forms of regulation.[57] But to look at this state presence from a different vantage point, it typically also creates an

53. Ibid., 67.
54. *Wall Street Journal*, 13 September 1984.
55. See Johnson, *MITI and the Japanese Miracle*, chap. 1, on the importance of this consensus for the "developmental" state.
56. Samuels, *Business of the Japanese State*, 8–9.
57. Offe, "Challenging the Boundaries," 68.

astonishing range of new and formal linkages between government and civil society. Civil advisory groups or panels are created to counsel legislators on what the disadvantaged or handicapped need or want. Grievance procedures are developed for appealing to the government when discrimination occurs, when military personnel misbehave, or when noise pollution levels from the local airport become unacceptable. It may be, as many writers suggest, that the expansion of government programs and services has engendered a sense of entitlement on the part of many formerly quiescent groups in society, a sense that all people have a stake in the distribution of benefits in society, and thus has spurred a rise in social demands as well as in pressures for increased political participation.[58] At the same time, however, an inevitable correlate of state expansion in the industrial democracies has been a proliferation of channels for airing views, articulating grievances, applying for benefits, and requesting governmental interventions—legitimate and formal new channels, in other words, for meeting human needs, redressing social grievances, and thus for channeling social conflicts.

In the early 1970s, with economic success achieved, a new consensus emerged in Japan backing the expansion of the public mandate, and the leadership finally began to look at ways to bring social policy more centrally into the "space of political concern." This reality of timing appears to be crucial for explaining how authorities in Japan have remained relatively insulated from many of the pressures that have effectively forced the opening up of social conflict elsewhere and led to the creation of an increasing number of institutionalized channels for dispute resolution. Thus, although there is no reason to assume that future developments in Japan will mirror those that occurred elsewhere, a major question is whether Japan will remain insulated from these same pressures. It is noteworthy that the adoption of key measures dealing with equality issues— the series of "special measures" laws concerning burakumin living conditions, and the 1985 Equal Employment Opportunity Law forbidding discrimination on the basis of sex—has been quite recent, occurring after the shift to social policy began. The current Burakumin Liberation League proposal for a new law that would actively involve the state in punishing those who discriminate against burakumin is another sign that new formal channels between state and society for resolving conflicts among competing social interests may yet emerge. Given its long historical roots, the Japanese preference for privatizing social conflict is not likely to diminish;

58. Crozier, Huntington, and Watanuki, *Crisis of Democracy*.

indeed, the approach would probably be elites' method of choice, whatever the country, if they had their way. Nevertheless, current trends indicate that Japanese authorities' record of success with the method may be reduced in the future.

The fourth and final condition reinforcing the Japanese approach to social conflict is the high level of economic performance that Japan's leadership has been able to deliver—a chief reason for the LDP's continued hold on power. Perhaps no other major country in the postwar era has been as successful as Japan in making a "spill-over" argument work. Unlike in countries such as Brazil, which have given business free rein only to increase economic inequality, Japan's economic growth has indeed trickled down to benefit ordinary people, including the workers who in the 1950s were willing to defer gratification in the name of economic recovery. The gap between rich and poor in Japan, with its probusiness stance and its record of privatizing social conflict, is not much greater than in Sweden, a country that has addressed social inequities with perhaps the most innovative range of social policies outside communist systems.[59] Though the gap in Japan was widening in the late 1980s, the achievement was nonetheless real.

A major task of groups undertaking status-based protests is to convince potential supporters and the public at large that the challenge they mount in their "offensive mobilization" warrants a change in the status quo. Yet any alteration in the fundamental arrangements in society carries a concomitant risk that the very fabric on which strong economic growth has been based will be reshaped. In Japan, the appeal of the status quo has been especially great for older generations who experienced war and poverty in their youth. Now that economic growth has leveled off and as the problems of a mature economy set in, it remains to be seen whether the formula of privatizing social conflict will continue to work, especially as affluent postwar generations come to the fore.

Costs of the Japanese Approach

The success of any particular strategy of conflict management can be judged from several perspectives. From the standpoint of authorities, success means, at a minimum, staying in power, preserving existing patterns of social relations, and restricting challenges to their preeminence. As protesters see it, a successful outcome in a social conflict ideally would entail accommodation by authorities to the protesters' specific demands, ac-

59. Verba et al., *Elites and the Idea of Equality*.

knowledgment of the legitimacy of their grievances, and the establishment or maintenance of satisfactory ways for handling future grievances.

Success can also be judged from a broader perspective. It is important, then, to look finally at the costs that Japan incurs as a democracy as a result of its approach to social conflict management in the domain considered here—equality struggles. Even if preemptive concessions provide a way for authorities to make minimal improvements in social conditions and thus to contain conflict in the long run, the fact remains that many status-related grievances in Japan are not addressed in a manner satisfactory to the protesters concerned. Individual conflict episodes often have no definitive resolution, owing especially to the authorities' fear that recourse to formal channels might generate new general principles with broad applicability to future similar cases. Lewis A. Coser has observed that for definitive conflict resolution to occur, two conditions must be satisfied: there must be an institutionally prescribed termination point (such as a court ruling), and "a shared universe of discourse" must grow out of the conflict.[60] Neither condition is satisfied in the pattern of social conflict resolution described in this book. To the extent that status-based conflicts do not find their way into existing channels for dispute resolution, the termination point is often ambiguous or the outcome unsatisfactory to the protesters.

As Charles Tilly's work suggests, the response of elites to protest over time structures the nature of protest itself.[61] The costs of the ultimate failure of Japanese authority figures to accommodate dissenters may therefore be quite high. For one thing, the very nature of the Japanese approach may actually force protest in Japan to the extremes of either the right or the left. By not opening up a dialogue with protesters or addressing grievances directly, authorities in Japan effectively spur the highly committed to become more radicalized. The presence in Japan of groups such as those involved in the Narita Airport protest, who are willing to devote a substantial portion of their lives to a protest, and the existence generally of an alienated left in the polarized politics of much of the postwar period may both arguably be linked to the particular style of Japanese conflict management. Another cost is apparent in the sense of dissatisfaction with government that the general public often voices in surveys. The view that elites and institutions somehow are not directly responsive to public needs may be traceable, at least in part, to patterns of conflict resolution that leave both underdogs and onlookers feeling vaguely dissatisfied.

60. Coser, *Continuities*, 37–38.
61. See Tilly, *From Mobilization to Revolution* and "Repertoires of Contention."

The Future

Privatization as a preferred and successful method of conflict management arose out of particular conditions in Japan, conditions uncharacteristic of any other major industrial country. The very contingency of this method, however, suggests that the pattern of response to conflict will likely change if those conditions alter. And in fact, we can identify at least four major forces that impinge on, and may affect, the Japanese response to conflict in the future.

The first of these is democratic ideology, which, together with Western-style egalitarianism, was introduced into Japan in the nineteenth and twentieth centuries, becoming official ideology as a result of the Allied Occupation. Even though at present their official status does not automatically insure their adoption by society as a whole, democracy and egalitarianism have become powerful normative resources for protesters in postwar Japan. Not only do they buttress all protesting groups' claims to the right of free political participation, but in the case of status-based protests specifically they provide crucial support to inferiors who must justify their challenge of the traditional prerogatives of seniors.

Over time, especially as generations educated wholly in the postwar era come to predominate in number, there is every reason to believe that the official ideology will become increasingly real. Many observers today argue that Japan is becoming ever more pluralist, and that support for democratic participatory values is increasing in the culture.[62] Value change that makes a nominal ideology actual is a crucial force, one that will inevitably affect both the resources available to protesters and the response to protest itself.

A second force affecting the conditions on which the Japanese approach to conflict rests is that of social change. Demographic shifts, urbanization, and the spread of the nuclear family, for example, will all certainly affect women in their struggle for equality. Japan's small family size and the gradual demise of the extended family system now mean that women spend an increasing part of their lives relatively free of child-rearing re-

62. Michio Muramatsu and Ellis S. Krauss, "Bureaucrats and Politicians in Policymaking: The Case of Japan," *American Political Science Review* 78 (March 1984): 126–146; McKean, *Environmental Protest and Citizen Politics*; Satō and Matsuzaki, *Jimintō seiken;* and Tsurutani, *Political Change in Japan.* Flanagan argues on the basis of survey data that Japanese are also becoming more "libertarian" (i.e., individualistic, self-assertive, and self-indulgent) and moving away from an "authoritarian" (austere, hierarchic, and group-oriented) focus; see "Changing Values," 409–410.

sponsibilities and available to engage in activities outside the home. The result has been a dramatic increase in the number of married women in the work force. Although women workers and bureaucrats, both established and incoming, today face much discrimination, as educational levels rise and better-educated women confront these conditions increased pressure for change is likely to occur. The steady growth of court cases over issues of sex discrimination since the mid 1960s point to such a trend.

The third force is economic: once the climate of prosperity changes, protest and the response to it among potential supporters, the public, and authorities are inevitably affected. To take but one example, consider the political cultural requirement that protest be motivated by dire necessity; as public expectations for what a person is due in life rise owing to generally greater affluence throughout society, it makes sense that this prerequisite would ease. In that regard the concerns underlying a tea pourers' rebellion become more immediately comprehensible, since the issue is not one of survival. The atmosphere of greater affluence is especially beneficial in the case of status-based conflicts, which, because they represent the "offensive" pursuit of new benefits and new rights, have had a particularly difficult time meeting the political cultural tests for a worthy protest. Even in the current atmosphere of minor retrenchments, moreover, it seems likely that these effects of increased prosperity will persist. In fact, the retrenchments themselves—especially to the extent that they keep authorities from the preemptive concession-making that the Japanese formula for conflict management so relies on—may even increase the level of social conflict.

Finally, the fourth key force with potential impact on Japanese conflict management is internationalization. Since the 1970s Japan has increasingly acknowledged a need to achieve major power status within the international community and to expand ties abroad. Many factors have influenced this change: Japan's growing foreign direct investment, the desire to move away from what has been seen as an overdependent relationship with the United States, foreign pressures to open Japanese markets, travel abroad of a population with greater economic resources, and the urgent practical need to train more Japanese to work effectively in an international context. The effects of Japan's greater identification with the other industrial democracies are profound. Few countries today are as preoccupied with their image abroad or more responsive to foreign pressure and criticism.[63]

63. See Herbert Passin, "Socio-Cultural Factors in the Japanese Perception of International Order," *Japan Institute of International Affairs Annual Review* (1971):

Indeed, in the past Japan's attentiveness to its international image has been an important factor in determining how the country responded to social issues and protests—occasionally with perverse results. For example, in 1951, when Japan was about to rejoin the international community and the country was gearing up for tourism, Kyoto city administrators, anxious that the poverty of a burakumin ghetto near the central train station would harm the city's image, built a board fence to screen the neighborhood from view; rather than address the ghetto's problems, in other words, they initiated a stark demonstration of conflict avoidance behavior.[64] More often, however, Japan's image concerns have been a spur to preemptive concessions, which in turn grew out of the authorities' sense that Japan was behind. The pollution cleanup in the early 1970s, for example, may have been spurred as much by Western media attention to the plight of Japanese pollution disease victims and Western criticism of Japan as a "polluter's paradise" as by citizens' protests.[65] Similarly, the Equal Employment Opportunity Law approved by the Diet in 1985 resulted almost totally because of international commitments made by the Japanese government.

Japan's concern with its international image is a major resource to protesters, who exploit it by building ties with protest groups abroad and by taking part in international conferences where foreign media attention can be directed to social problems in Japan. Today, as Japan rises in status as a major power and a role model to other countries, the pressure on Japan's leadership to address the country's social problems and accommodate social protest can only grow. Meeting the challenge of status conflict will be only one of the tasks of the 1990s.

51–75, which analyzes the sources of the Japanese preoccupation with their international image and status.

64. Muraoka Sukeyuki, interview with author, Kyoto branch office, Buraku Liberation League, 12 July 1978. For an account of the city's subsequent efforts to address the problem, see Yoshino and Murakoshi, *The Invisible Visible Minority*, 57–58.

65. Susan J. Pharr and Joseph L. Badaracco, Jr., "Coping with Crisis: Environmental Regulation," in *America Versus Japan*, ed. Thomas K. McCraw, 229–259 (Boston: Harvard Business School Press, 1986).

BIBLIOGRAPHY

Abegglen, James C. *The Japanese Factory.* Glencoe, Ill.: Free Press, 1958.

Abramson, Paul R. "Social Class and Political Change in Western Europe: A Cross-National Longitudinal Analysis." *Comparative Political Studies* 4 (1971): 131–155.

Akasaka Tarō. "'Kōno shintō' hataage no shokku" (A shock caused by the establishment of Kōno's new political party). *Bungei Shunjū* 54 (August 1976): 254–258.

———. "Shin Jiyū Kurabu 18 nin no shinjō chōsa" (Investigation of 18 New Liberal Club members). *Bungei Shunjū* 55 (March 1977): 210–214.

Allardt, Erik. "Past and Emerging Political Cleavages." In *Party Organization and the Politics of the New Masses,* edited by Otto Stammer, 66–74. Berlin: Institute of Political Science at the Free University, 1968.

Amino Yoshihiko. *Nihon chūsei no minshūzō* (Images of the Japanese common people in the Middle Ages). Tokyo: Iwanami Shoten, 1980.

Aoki Kōji. *Hyakushō ikki no sōgō nenpyō* (A comprehensive chronology of peasant uprisings in the Tokugawa period). Tokyo: San'ichi Shobō, 1971.

Apter, David E., and Nagayo Sawa. *Against the State: Politics and Social Protest in Japan.* Cambridge, Mass.: Harvard University Press, 1984.

Ash, Roberta. *Social Movements in America.* Chicago: Markham, 1972.

Austin, Lewis. *Saints and Samurai: The Political Culture of American and Japanese Elites.* New Haven: Yale University Press, 1975.

Baerwald, Hans H. *Party Politics in Japan.* London: Allen Unwin, 1986.

Bailey, F. G. *Stratagems and Spoils: A Social Anthropology of Politics.* Oxford: Basil Blackwell, 1969.

Barnes, Samuel H., Max Kaase, et al. *Political Action: Mass Participation in Five Western Democracies.* Beverly Hills, Calif.: Sage, 1979.

Bayley, David H. *Forces of Order.* Berkeley and Los Angeles: University of California Press, 1976.

———. "Public Protest and the Political Process in India." In *Protest, Reform, and Revolt,* edited by Joseph R. Gusfield, 298–308. New York: John Wiley, 1970.

Befu, Harumi. "Power in Exchange: Strategy of Control and Patterns of Compliance in Japan." *Asian Profile* 2 (December 1974): 601–622.

Beer, Samuel H. "Federalism, Nationalism, and Democracy in America." *American Political Science Review* 72 (March 1978): 9–21.

———. "The Modernization of American Federalism." *Publius* (Fall 1973): 48–95.

———. "Political Overload and Federalism." *Polity* 10 (1977): 5–17.

Bell, Daniel. *The Coming of Post-industrial Society.* New York: Basic Books, 1973.

———. *The Cultural Contradiction of Capitalism.* New York: Basic Books, 1976.

Bendix, Reinhard. "The Lower Classes and the 'Democratic Revolution.'" In *Protest, Reform, and Revolt,* edited by Joseph R. Gusfield, 195–213. New York: John Wiley, 1970.

———. "Preconditions of Development: A Comparison of Japan and Germany." In *Aspects of Social Change in Modern Japan,* edited by Ronald P. Dore, 27–68. Princeton: Princeton University Press, 1967.

———, ed. *State and Society.* Boston: Little, Brown, 1968.

Benedict, Ruth. *The Chrysanthemum and the Sword.* Boston: Houghton Mifflin, 1946.

Benjamin, Roger W. "Images of Conflict Resolution and Social Control: American and Japanese Attitudes Toward the Adversary System." *Journal of Conflict Resolution* 19 (March 1975): 123–137.

Bennett, John, and Iwao Ishino. *Paternalism in the Japanese Economy: Anthropological Studies of Oyabun-Kobun Patterns.* Minneapolis: University of Minnesota Press, 1963.

Berger, Gordon. *Parties out of Power in Japan, 1931–1941.* Princeton: Princeton University Press, 1977.

Berger, Peter L., and Thomas Luckmann. *The Social Construction of Reality.* Garden City, N.Y.: Doubleday, 1966.

Birnbaum, Norman. *The Crises of Industrial Society.* New York: Oxford University Press, 1969.

Blaker, Michael. *Japanese International Negotiating Style.* New York: Columbia University Press, 1977.

Blau, Peter M. *Exchange and Power in Social Life.* New York: John Wiley, 1964.

Bowen, Roger. *Rebellion and Democracy in Meiji Japan.* Berkeley and Los Angeles: University of California Press, 1981.

Bright, Charles, and Susan Harding, eds. *Statemaking and Social Move-*

ments: Essays in History and Theory. Ann Arbor: University of Michigan Press, 1984.

Broadbent, Jeffrey. "Environmental Movements in Japan: Citizen Versus State Mobilization." Paper presented at the annual meeting of the American Sociological Association, 1983.

Brooks, William Lyman. "Outcaste Society in Early Modern Japan." Ph.D. diss., Columbia University, 1976.

Buraku Kaihō Dōmei (Buraku Liberation League). Konnichi no buraku (Buraku today). Osaka: Kaihō Shuppansha, 1987.

Buraku Kaihō Kenkyūsho (Buraku Liberation Research Institute), ed. Long-suffering Brothers and Sisters, Unite! Osaka: Kaihō Shuppansha, 1981.

Buraku Kaihō Newsletter. 1984.

Buraku Mondai Kenkyūjo (Buraku Problems Institute). Dōwa Kyōiku Undō kikan (Dōwa Education Movement quarterly) (Kobe) 7 (Winter 1975).

Butler, David, and Donald Stokes. Political Change in Britain. 2d ed. New York: St. Martin's Press, 1976.

Calista, Donald J. "Postmaterialism and Value Convergence: Value Priorities of Japanese Compared with Their Perceptions of American Values." Comparative Political Studies 16 (January 1984): 529–555.

Campbell, John Creighton. "Policy Conflict and Its Resolution Within the Governmental System." In Conflict in Japan, edited by Ellis S. Krauss, Thomas P. Rohlen, and Patricia G. Steinhoff, 294–334. Honolulu: University of Hawaii Press, 1984.

"'Chūdō' ni maibotsu sezu kakki aru kōdō e doryoku" (We are not satisfied with being equal to the "Middle-of-the-Roaders"; instead let's try to be active). Interview with New Liberal Club chief representative Kōno Yōhei. Asahi Shinbun, 20 July 1979.

"'Chūdō' tono kankei ni gokai" (Misunderstandings concerning our relationship with the "Middle-of-the-Roaders"). Interview with Kōno Yōhei. Asahi Shinbun, 6 February 1979.

Chūma Kōki (NLC Representative). Kokkai katsudō repōto (Diet activities report). Osaka: Chūma Kōki Kōenkai, 1977.

"Chūō no taiō o chūshi: Nishioka shi ritō, Shin Jiyū Kurabu chihō soshiki" (New Liberal Club local organizations are watching how the head office reacts to the Nishioka separation). Asahi Shinbun, 18 July 1979.

Clark, Rodney. The Japanese Company. Tokyo: Charles E. Tuttle, 1979.

Cole, Robert E. "Changing Labor Force Characteristics and Their Impact on Japanese Industrial Relations." In Japan: The Paradox of Progress, edited by Lewis Austin, 165–213. New Haven: Yale University Press, 1976.

———. "Diffusion of Participatory Work Structure." In Change in Organizations, edited by Paul S. Goodman and Associates. San Francisco: Jossey-Bass, 1982.

———. Japanese Blue Collar. Berkeley and Los Angeles: University of California Press, 1971.

Coleman, James S. *Community Conflict*. New York: Free Press, 1957.

Collins, Randall. *Conflict Sociology: Toward an Explanatory Science*. New York: Academic Press, 1975.

Cook, Alice H., and Hiroko Hayashi. *Working Women in Japan: Discrimination, Resistance, and Reform*. Ithaca, N.Y.: Cornell University Press, 1980.

Coser, Lewis A. *Continuities in the Study of Social Conflict*. New York: Free Press, 1967.

————. *The Functions of Social Conflict*. New York: Free Press, 1956.

Crewe, Ivor, Bo Sarlvik, and James Alt. "Partisan Dealignment in Britain 1964–1975." *British Journal of Political Science* 7 (1977): 129–190.

Crozier, Michel, Samuel P. Huntington, and Watanuki Joji. *The Crisis of Democracy*. New York: New York University Press, 1975.

Cummings, William K. *Education and Equality in Japan*. Princeton: Princeton University Press, 1980.

Curtis, Gerald L. *The Japanese Way of Politics*. New York: Columbia University Press, 1988.

Daalder, Hans, ed. *Party Systems in Denmark, Austria, Switzerland, the Netherlands, and Belgium*. New York: St. Martin's Press, 1987.

Dahl, Robert A., and Charles E. Lindblom. *Politics, Economics, and Welfare*. Chicago: University of Chicago Press, 1976.

Dahrendorf, Ralf. *Class and Class Conflict in Industrial Society*. Stanford: Stanford University Press, 1959.

————. *Conflict After Class: New Perspectives in the Theory of Social and Political Conflict*. London: Longmans, Green, 1967.

————. "Conflict and Liberty: Some Remarks on the Social Structure of German Politics." In *State and Society*, edited by Reinhard Bendix, 378–390. Boston: Little, Brown, 1968.

————. "Towards a Theory of Social Conflict." *Conflict Resolution* 2 (June 1958): 170–183.

Dalton, Russell J. "Was There a Revolution? A Note on Generational Versus Life-Cycle Explanations of Value Differences." *Comparative Political Studies* 9 (1977): 459–473.

Davies, Derek. "Japan's Great Debate." *Far Eastern Economic Review* 98 (4 November 1977): 20–25.

Deutsch, Morton. *The Resolution of Conflict: Constructive and Destructive Processes*. New Haven: Yale University Press, 1973.

DeVos, George, and Hiroshi Wagatsuma. *Japan's Invisible Race: Caste in Culture and Personality*. Berkeley and Los Angeles: University of California Press, 1966.

DiPalma, Giuseppe. *The Study of Conflict in Western Society*. Morristown, N.J.: General Learning Press, 1973.

Doi, Takeo. *The Anatomy of Dependence*. Tokyo: Kōdansha, 1973.

————. "Higaisha-ishiki: The Psychology of Revolting Youth in Japan." In

Japanese Culture and Behavior, edited by Takie Sugiyama Lebra and William P. Lebra, 450–457. Honolulu: University of Hawaii Press, 1974.

Donoghue, John D. *Pariah Persistence in Changing Japan*. Washington, D.C.: University Press of America, 1977.

Dore, Ronald P. *British Factory—Japanese Factory*. Berkeley and Los Angeles: University of California Press, 1973.

―――, ed. *Aspects of Social Change in Modern Japan*. Princeton: Princeton University Press, 1967.

Douglas, Mary. *Natural Symbols*. New York: Vintage Books, 1973.

Duke, James T. *Conflict and Power in Social Life*. Provo, Utah: Brigham Young University Press, 1976.

Dumont, Louis. *Homo Hierarchicus*. Chicago: University of Chicago Press, 1966.

Duncan, William. *Doing Business with Japan*. Epping, Eng.: Gower Press, 1976.

Duus, Peter. "Liberal Intellectuals and Social Conflict in Taishō Japan." In *Conflict in Modern Japanese History: The Neglected Tradition*, edited by Tetsuo Najita and J. Victor Koschmann, 412–440. Princeton: Princeton University Press, 1982.

Edelman, Murray. *Political Language: Words That Succeed and Policies That Fail*. New York: Academic Press, 1977.

―――. *Politics as Symbolic Action: Mass Arousal and Quiescence*. New York: Academic Press, 1971.

―――. *The Symbolic Uses of Politics*. Urbana: University of Illinois Press, 1964.

Edinger, Lewis J. *Politics in Germany*. Boston: Little, Brown, 1968.

Etzioni, Amitai. *The Active Society*. New York: Free Press, 1968.

Evans, Robert R. *Readings in Collective Behavior*. Chicago: Rand McNally, 1969.

Fanon, Franz. *The Wretched of the Earth*. New York: Grove Press, 1968.

Feierabend, Ivo K., Rosalind L. Feierabend, and Ted Robert Gurr. *Anger, Violence, and Politics*. Englewood Cliffs, N.J.: Prentice-Hall, 1972.

Fireman, Bruce, and William A. Gamson. "Utilitarian Logic in the Resource Mobilization Perspective." In *The Dynamics of Social Movements*, edited by Mayer N. Zald and John D. McCarthy, 8–44. Cambridge, Mass.: Winthrop, 1979.

Flanagan, Scott C. "Changing Values in Advanced Industrial Societies: Inglehart's Silent Revolution from the Perspective of Japanese Findings." *Comparative Political Studies* 14 (January 1982): 403–444.

Flanagan, Scott C., and Bradley M. Richardson. "Political Disaffection and Political Stability: A Comparison of Japanese and Western Findings." In *Comparative Social Research*, edited by Richard H. Tomasson, vol. 3. Greenwich, Conn.: JAI Press, 1980.

Flora, Peter, and Arnold J. Heidenheimer, eds. *The Development of Welfare States in Europe and America.* New Brunswick, N.J.: Transaction Books, 1981.

Franklin, Mark N., and Anthony Mughan. "The Decline of Class Voting in Britain: Problems of Analysis and Interpretation." *American Political Science Review* 72 (1978): 523–534.

Freeman, Jo. *The Politics of Women's Liberation.* New York: David McKay, 1975.

Fukuda, K. John. *Japanese-Style Management Transferred: The Experience of East Asia.* London: Routledge and Kegan Paul, 1988.

Gale, Roger W. "The 1976 Election and the LDP: Edge of a Precipice?" *The Japan Interpreter* 11 (Spring 1977): 433–447.

Galtung, Johan. "Institutionalized Conflict Resolution: A Theoretical Paradigm." *Journal of Peace Research* 4 (1965): 348–397.

Gamson, William A. *Power and Discontent.* Homewood, Ill.: Dorsey Press, 1968.

———. *The Strategy of Social Protest.* Homewood, Ill.: Dorsey Press, 1975.

Goffman, Erving. *Interaction Ritual: Essays on Face to Face Behavior.* Garden City, N.Y.: Anchor Books, 1967.

———. *The Presentation of Self in Everyday Life.* Garden City, N.Y.: Anchor Books, 1959.

Gordon, Andrew. *The Evolution of Labor Relations in Japan: Heavy Industry, 1853–1955.* Cambridge, Mass.: Harvard University Press, 1985.

Groth, David E. "Biting the Bullet: The Politics of Grass-Roots Protest in Contemporary Japan." Ph.D. diss., Stanford University, 1986.

Gurr, Ted R. *Why Men Rebel.* Princeton: Princeton University Press, 1970.

Gusfield, Joseph R. *Symbolic Crusade: Status Politics and the American Temperance Movement.* Urbana: University of Illinois Press, 1966.

Hah, Chong-do, and Christopher C. Lapp. "Japanese Politics of Equality in Transition: The Case of the Burakumin." *Asian Survey* 18 (May 1978): 487–504.

"Haiiro Jimintō no 'hanran gun' to yū meiyo o kaketa, nisei giin tachi no jitsuryoku" (The real ability of young juniors who gamble their honor in the name of the "rebel army" of the gray Liberal Democratic party). *Shūkan Shinchō* 21 (24 June 1976): 132–135.

Hall, John, and Marius B. Jansen, eds. *Studies in the Institutional History of Early Modern Japan.* Princeton: Princeton University Press, 1968.

Hall, Peter. *Governing the Economy.* Cambridge: Polity Press, 1986.

Hanami, Tadashi. "Equality and Prohibition of Discrimination in Employment—The Japanese Case." N.d. Photocopy.

———. *Labor Relations in Japan Today.* Tokyo: Kōdansha, 1979.

Hanami Tadashi and Akamatsu Ryōko, with Watanabe Mayumi. *Josei to kigyō no shinjidai* (A new era for women and enterprises). Tokyo: Yūhikaku, 1986.

Handa Takashi. "Yōhei basu wa gasorin dai 2-oku en o chōtatsu dekiruka" (Will the Kōno party be able to raise the 200 million yen required to manage a substantial party [of influence]?) *Shūkan Asahi*, 2 July 1976, 21–23.

Hane, Mikiso. *Peasants, Rebels, and Outcastes: The Underside of Modern Japan*. New York: Pantheon Books, 1982.

Harada Tomohiko. *Hi-sabetsu buraku no rekishi* (History of the discriminated-against outcaste hamlets). Tokyo: Asahi Shinbunsha, 1975.

———. "Sengo no buraku kaihō undō" (Postwar buraku liberation movement). In *Buraku mondai gaisetsu* (Outline of buraku problems), edited by Buraku Kaihō Kenkyūsho, 189–212. Osaka: Kaihō Shuppansha.

Hashimoto Akikazu. "Kōnō shintō o sasaeru kiban wa aruka: 'Kikentō' no konnichi teki bunseki" (Is there any base of support for the new Kōno party? A contemporary analysis of "absentees"). *Asahi Jānaru* 18 (2 July 1976): 12–16.

Hayashi, Chikio. "Changes in Japanese Thought During the Past Twenty Years." In *Text of Seminar on "Changing Values in Modern Japan,"* edited by Nihonjin Kenkyūkai, 3–57. Tokyo: Nihonjin Kenkyūkai, 1977.

Hayashiya Tatsusaburō. "Chayoriai to sono dentō" (The tea party and its tradition). *Bungaku* 19 (May 1954): 34–40.

———. *Nihon geinō no sekai* (The world of Japanese performing arts). Tokyo: Nihon Hōsō Shuppan Kyōkai, 1973.

Heisler, Martin O. "Political Economy Aspects of Ethnic and Regional Conflict." Paper presented at the XI World Congress of the International Political Science Association, Moscow, 12–18 August 1979.

Hijikata Tetsu. *Hi-sabetsu buraku no tatakai* (The struggle by discriminated-against outcaste hamlets). Tokyo: Shinsensha, 1973.

Hildebrandt, Kai, and Russell J. Dalton. "The New Politics: Political Change or Sunshine Politics?" In *German Political Studies: Elections and Parties*, edited by Klaus von Beyme and Max Kaase, vol. 3. London: Sage, 1978.

Hirasawa, Yasumasa. "Buraku Liberation Movement and Its Implications for Dōwa Education: A Critical Analysis of the Literature." Harvard University, Graduate School of Education, 1984. Photocopy.

———. "Review and Analysis of the Yata Case." Harvard University, 1982. Photocopy.

"Hirosugita dohyō daga seika wa atta" (The fighting ring was too large, but we did manage to get some results). Interview with Kōno Yōhei. *Asahi Jānaru* 19 (22 July 1977): 16–17.

"Hōhōron de giron wa atta ga . . ." (We in fact had debates over methods, but . . .). Interview with Kōno Yōhei by Ishikawa Masumi. *Asahi Shinbun*, 8 July 1979.

Horowitz, Irving L. "Consensus, Conflict, and Cooperation: A Sociological Inventory." *Social Forces* 41 (December 1962): 177–188.

Hosojima Izumi. "Hoshu yurugasu Kōno shintō" (The new Kōno party that shook the conservatives). *Ekonomisuto* 54 (29 June 1976): 10–14.

Howes, John F., and Nobuya Bamba, eds. *Pacifism in Japan: The Christian and Socialist Tradition.* Vancouver: University of British Columbia Press, 1978.

Hrebenar, Ronald J. *The Japanese Party System: From One-Party Rule to Coalition Government.* Boulder, Colo.: Westview Press, 1986.

Huddle, Norie, and Michael Reich. *Island of Dreams: Environmental Crisis in Japan.* New York: Autumn Press, 1975.

Huntington, Samuel P. *American Politics: The Promise of Disharmony.* Cambridge, Mass.: Harvard University Press, 1981.

Hyōgoken Kōkyōso Yōka Kōkō Bunkai (Yōka High School Branch of the High School Teachers' Union of Hyōgo Prefecture). *Yōka kara zenkoku e zenkoku kara Yōka e* (From Yōka to the whole country, from the whole country to Yōka). Kyoto: Chōbunsha, 1975.

————. *Yōka Kōkō jiken: Kaidō Asada-ha no kyōikuhakai to jyūminshihai no jittai* (The incident of Yōka High School: The destruction of education and the control of local people by the Kaidō Asada group). Kobe: Buraku Mondai Kenkyūjo, 1976.

Hyōgoken Kōtōgakkō Kyōshokuin Kumiai Yōka Kōkō Bunkai (Hyōgo Prefectural High School Teachers' Union, Yōka High School Section). *Yagigawa, hiroku fukaki nagareni: Yōka Kōkō jiken sanshūnen kinen shashinshū* (Yagigawa, a wide and deep stream: The third-anniversary memorial photo album of the Yōka High School incident). Kobe: Yōka Asago Bōryoku Jiken Sanshūnen-kinen Jigyō Jikkōiinkai, 1977.

Ike, Nobutaka. "Economic Growth and Intergenerational Change in Japan." *American Political Science Review* 67 (December 1973): 1194–1203.

Ima . . . Tajima de okotte iru koto: Bōryoku shūdan—Asada ippa no kyōikuhakai (Now . . . what's been happening in Tajima: The violent group—the destruction of education by the Asada group). Kobe: Nihon Kyōsantō Hyōgoiinkai, 1974.

Imai Hisao. *Jūsan nin no saishō kōhosha tachi* (Thirteen candidates for the [Liberal Democratic party] presidency). Tokyo: Keizai Ōraisha, 1980.

Imai, Masaaki. *Never Take Yes for an Answer: An Inside Look at Japanese Business for Foreign Businessmen.* Tokyo: Simul Press, 1975.

Imaizumi, Akio. *Dōwa Problem: Present Situation and Government Measures.* Tokyo: Prime Minister's Office, 1977.

Inaba Michio. "Ochikobore shimin kara no chōyaku" (A boost from citizens at the fringe). *Ekonomisuto* 55 (2 August 1977): 18–23.

Inglehart, Ronald. "Changing Values in Japan and the West." *Comparative Political Studies* 14 (1982): 445–479.

————. "Political Dissatisfaction and Mass Support for Social Change in

Advanced Industrial Society." *Comparative Political Studies* 10 (1977): 455–472.

———. *The Silent Revolution: Changing Values and Political Styles Among Western Publics.* Princeton: Princeton University Press, 1977.

———. "The Silent Revolution in Europe: Intergenerational Change in Post-industrial Societies." *American Political Science Review* 65 (December 1971): 991–1017.

———. "Values, Objective Needs, and Subjective Satisfaction Among Western Publics." *Comparative Political Studies* 9 (1977): 429–458.

Inoguchi, Takashi. "Explaining and Predicting Japanese General Elections, 1960–1980." *Journal of Japanese Studies* 7 (Summer 1981): 285–318.

———, ed. *Shin hoshushugi no taitō* (The rise of neoconservatism). *Leviathan*, no. 1 (Autumn 1987) (special issue). Tokyo: Bokutakusha, 1987.

Irokawa, Daikichi. "The Survival Struggle of the Japanese Community." *Japan Interpreter* 9 (Spring 1975): 466–494.

Ishida, Takeshi. "Conflict and Its Accommodation: *Omote-Ura* and *Uchi-Soto* Relations." In *Conflict in Japan*, edited by Ellis S. Krauss, Thomas P. Rohlen, and Patricia G. Steinhoff, 16–38. Honolulu: University of Hawaii Press, 1984.

———. *Gendai soshikiron* (Contemporary organization). Tokyo: Iwanami Shoten, 1961.

———. *Japanese Political Culture: Change and Continuity.* New Brunswick, N.J.: Transaction Books, 1983.

Itō Masaya. *Jimintō sengokushi* (Turbulent era for the Liberal Democratic party). 2 vols. Tokyo: Asahi Sonorama, 1982–1983.

Iwami Takao. "Kōno Yōhei: Taishū mitchaku rosen wa seikō suruka" (Kōno Yōhei: Will these popular strategies be successful?). *Bungei Shunjū* 54 (October 1976): 202–206.

———. "Wakate giin no kekki" (The rise of young congressmen). Portion of article entitled "Jimintō wa kanarazu bunretsu suru" (Liberal Democratic party will surely split). *Ekonomisuto* 54 (22 June 1976): 29 (full article 25–29).

Iwao, Sumiko. "A Full Life for Modern Japanese Women." In *Text of Seminar on Changing Values in Modern Japan*, edited by Nihonjin Kenkyūkai, 95–111. Tokyo: Nihonjin Kenkyūkai, 1977.

Jamieson, K. M. "Antecedent Genre as Rhetorical Constraint." *Quarterly Journal of Speech* 61 (1975): 406–415.

———. "Generic Constraints and the Rhetorical Situation." *Philosophy and Rhetoric* 6 (1973): 162–170.

Janowitz, Morris. "Sociological Theory and Social Control." *American Journal of Sociology* 80 (July 1975): 82–108.

Japan. *Seminar in* [sic] *Public Administration Officers on Women's Problems.* Tokyo, 1973 and 1975.

————. Economic Planning Agency. *Kokumin seikatsu hakusho* (White paper on national life). Tokyo, 1971.

————. Management and Coordination Agency. Director-General's Secretariat, Office of Dōwa Projects. *Dōwa mondai no genkyō, 1987* (The status of dōwa problems, 1987). Tokyo, 1987.

————. Management and Coordination Agency. Statistics Bureau. *Statistical Handbook of Japan 1988.* Tokyo, 1988.

————. Ministry of Foreign Affairs. *Status of Women in Modern Japan.* Tokyo, 1975.

————. Ministry of Labor. "The Labor Conditions of Women 1987—Summary." Tokyo: Foreign Press Center, 1988.

————. "Survey on Personnel Management of Women Workers." Tokyo, 1981.

————. Women's and Minors' Bureau. *The Status of Women in Japan.* Tokyo, 1968, 1973, and 1977.

————. Women's and Young Workers' Bureau. *Fujin rōdō no jitsujō, 1985* (The status of women workers, 1985). Tokyo, 1985.

————. *The Status of Women in Japan.* Tokyo, 1983.

Japan External Trade Organization. "Female Employment in Japan." *Now in Japan* 19 (December 1975): 1–25.

Japan Institute of Labor. *Japan Labor Bulletin.*

Japan 1988: An International Comparison. Tokyo: Keizai Kōhō Center, 1988.

Japanese Women Yesterday and Today. Tokyo: Foreign Press Center, 1986.

Jiji nenkan (Jiji almanac). 1968–1977. Tokyo: Jiji Tsūshinsha, 1967–1976.

"Jikengo sannenkan no tatakai" (The battle three years after the incident). *Buraku Kaihō*, June 1978, 129–134.

"Jimintō ikōru kokka dewa nai jidai" (The age in which the Liberal Democratic party is no longer coterminous with the nation). Editorial. *Ekonomisuto* 55 (5 July 1977): 34.

"Jimintō no 150 nichi" (150 days of the Liberal Democratic party). *Sekai*, no. 369 (August 1976): 196–208.

"Jimintō zanpai de seikyoku kinpaku" (Crushing defeat of the Liberal Democratic party brings tension to political situation). *Asahi Shinbun* (evening edition), 8 October 1979.

Johnson, Chalmers. *MITI and the Japanese Miracle.* Stanford: Stanford University Press, 1982.

Kahn, Herman. *The Emerging Japanese Superstate: Challenge and Response.* Englewood Cliffs, N.J.: Prentice-Hall, 1970.

Kaji, Etsuko. "The Invisible Proletariat: Working Women in Japan." *AMPO* 18 (Autumn 1973): 48–58.

Kanter, Rosabeth. "Women and Hierarchies." Paper presented at the annual meeting of the American Sociological Association, San Francisco, 1975.

————. *Women and Organization.* Englewood Cliffs, N.J.: Prentice-Hall, 1976.

Karsh, Bernard. "The Development of a Strike." In *Protest, Reform, and Revolt*, edited by Joseph R. Gusfield, 313–333. New York: John Wiley, 1970.

Kase Hideaki. "Kōno Yōhei ni aete tou—Anata no kinmyaku wa yogorete inaika" (May I be so direct, Yōhei Kōno—Are your money and personal connections free from dirt?). *Gendai* 11 (May 1977): 56–79.

Kawashima Takeyoshi. *Nihon shakai no kazokuteki kōsei* (The family-like structure of Japanese society). Tokyo: Nihon Hyōronsha, 1950.

Kelly, William W. *Deference and Defiance in Nineteenth-Century Japan.* Princeton: Princeton University Press, 1985.

Kishima, Takako. "Political Life Reconsidered: A Poststructuralist View of the World of Man in Japan." Ph.D. diss., University of Wisconsin–Madison, 1987.

Kishimoto Kōichi. "Kōnoke no hitobito" (The Kōno family). *Chūō Kōron* 91 (August 1976): 200–208.

Klapp, Orrin E. *Currents of Unrest: An Introduction to Collective Behavior.* New York: Holt, Rinehart and Winston, 1972.

————. "Dramatic Encounters." In *Protest, Reform, and Revolt*, edited by Joseph R. Gusfield, 377–393. New York: John Wiley, 1970.

Koizuka Fumihiro. "Jimintō banare suru wakate" (The young [congressmen] are leaving the Liberal Democratic party). Portion of article entitled "Jiko shuchō suru wakate kanryo no yukue" (The future of these self-asserting young bureaucrats). *Ekonomisuto* 55 (19 July 1977): 40–41 (full article 36–41).

Kolinsky, Eva, ed. *Opposition in Western Europe.* New York: St. Martin's Press, 1987.

Konishi Yaichirō. "Hyōgo Yōka Kōkō jiken no shinsō" (The truth about the Yōka High School incident in Hyōgo). *Buraku Kaihō*, February 1975, 42–56.

"Konna kotode hetabatte tamaru monoka!" (Such an adversary will never crush me!). Interview with Kōno Yōhei by Horiguchi Akio. *Shūkan Asahi* 84 (26 October 1979): 24–25.

Kōno Kenzō. *Gichō ichidai* (My years as House speaker). Tokyo: Asahi Shinbunsha, 1978.

"Kōno kun fumarete tsuyoku naritamae" ([Young] Mr. Kōno, may you become stronger through your experiences). Interview with Utsunomiya Tokuma of the Liberal Democratic party. *Ekonomisuto* 54 (29 June 1979): 15–19.

Kōno Shin Jiyū Kurabu daihyō ga jinin" (New Liberal Club chief representative Kōno resigns). *Asahi Shinbun*, 27 November 1979.

Kōno Yōhei. "Hoshu o sasaeru tame ni saru" (We leave in order to support conservatism). *Chūō Kōron* 91 (August 1976): 193–199.

————. "Jimintō yo saraba: Hyaku no giron yori mo mazu kōdō o—sore ga wareware rokunin no shinjō da" (Good-bye, LDP: Let's act now, instead of having a hundred debates—that is how the six of us feel). *Bungei Shunjū* 54 (August 1976): 94–102.

Krauss, Ellis S. "Japanese Parties and Parliament: Changing Leadership Role and Role Conflict." In *Political Leadership in Contemporary Japan*, edited by Terry Edward MacDougall, 93–114. Michigan Papers in Japanese Studies, no. 1. Ann Arbor: University of Michigan, 1982.

————. *Japanese Radicals Revisited: Student Protest in Postwar Japan*. Berkeley and Los Angeles: University of California Press, 1974.

Krauss, Ellis S., and Bradford L. Simcock. "Citizens' Movements: The Growth and Impact of Environmental Protest in Japan." In *Political Opposition and Local Politics in Japan*, edited by Kurt Steiner, Ellis S. Krauss, and Scott C. Flanagan, 187–227. Princeton: Princeton University Press, 1980.

Krauss, Ellis S., Thomas P. Rohlen, and Patricia G. Steinhoff. "Conflict and Its Resolution in Postwar Japan." In *Conflict in Japan*, edited by Krauss, Rohlen, and Steinhoff, 377–397. Honolulu: University of Hawaii Press, 1984.

Kreps, Juanita M., ed. *Women and the American Economy*. Englewood Cliffs, N.J.: Prentice-Hall, 1976.

Krieger, Leonard. *The German Idea of Freedom*. Boston: Beacon Press, 1957.

Kriesberg, Louis. *The Sociology of Social Conflicts*. Englewood Cliffs, N.J.: Prentice-Hall, 1973.

"Kunitori e jitto matsu" (An enduring dream for power). *Yomiuri Shinbun*, 8 March 1979.

Kurimoto Shin'ichirō. *Gensō to shite no keizai* (Economy as illusion). Tokyo: Seidosha, 1980.

Kuroda, Yasumasa. *Reed Town, Japan*. Honolulu: University of Hawaii Press, 1974.

Kurosawa, Akira. *Something Like an Autobiography*. New York: Alfred Knopf, 1982.

"Kyosen no shingen shōbu" (An honest conversation with Kyosen). Interview with Kōno Yōhei by Ōhashi Kyosen. *Shūkan Asahi* 76 (10 December 1971): 46–50.

La Palombara, Joseph. *Democracy, Italian Style*. New Haven: Yale University Press, 1987.

Lawler, Edward J. "The Impact of Status Differences on Coalitional Agreements." *Journal of Conflict Resolution* 19 (June 1975): 271–85.

Lebra, Joyce, Joy Paulson, and Elizabeth Powers, eds. *Women in Changing Japan*. Boulder, Colo.: Westview Press, 1976.

Lebra, Takie Sugiyama. "Intergenerational Continuity and Discontinuity in Moral Values Among Japanese." In *Japanese Culture and Behavior: Se-*

lected Readings, edited by Takie Sugiyama Lebra and William P. Lebra. Honolulu: University of Hawaii Press, 1974.

————. *Japanese Patterns of Behavior*. Honolulu: University of Hawaii Press, 1976.

————. *Japanese Women: Constraint and Fulfillment*. Honolulu: University of Hawaii Press, 1984.

Lee, Changsoo, and George DeVos. *Koreans in Japan: Ethnic Conflict and Accommodation*. Berkeley and Los Angeles: University of California Press, 1981.

Leichter, Howard M. *American Public Policy in a Comparative Context*. New York: McGraw-Hill, 1984.

————. *A Comparative Approach to Policy Analysis*. Cambridge: Cambridge University Press, 1979.

Leiserson, Michael. "Factions and Coalitions in One-Party Japan: An Interpretation Based on the Theory of Games." *American Political Science Review* 62 (September 1986): 770–787.

Levine, Solomon. "Labor in Japan." In *Business and Society in Japan*, edited by Bradley M. Richardson and Taizō Ueda. New York: Praeger, 1981.

Lewin, Kurt. *Resolving Social Conflicts*. New York: Harper and Row, 1948.

Lindberg, Leon N. *Politics and the Future of Industrial Society*. New York: David McKay, 1976.

Lindblom, Charles E. *Politics and Markets*. New York: Basic Books, 1977.

Lipset, Seymour M., and Stein Rokkan. "Cleavage Structure, Party Systems, and Voter Alignments: An Introduction." In *Party Systems and Voter Alignments*, edited by Lipset and Rokkan, 1–64. New York: Free Press, 1967.

Lipset, Seymour M., Martin Trow, and James S. Coleman. *Union Democracy*. Glencoe, Ill.: Free Press, 1956.

Lipsky, Michael. *Protest in City Politics*. Chicago: Rand McNally, 1970.

Lloyd, P. C. *Africa in Social Change*. Baltimore: Penguin Books, 1967.

Longworth, John. *Beef in Japan*. St. Lucia Queensland, Australia: University of Queensland Press, 1983.

McCarthy, John D., and Mayer N. Zald. "Resource Mobilization and Social Movements: A Partial Theory." *American Journal of Sociology* 82 (May 1977): 1212–1241.

MacDougall, Terry Edward, ed. *Political Leadership in Contemporary Japan*. Michigan Papers in Japanese Studies, no. 1. Ann Arbor: University of Michigan, 1982.

Machiavelli, Niccolò. *The Prince and the Discourses*. New York: Modern Library, 1950.

Mack, Raymond W., and Richard C. Snyder. "The Analysis of Social Conflict—Towards an Overview and Synthesis." *Journal of Conflict Resolution* 1 (1957): 212–248.

McKean, Margaret A. *Environmental Protest and Citizen Politics in Japan.* Berkeley and Los Angeles: University of California Press, 1981.

————. "Political Socialization Through Citizens' Movements." In *Political Opposition and Local Politics in Japan,* edited by Kurt Steiner, Ellis S. Krauss, and Scott Flanagan, 228–273. Princeton: Princeton University Press, 1980.

McNeil, Elton B. *The Nature of Human Conflict.* Englewood Cliffs, N.J.: Prentice-Hall, 1965.

Mainichi Shinbunsha Seijibu. *Seihen* (Political change). Tokyo: Mainichi Shinbunsha, 1975.

Maki Tarō. "Nakasone 'anrakushi' o takuramu Miyazawa vs. Takeshita no yamiuchi." (A surprise attack by rivals Miyazawa and Takeshita, both of whom have a desire to replace [Prime Minister] Nakasone). *Gendai* 18 (March 1984): 122–139.

Marx, Gary T. "External Efforts to Damage or Facilitate Social Movements: Some Patterns, Explanations, Outcomes, and Complications." In *The Dynamics of Social Movements: Resource Mobilization, Social Control, and Tactics,* edited by Mayer N. Zald and John D. McCarthy, 94–125. Cambridge, Mass.: Winthrop, 1979.

Matsushita, Keiichi. "A Japanese Tea Ceremony." *Asahi Shinbun,* 15 November 1982.

Mellen, Joan. *The Waves at Genji's Door: Japan Through Its Cinema.* New York: Pantheon Books, 1976.

Merelman, Richard M. *Making Something of Ourselves: On Culture and Politics in the United States.* Berkeley and Los Angeles: University of California Press, 1984.

"Michi kewashi mini seitō" (Minor political parties are in difficulty). *Asahi Shinbun,* 10 October 1979.

"Miki shi ga kōkei sōsai ni" (Mr. Miki takes office as [LDP] president). *Yomiuri Shinbun,* 2 December 1974.

Milkis, Sidney, and Thomas Baldino. "The Future of the Silent Revolution: A Reexamination of Intergenerational Change in Western Europe." Paper delivered at the annual meeting of the Midwest Political Science Association, Chicago, 1978.

Milner, James W., ed. *Prologue to the Future: The United States and Japan in the Postindustrial Age.* Lexington, Mass.: D. C. Heath, 1974.

Moe, Terry M. *The Organization of Interests: Incentives and the Internal Dynamics of Political Interest Groups.* Chicago: University of Chicago Press, 1980.

"'Mōichido chōsen shitai' Kōno-san fushime gachi" ("I wish to try once again," says Mr. Kōno with downcast eyes). *Asahi Shinbun* (evening edition), 8 October 1979.

Moore, Barrington, Jr. *Authority and Inequality Under Capitalism and So-*

cialism: U.S.A., U.S.S.R., and China. Oxford: Oxford University Press, 1987.

———. *Injustice: The Social Bases of Obedience and Revolt.* White Plains, N.Y.: M. E. Sharpe, 1978.

Murakami, Yasusuke. "The Age of New Middle Mass Politics: The Case of Japan." *Journal of Japanese Studies* 8 (Winter 1982): 29–72.

———. "The Reality of the New Middle Class." *Japan Interpreter* 1 (Winter 1978): 1–15.

Murakawa Ichirō. *Nihon hoshutō shōshi: Jiyū minken to seitō seiji* (Short history of Japanese conservative parties: Civil liberties and party politics). Tokyo: Kyōikusha, 1978.

Murakoshi Sueo and Miwa Yoshi, eds. *Konnichi no buraku sabetsu* (Discrimination against burakumin today). Osaka: Kaihō Shuppansha, 1987.

Muramatsu, Michio, and Ellis S. Krauss. "Bureaucrats and Politicians in Policymaking: The Case of Japan." *American Political Science Review* 78 (1984): 126–146.

Myrdal, Gunnar, with Richard Sterner and Arnold Rose. *An American Dilemma: The Negro Problem and Modern Democracy.* 2 vols. New York: Harper, 1944.

Nagayama Yoshitaka. "Hato basu ka taka basu ka. Kōno shokku de mōichidai no maikuro basu wa shuppatsu suruka" (After its shocking breakaway from the Liberal Democratic party, will this [new party] veer to the left or to the right? Will more congressmen leave the party en masse?). *Shūkan Asahi* 81 (2 July 1976): 18–20.

Najita, Tetsuo, and J. Victor Koschmann, eds. *Conflict in Modern Japanese History: The Neglected Tradition.* Princeton: Princeton University Press, 1982.

Nakane, Chie. *Japanese Society.* Berkeley and Los Angeles: University of California Press, 1970.

Nelkin, Dorothy, and Michael Pollak. *The Atom Besieged: Extraparliamentary Dissent in France and Germany.* Cambridge, Mass.: MIT Press, 1981.

New Liberal Club. *Chūshō kigyō seisaku* (A small enterprise policy). Ser. 4. Tokyo, 1977.

———. *Enerugī seisaku* (An energy policy). Ser. 3. Tokyo, 1977.

———. *Shin Jiyū Kurabu kara anata e* (To you from the New Liberal Club). Ser. 2. Tokyo, 1977.

———. *Shin Jiyū Kurabu zenkoku rengō kaisoku* (New Liberal Club federal regulations). Tokyo, 1978.

———. *Wareware no kihon rinen: Atarashii jiyū shakai o tsukuru tame ni* (Our principles: To create a new free society). Tokyo, 1977.

New Liberal Club and Council of Tokyo Citizens (Tomin Kaigi). *"Katsuryoku aru jichitai" o mezasu Shin Jiyū Kurabu no Tokyo seisaku* (The NLC's Tokyo policy for the realization of "active autonomy"). Tokyo, 1977.

Nihon Seikei Shinbun, ed. *Kokkai binran* (Diet handbook). Tokyo: Nihon Seikei Shinbunsha, 1956, 1960, 1966, 1975, 1976, 1978, and 1987.

Ninomiya, Shigeaki. "An Inquiry Concerning the Origin, Development, and Present Situation of the Eta in Relation to the History of Social Classes in Japan." *Transactions of the Asiatic Society of Japan*, 2d ser., 10 (1933): 47–154.

Nishihira, Shigeki. "Political Opinion Polling in Japan." In *Political Opinion Polling: An International Review*, edited by Robert M. Worcester, 152–168. New York: St. Martin's Press, 1983.

"Nishioka kanjichō ga ritō" (Secretary-General Nishioka departs). *Asahi Shinbun*, 17 July 1979.

"NLC hopes to play stronger role." Interview with Kōno Yōhei. *Asahi Evening News*, 25 February 1978.

Nordlinger, Eric A. *On the Autonomy of the Democratic State*. Cambridge, Mass.: Harvard University Press, 1981.

Obershall, Anthony. *Social Conflict and Social Movements*. Englewood Cliffs, N.J.: Prentice-Hall, 1973.

Offe, Claus. "Challenging the Boundaries of Institutional Politics: Social Movements Since the 1960s." In *Changing Boundaries of the Political*, edited by Charles Maier, 63–105. Cambridge: Cambridge University Press, 1987.

Ohnuki-Tierney, Emiko. *The Monkey as Mirror: Symbolic Transformations in Japanese History and Ritual*. Princeton: Princeton University Press, 1987.

Olson, Mancur. *The Logic of Collective Action*. Cambridge, Mass.: Harvard University Press, 1975.

Ostrom, Vincent. "Nonhierarchical Approaches to the Organization of Public Activity." *Annals of the American Academy of Political and Social Science*, no. 466 (March 1983): 135–148.

Packard, George R., III. *Protest in Tokyo*. Princeton: Princeton University Press, 1966.

Passin, Herbert. "Socio-Cultural Factors in the Japanese Perception of International Order." *Japanese Institute of International Affairs Annual Review* (1971): 51–75.

———. "The Sources of Protest in Japan." *American Political Science Review* 56 (June 1962): 391–403.

———. "Untouchability in the Far East." *Monumenta Nipponica* 11 (October 1955): 27–47.

Pempel, T. J. *Policy and Politics in Japan: Creative Conservatism*. Philadelphia: Temple University Press, 1982.

Perry, Linda. "Mothers, Wives, and Daughters in Osaka: Autonomy, Alliance, and Professionalism." Ph.D. diss., University of Pittsburgh, 1976.

Pharr, Susan J. "In Search of Equality: A Case of Burakumin Protest."

Paper presented at the Midwest Regional Seminar on Japan, Columbia, Missouri, 2 October 1981.

———. "Japan: Historical and Contemporary Perspectives." In *Women: Role and Status in Eight Countries*, edited by Janet Z. Giele and Audrey C. Smock, 219–255. New York: John Wiley, 1977.

———. "The Japanese Women: Evolving View of Life and Role." In *Japan: The Paradox of Progress*, edited by Lewis Austin, 301–327. New Haven: Yale University Press, 1976.

———. "Liberal Democrats in Disarray: Intergenerational Conflict in the Conservative Camp in Japan." In *Political Leadership in Modern Japan*, edited by Terry Edward MacDougall, 29–50. East Asian Monograph Series, no. 1. Ann Arbor: University of Michigan Press, 1982.

———. *Political Women in Japan*. Berkeley and Los Angeles: University of California Press, 1981.

———. "The Politics of Women's Rights." In *Democratizing Japan: The Allied Occupation*, edited by Robert E. Ward and Sakamoto Yoshikazu, 221–252. Honolulu: University of Hawaii Press, 1987.

———. "Status Conflict: The Rebellion of the Tea Pourers." In *Conflict in Japan*, edited by Ellis S. Krauss, Thomas P. Rohlen, and Patricia G. Steinhoff, 214–240. Honolulu: University of Hawaii Press, 1984.

Pharr, Susan J., and Joseph L. Badaracco, Jr. "Coping with Crisis: Environmental Regulation." In *America Versus Japan*, edited by Thomas K. McCraw, 229–259. Boston: Harvard Business School Press, 1986.

Pirages, Dennis. *Managing Political Conflict*. New York: Praeger, 1976.

Plath, David W. *Long Engagements: Maturity in Modern Japan*. Stanford: Stanford University Press, 1980.

———. *Work and Lifecourse in Japan*. Albany: State University of New York Press, 1983.

Problems of Working Women. Tokyo: Japan Institute of Labor, 1986.

Rae, Douglas. *Equalities*. Cambridge, Mass.: Harvard University Press, 1981.

Rappoport, Anatol. *Fights, Games, and Debates*. Ann Arbor: University of Michigan Press, 1960.

Richardson, Bradley M. *The Political Culture of Japan*. Berkeley and Los Angeles: University of California Press, 1974.

Richardson, Bradley M., and Scott C. Flanagan. *Politics in Japan*. Boston: Little, Brown, 1984.

Rimlinger, Gaston V. "The Legitimation of Protest: A Comparative Study in Labor History." In *Protest, Reform, and Revolt*, edited by Joseph R. Gusfield, 363–376. New York: John Wiley, 1970.

"Ritō o omoitodomatta Yamaguchi Toshio kokutai iinchō o kakaete Shin Jiyū Kurabu wa kōnaru to yū mikata" (Some thoughts about the future of the New Liberal Club whose Diet Policy Committee chairman,

Yamaguchi Toshio, just gave up his position). *Nikkan Gendai*, 21 July 1979.

Rogowski, Ronald. *Rational Legitimacy: A Theory of Political Support*. Princeton: Princeton University Press, 1974.

Rohlen, Thomas P. *For Harmony and Strength: Japanese White Collar Organization in Anthropological Perspective*. Berkeley and Los Angeles: University of California Press, 1974.

———. "Violence at Yoka High School: The Implications for Japanese Coalition Politics of the Confrontation Between the Communist Party and the Buraku Liberation League." *Asian Survey* 16 (July 1976): 682–699.

Rose, Richard. *Challenge to Governance*. London: Sage, 1980.

———. *Understanding Big Government*. London: Sage, 1984.

Roth, Guenther. *The Social Democrats in Imperial Germany: A Study in Working-Class Isolation and National Integration*. Totowa, N.J.: Bedminster Press, 1963.

Ruyle, Eugene E. "Conflicting Japanese Interpretations of the Outcaste Problem (*buraku mondai*)." *American Ethnologist* 6 (February 1979): 55–72.

Rustow, Dankwart. *A World of Nations: Problems of Political Modernization*. Washington, D.C.: Brookings Institution, 1967.

"Sain wa 'mate' daga, watashi wa utta" (The public expected me to wait, yet I dared to take action). Interview with Kōno Yōhei by Ōsuma Mizuo. Portion of article entitled "Shin Jiyū Kurabu kaimetsu no kiki o ou" (Survey of the New Liberal Club's critical situation). *Sandē Mainichi*, 2 December 1979, 19–22 (full article 16–22).

Samuels, Richard J. *The Business of the Japanese State: Energy Markets in Comparative and Historical Perspective*. Ithaca, N.Y.: Cornell University Press, 1987.

Satake Akihiro. *Gekokujō no bungaku* (Literature on gekokujō). Tokyo: Chikuma Shobō, 1970.

Satō Seizaburō and Matsuzaki Tetsuhisa. *Jimintō seiken* (Rule by the Liberal Democratic party). Tokyo: Chūō Kōronsha, 1986.

Scalapino, Robert A. *Democracy and the Party Movement in Prewar Japan: The Failure of the First Attempt*. Berkeley and Los Angeles: University of California Press, 1953.

———. *Parties and Politics in Contemporary Japan*. Berkeley and Los Angeles: University of California Press, 1962.

Scalapino, Robert, and Junnosuke Masumi. "The Crisis of May–June 1960—A Case Study in Japanese Politics." In *Protest, Reform, and Revolt: A Reader in Social Movements*, edited by Joseph R. Gusfield, 274–298. New York: John Wiley, 1970.

Schattschneider, E. E. *The Semi-sovereign People: A Realist's View of Democracy in America*. New York: Holt, Reinhart and Winston, 1967.

Scheiner, Irwin. "Benevolent Lords and Honorable Peasants: Rebellion and Peasant Consciousness in Tokugawa Japan." In *Japanese Thought in the Tokugawa Period, 1600–1868*, edited by Tetsuo Najita and Irwin Scheiner, 39–62. Chicago: University of Chicago Press, 1978.

Scheingold, Stuart A. *The Politics of Rights: Lawyers, Public Policy, and Political Change.* New Haven: Yale University Press, 1974.

Schelling, Thomas. *The Strategy of Conflict.* Cambridge, Mass.: Harvard University Press, 1963.

"Seiji fuan koso nozomashii" (It is better to have political instability). Interview with Kōno Yōhei. *Ekonomisuto* 54 (7 September 1976): 26–29.

"Shiken tōan to shite wa rakudai da" (Their answers in an interview are not satisfactory at all). *Bungei Shunjū* 55 (June 1976): 124–130.

"Shin Jiyū Kurabu" (New Liberal Club). In *Asahi Nenkan, 1977* (Asahi Yearbook, 1977), 337. Tokyo: Asahi Shinbunsha, 1977.

"Shin Jiyū Kurabu naifun o shūshū" (Discord within the New Liberal Club has been handled). *Asahi Shinbun*, 20 July 1979.

"Shin Jiyū Kurabu sōdō de Jimin, Chūdō tsunahiki" (The Liberal Democratic and the Middle-of-the-Road parties both wish to take advantage of the New Liberal Club discord). *Asahi Shinbun*, 19 July 1979.

"Shin Jiyū Kurabu sōkai no yaritori" (Give and take at the general meeting of New Liberal Club). *Asahi Shinbun*, 19 July 1979.

"Shin Jiyū Kurabu tetsuya no rosen ronsō: Yuzuranu daihyō, kanjichō" (Overnight debate on the New Liberal Club party line: Neither Chief Representative [Kōno] nor Secretary-General [Nishioka] compromises). *Asahi Shinbun*, 17 June 1979.

"Shin Jiyū Kurabu tettei kenkyū" (Thorough research on the New Liberal Club). *Bungei Shunjū* 55 (June 1977): 92–121.

Shitō Kineo. "Yōhei no ichiban nagai hi" (The longest day of [Kōno] Yōhei). *Shūkan Posuto* 11 (14 December 1979): 44.

"Shōgen ga kataru jūichigatsu nijūninichi no shinsō: Nihon Kyōsantō wa ikani detchiagetaka" (The truth about November 22, as told by witnesses: How the Japan Communist party fabricated things). *Buraku Kaihō*, March 1975, 64–85.

Simons, Herbert W., and Elizabeth W. Mechling. "The Rhetoric of Political Movements." In *Handbook of Political Communications*, edited by Dan D. Nimmo and Keith R. Sanders, 417–444. Beverly Hills, Calif.: Sage, 1981.

Skinner, Quentin. *The Foundation of Modern Political Thought.* Cambridge: Cambridge University Press, 1978.

Smelser, Neil J. *Theory of Collective Behavior.* New York: Free Press, 1963.

Smith, Henry Dewitt, II. *Japan's First Student Radicals.* Cambridge, Mass.: Harvard University Press, 1972.

Smith, Robert J. *Japanese Society: Tradition, Self, and the Social Order.* Cambridge: Cambridge University Press, 1983.

Smith, Thomas C. *The Agrarian Origins of Modern Japan*. Stanford: Stanford University Press, 1959.

Spiegel, Hans, and Janice Perlman. "Docklands and Coventry: Two Citizen Action Groups in Britain's Economically Declining Areas." In *Paternalism, Conflict, and Coproduction: Learning from Citizen Action and Citizen Participation in Western Europe*, edited by Lawrence Susskind, Michael Elliot, and Associates. New York: Plenum Press, 1983.

Steinhoff, Patricia G. "Student Conflict." In *Conflict in Japan*, edited by Ellis S. Krauss, Thomas P. Rohlen, and Patricia G. Steinhoff, 174–213. Honolulu: University of Hawaii Press, 1984.

Stevens, Evelyn P. *Protest and Response in Mexico*. Cambridge, Mass.: MIT Press, 1974.

Stockwin, J. A. A. *Japan: Divided Politics in a Growth Economy*. New York: W. W. Norton, 1982.

Strauss, Anselm. *Negotiations: Varieties, Contexts, Processes, and Social Order*. San Francisco: Jossey-Bass, 1978.

Strayer, Joseph R. "The Tokugawa Period and Japanese Feudalism." In *Studies in the Institutional History of Early Modern Japan*, edited by John Whitney Hall and Marius B. Jansen, 3–14. Princeton: Princeton University Press, 1968.

Sugio Toshiaki, ed. *Shiryō—Yōka Kōkō no dōwa kyōiku* (Collected materials—Dōwa education at Yōka High School). Kobe: Buraku Mondai Kenkyūjo, 1975.

Szalai, Alexander. *The Situation of Women in the United Nations*. Research Report no. 18. New York: United Nations Institute for Training and Research, 1973.

Tagami Kazuyoshi. "1989–nendo chiiki kaizen taisaku yosan omiru" (Looking over the 1989 budget for dōwa projects). *Buraku* 41 (March 1989): 45–51.

Tagawa Seiichi. *Dokyumento Jimin dattō* (Documenting the breakaway from the Liberal Democrats). Tokyo: Tokuma Shoten, 1983.

Takabatake Michitoshi. "Hachijū nendai no seiji kiryū" (The political stream in the eighties). *Mainichi Shinbun*, 24 June 1980.

———. "Jimintō gosan to jikai no kōzō" (Miscalculation and self-discipline in the Liberal Democratic Party). *Ekonomisuto* 62 (3 January 1984): 10–21.

———. "Mass Movements: Change and Diversity." In *Annals of the Japan Political Science Association 1977: The Political Process in Modern Japan*, edited by the Japan Political Science Association, 323–359. Tokyo: Iwanami Shoten, 1979.

———. "San'in sen, sokojikara miseta Jimintō" (The Upper House election: The Liberal Democratic party demonstrates its fundamental strength). *Ekonomisuto* 55 (26 July 1977): 22–28.

Takahashi Akira. "Nihon gakusei undō no shisō to kōdō" (Thoughts and behavior in the Japanese student movement). *Chūō Kōron* 5 (May 1968); 6 (June 1968); 8 (August 1968); and 9 (September 1968).

Tawara Kotarō. "Jimintō dai ikki, niki kōkeisha" (The first- and second-phase successors of the Liberal Democratic party). *Seiron*, March 1977, 38–49.

"Tayōka shakai ni taiō" (We are considering how to deal with these multiple dimensions of modern society). Interview with Kōno Yōhei by Hara Takafumi. *Yomiuri Shinbun*, 18 March 1979.

Thayer, Nathaniel B. *How the Conservatives Rule Japan.* Princeton: Princeton University Press, 1969.

Thompson, E. P. *The Making of the English Working Class.* New York: Vintage Books, 1963.

Tilly, Charles. *From Mobilization to Revolution.* Reading, Mass.: Addison-Wesley, 1978.

———. "Repertoires of Contention in America and Britain, 1750–1830." In *The Dynamics of Social Movements*, edited by Mayer N. Zald and John D. McCarthy, 126–155. Cambridge, Mass.: Winthrop, 1979.

Titus, David Anson. *Palace and Politics in Prewar Japan.* New York: Columbia University Press, 1974.

Tocqueville, Alexis de. "The Old Regime and the French Revolution." In *Protest, Reform, and Revolt*, edited by Joseph R. Gusfield, 68–84. New York: John Wiley, 1970.

"Todai Students Like the LDP." *Asahi Evening News*, 1 July 1978.

Togawa Isamu. *Shōsetsu Yoshida gakkō* (The story of the Yoshida school). Vol. 2. Tokyo: Kadokawa Shoten, 1980.

"Tōnai atsureki fukamaru Shin Jiyū Kurabu" (A growing strain within the New Liberal Club). *Asahi Shinbun*, 6 March 1979.

Totten, George O. *The Social Democratic Movement in Prewar Japan.* New Haven: Yale University Press, 1966.

"Tsuini jinin! Ochita gūzō Kōno Yōhei ni koredake no hinan" (Kōno Yōhei, at last resigned! These criticisms of a broken idol). *Shūkan Bunshun* 21 (6 December 1979): 24–28.

Tsurumi, Kazuko. *Social Change and the Individual: Japan Before and After Defeat in World War II.* Princeton: Princeton University Press, 1970.

———. "Social Structure: A Mesh of Hierarchical and Coequal Relationships in Villages and Cities." Part 1 of a 3-part series, "Aspects of Endogenous Development in Modern Japan." Research Papers of the Institute of International Relations, Sophia University, Series A-36. Tokyo, 1979.

Tsurushima, Setsurei. "Minority Protests: The Burakumin." Paper presented at the Conference on Contemporary Social Problems: Institutions for Change in Japanese Society, Berkeley, 17–18 November 1982.

Tsurutani, Taketsugu. *Political Change in Japan.* New York: David McKay, 1977.

Turner, Ralph H., and Lewis M. Killian. *Collective Behavior.* Englewood Cliffs, N.J.: Prentice-Hall, 1972.

Turner, Victor W. *The Ritual Process: Structure and Anti-Structure.* Chicago: Aldine, 1969.

Uchiyama Hideo, Uchida Mitsuru, and Iwami Takao. "'Hakuchū seiji' e no kitai to fuan" (Hope and anxiety for "balance of power" politics). *Ekonomisuto* 62 (17 January 1984): 10–19.

Upham, Frank K. *Law and Social Change in Postwar Japan.* Cambridge, Mass.: Harvard University Press, 1987.

———. "Ten Years of Affirmative Action for Japanese Burakumin: A Preliminary Report on the Law on Special Measures for Dōwa Projects." *Law in Japan: An Annual* 13 (1980): 39–73.

Verba, Sidney, Norman H. Nie, and Jae-on Kim. *Participation and Political Equality: A Seven-Nation Comparison.* Cambridge: Cambridge University Press, 1978.

Verba, Sidney, Steven Kelman, Gary R. Orren, Miyake Ichirō, Watanuki Joji, Kabashima Ikuo, and G. Donald Ferree, Jr. *Elites and the Idea of Equality: A Comparison of Japan, Sweden, and the United States.* Cambridge, Mass.: Harvard University Press, 1987.

Vlastos, Stephen. *Peasant Protests and Uprisings in Tokugawa Japan.* Berkeley and Los Angeles: University of California Press, 1986.

Vogel, Ezra F. *Japan as Number One: Lessons for America.* Cambridge, Mass.: Harvard University Press, 1979.

———, ed. *Modern Japanese Organization and Decision-Making.* Berkeley and Los Angeles: University of California Press, 1975.

Wagatsuma, Hiroshi. "Political Problems of a Minority Group in Japan." In *Case Studies on Human Rights and Fundamental Freedom*, edited by William A. Veenhoven and Winifred Crum Ewing, 3: 243–273. The Hague: Martinus Nijhoff, 1976.

Wagatsuma Sakae, ed. *Roppō zensho* (Compendium of laws). Tokyo: Yūhikaku, 1967.

Wald, Kenneth. "The Rise of Class-based Voting in London." *Comparative Politics* 9 (1977): 219–229.

Ward, Robert E. *Japan's Political System.* Englewood Cliffs, N.J.: Prentice-Hall, 1978.

Watanuki Joji. *Politics in Postwar Japanese Society.* Tokyo: University of Tokyo Press, 1977.

White, Harrison. "Notes on the Constituents of Social Structure." Harvard University, n.d. Photocopy.

White, James W. "Civic Attitudes, Political Participation, and System Stability in Japan." *Comparative Political Studies* 14 (October 1981): 371–400.

White, Merry I., and Barbara Molony, eds. *Proceedings of the Tokyo Symposium on Women*. Tokyo: International Group for the Study of Women, 1979.

Whyte, Martin K. *Small Groups and Political Rituals in China*. Berkeley and Los Angeles: University of California Press, 1974.

Williams, Robin M. *The Reduction of Intergroup Tensions*. Social Science Research Council Bulletin no. 57. New York: SSRC, 1947.

Wilson, John. *Introduction to Social Movements*. New York: Basic Books, 1973.

Yagi Kōsuke. *Sabetsu kyūdan: Sono shisō to rekishi* (Discrimination *kyūdan*: Its ideology and history). Tokyo: Hihyōsha, 1976.

"Yahari hiyowa na seiken" (The government is still fragile). *Ekonomisuto* 55 (26 July 1977): 29.

Yamaguchi Yasushi. "Jōkyō e no shindan" (A diagnosis of the current situation). *Sekai*, no. 369 (August 1976): 184–195.

Yamazaki Masakazu. "Atarashii kojin shugi no yochō" (Signs of a new individualism). *Chūō Kōron* 98 (August 1983): 62–88.

"Yōka Kōkō no konran no genkyō wa Nikkyō sabetsusha shūdan Miyamoto ippa da!" (The original cause behind the Yōka High School turmoil is the Miyamoto group, that discriminatory faction within the Japan Communist party!). *Sayama Sabetsu Saiban* 14 (September 1974): 2–15.

Yōka Kōkō sabetsu kyōiku kyūdan tōsō: Sabetsu kyanpein o haishi jijitsu o tashikameru tameni (The *kyūdan* struggle against the discriminatory education of Yōka High School: Clearing away the discriminatory campaign to get at the facts). Kobe: Buraku Kaihō Dōmei, Hyōgo-ken Rengō-kai, 1975.

Yōka no Shinjitsu o Mamorukai. *Yōka Kōkō jiken no shinjitsu* (The truth behind the Yōka High School incident). Kyoto: Buraku Mondai Kenkyūjo Shuppanbu, 1978.

"Yōka tōsō no keika" (The process of the Yōka struggle). *Sayama Sabetsu Saiban* 14 (September 1974): 45–48.

Yokoi Kiyoshi. *Chūsei minshū no seikatsu bunka* (The life of the common people during the Middle Ages). Tokyo: Tōkyō Daigaku Shuppankai, 1975.

Yomiuri Nenkan (Yomiuri Yearbook), 1968–1977. Tokyo: Yomiuri Shinbunsha, 1967–1976.

Yoshino, Roger I., and Sueo Murakoshi. *The Invisible Visible Minority: Japan's Burakumin*. Osaka: Buraku Kaihō Kenkyūsho, 1977.

Youth Division of Sōka Gakkai. *Cries for Peace: Experiences of Japanese Victims of World War II*. Tokyo: Japan Times, 1974.

Zald, Mayer N., and John D. McCarthy, eds. *The Dynamics of Social Movements: Resource Mobilization, Social Control, and Tactics*. Cambridge, Mass.: Winthrop, 1979.

INDEX

Compositor: G&S Typesetters, Inc.
Text: 10/13 Janson
Display: Janson
Printer: Maple-Vail Book Mfg. Group
Binder: Maple-Vail Book Mfg. Group